The Paley's Place Cookbook

The Paley's Place Cookbook

RECIPES AND STORIES FROM THE PACIFIC NORTHWEST

Vitaly Paley and Kimberly Paley

with Robert Reynolds

Photography by John Valls

TEN SPEED PRESS
Berkeley | Toronto

For Merle Clinton Brown

Ten Speed Press
PO Box 7123
Berkeley, California 94707
www.tenspeed.com

Distributed in Australia by Simon and Schuster Australia,
in Canada by Ten Speed Press Canada, in New Zealand by
Southern Publishers Group, in South Africa by Real Books,
and in the United Kingdom and Europe by Publishers
Group UK.

Cover and text design by Betsy Stromberg

Library of Congress Cataloging-in-Publication Data

Paley, Vitaly.
  The Paley's Place cookbook : recipes and stories from the
Pacific Northwest / Vitaly Paley and Kimberly Paley, with
Robert Reynolds ;   photography by John Valls.
     p. cm.
  Includes index.
  ISBN-13: 978-1-58008-830-5
  ISBN-10: 1-58008-830-9
  1. Cookery, American—Pacific Northwest style. 2. Paley's
Place Bistro and Bar. I. Paley, Kimberly. II. Reynolds,
Robert. III. Title.
  TX715.2.P32P3157 2008
  641.59795—dc22

                                            2008021668

Printed in China
First printing, 2008

1 2 3 4 5 6 7 8 9 10 — 12 11 10 09 08

Contents

Introduction

Close to Home: Cooking in the Pacific Northwest

by **VITALY PALEY**

The story of Paley's Place began in New York, where Kimberly and I met. She was a dancer who had come from California to study at the Martha Graham School. Born in Russia, I had come to New York as a teenager and now, in the eighties, was studying music at Juilliard. Like many of our friends, we subsidized our art by working in the food world, and we met when we were both managers for a dinner cruise company. One July Fourth—the 100th birthday of the Statue of Liberty—when our work was done for the night, we wound up making out in the shadows of the torch the old Dame held high. We remember fireworks.

Looking back, we think we chose food over art, but perhaps it was fate, and food chose us. I went to the French Culinary Institute in New York, and together we moved to France to work and learn together at a Michelin-starred restaurant called Au Moulin de la Gorce, near Limoges. Back in New York, we worked with the best, including Tom Valenti at Alison on Dominick, David Bouley of Bouley, Michael Romano and Danny Meyer of Union Square Café, and David and Karen Waltuck of Chanterelle. Kimberly studied with Kevin Zraly at Windows on the World, Andrea Immer, and master sommelier Roger Dagorn.

But it was in our tiny Bleecker Street apartment that our vision for the restaurant that would become Paley's Place began to shape itself. In the spirit of collaboration that we still share, we invited friends and family to dinners—and not just any dinners. On each occasion, we created experiences that reflected whatever inspired us about a particular menu. We wrote invitations, specifying a dress code for the evening—informal or jacket and tie. Kimberly's hospitality was unstinting, her eye for detail meticulous. She set the stage, making menus by hand and dressing the table with silverware arranged face down, as she learned to do in France and as she still does in the restaurant. If I plucked basil from clay pots on the fire escape, Kimberly described it on the menu as "local," a nod to the lessons we learned in France and a sweet gesture toward our yet-unwritten future in Portland, in the cool, open West.

After one summer too many in hot, airless, underground restaurant kitchens (me) and coping with the behind-the-scenes madness of restaurant dining rooms (Kimberly), we sold our apartment on Bleecker Street, packed up, and left New York knowing two things: we wanted our own restaurant, and we wanted it to be in Oregon.

1

Oregon reminded us of France, where ingredients are stars. In New York's kitchens, I saw you could get anything at any time. I also noticed that not much came from close by. While Kimberly and I didn't necessarily want ours to be a French restaurant, we knew we wanted to sustain what we learned in France about being closer to the sources of food. In Portland, we see not only where food comes from, but who grows it. Here, our food is shaped by connections with people and the ingredients they bring to the restaurant's door—mushrooms, potatoes, truffles, chestnuts. A signature reference on our menu to "George's Gathered Greens" (page 60) doesn't refer to the chef, but to the farmer, George Weppler.

In anticipation of moving to Oregon, we had already made connections with winemakers Ken Wright (then of Panther Creek and now of Ken Wright Cellars) and Russ Raney of Evesham Wood. Once here, we discovered food producers—like George Weppler and cheesemaker Pierre Kolish of Juniper Grove Farm in Redmond—who we feel are visionaries.

Over the years since we opened Paley's Place, we have come to feel that we have not just created a restaurant, but are participating in a bigger movement to establish the uniqueness of Oregon, a region that has figured out how to sustain the integrity of its agricultural traditions. Unlike France, Oregon doesn't have an *Appellation d'origine contrôlée* (AOC) system as a guarantee of superior quality. But Oregon's producers make a certain kind of promise among themselves: when they say the berries are good, they mean it.

In this book, as in our restaurant, we have tried to bring out the stories of the people who provide us with impeccable ingredients. Their stories reflect the way we strive to do business; their engagement matches ours, and therefore fosters respect each time we touch what they provide. In these pages you will get a glimpse of the growers, foragers, fishermen, and artisan producers who provide us with lamb, mushrooms, potatoes, greens, nuts, cheese, salmon, and more. Other stories in these pages are meant to shed light on some of the culinary techniques and influences, hospitable spirit, and threads of memory that tie our past experiences to our present.

Our approach to food and wine and the dining experience is deeply personal. The recipes and stories in this book reflect how and why we do what we do with these products in this place. In the end, it is all about relationships. It starts with Kimberly and me—our collaboration is an endless source of inspiration for both of us. Our relationships with our customers, our purveyors, and our staff are gifts. Without them, this story would be very different.

Cooking seasonally does not come naturally to most of us. We can buy anything at any time of year, and that path of lesser resistance is always easier to follow. The foods we buy have to be seasonal somewhere, right? But defrosted fish is not the same as fresh off the boat, and an out of season tomato or ear of corn can never compare to just picked. Let your senses guide you to what smells and feels real rather than what looks shiny and flawless. If you search out locally produced and grown goods whenever possible, chances are they will be seasonal as well.

In the kitchen, trust your senses to help you take a dish to its logical conclusion rather than blindly following the recipe. Experience has taught me that achieving a perfect balance of flavors is a learned skill. Each dish can attain a "sweet spot," however elusive it might be, and you learn where it is by tasting.

I am constantly reminded of my final exam in cooking school, where I had to reproduce several classic French recipes. I was a good student and I knew them all by heart, so making them was easy, I thought. When I presented the finished dishes to the panel of judges, I received a less-than-enthusiastic critique. I had followed the recipes exactly as I had been taught to do them. So what went wrong? One judge asked me if I'd tasted what I made. There and then it all made sense. I've never forgotten that lesson. I urge you to taste, taste, and taste what you're cooking at every stage. Learning to follow flavors as they unfold will help you navigate through written instructions and will eventually educate your senses and produce impressive results.

Now for a few words about preparing the recipes in this book:

• Use kosher salt for general seasoning. Use a coarse sea salt of any kind (I prefer *fleur de sel*) for finishing a dish. Do not use generic table salt. It is full of iodine and added chemicals to mask its unpleasant flavor. When it comes to pepper, I only use black. It simply tastes better than white. Grind it fresh every time you use it. Be liberal with your seasoning when cooking, and you and your guests will appreciate the results.

• Use extra-virgin olive oil for vinaigrettes and to sauté vegetables. Use grapeseed or canola oils to cook meat, poultry, and seafood unless the recipe calls for something else.

• Use only unsalted butter, as it has the taste of cream. Salted butter is usually of lesser quality, and using it will prevent you from seasoning the dish correctly.

For me, cooking is about both soulful searching and rigorous technique. It is influenced by mood and memories, yet it also requires constant repetition and a tireless quest for both perfection and consistency alongside a readiness to adjust on the fly. Cooking is an art whose disciplined performance must retain what I like to call a fresh drop of blood—the ability to be new and exciting and to inspire every time you do it. May this book inspire you to cook with care and add to your joy in making food.

If It's Wine You Like, Drink It

by KIMBERLY PALEY

In the very beginning, I told Vitaly, "If I had my way, everything we do would be served with Bandol Rosé from Domaine Tempier." I like to say I lost my virginity the first time I tasted rosé from Tempier—it was the beginning of my wine education.

In the early eighties, I was hired to teach jazz dance at a summer workshop in Montpellier, France. When the job ended, I used my paycheck to travel and stay in the south of France for the summer. One pivotal stop I made during my travels was in the small village of Bandol. It was there, in the nearby hilly vineyards, that I had my first *liason dangereuse* with Domaine Tempier. It was love at first sensation. My memory of the place is of heat, bramble, scrub, and thirsty olive trees. The rosé was at once fruity, yet dry. It was fresh and quenched my thirst. It tasted like summer. The blanc was unique and radiant. It was easy to drink and its golden yellow color reminded me of the most perfect sunflower. And before I ever took a sip of the red, the aromas of spice, eucalyptus, scrub brush, and dry leaves filled my nostrils. When I swirled it in my mouth, my gums buzzed from the inky tannins and the flavors exploded across my palate. It was an emotional experience that began my journey into the world of wine.

The second pivotal event in my wine education happened much later, in 1992, and also in France. Vitaly and I were doing a stage (apprenticeship) at a Michelin-starred restaurant near Limoges, in the geographic center of France. The ambience at the restaurant, housed in a château, involved fine china, sterling silver, tuxedo-clad servers, and serious work. One evening, diners at one table ordered a rare vintage of Château Margaux. Working with the sommelier, I was responsible for fetching wines from the wine cellar. Because the château dated from the fifteenth century, the cellar was cloaked in damp darkness, the wine organized in dusty rows. To find my way, I had to light a wine-cellar candle that seemed left over from medieval times. Returning upstairs with the precious bottle, I decanted the velvety red liquid into a gorgeous gooseneck crystal vessel. One person at the table was a fourteen-year-old boy, who swirled and smelled the wine before taking a tiny sip. When his father asked what it was, the lad nailed it as an old Bordeaux. I was dumbfounded, and felt at once how much I had to learn.

Upon my return to New York City, I continued to read and study, and to taste everything I could. I was privileged to learn from the likes of Master Sommelier Roger Dagorn, Kevin Zraly at Windows on the World, and Andrea Immer. These great educators, each with a particular point of view, all led me to understand one thing of utmost importance: if you like the wine, drink it. Trust your senses.

When we moved to Portland, my wine education entered a whole new phase. We met the granddads of the Oregon wine industry—David Lett of Eyrie Vineyards, Dick Ponzi of Ponzi Vineyards, Dick Erath of Erath Vineyards, and David Adelsheim of Adelsheim Vineyards.

These were the visionaries who believed in what they saw in Oregon's soil and made prize-winning wines that attracted world attention from the grapes grown in it. We saw the spirit demonstrated by these men as uniquely Oregonian. It was a spirit we wanted to be part of. Our collaboration with these and other winemakers—including John Paul of Cameron Winery, Doug Tunnell of Brickhouse Vineyard, and Patti Green and Jim Anderson of Patricia Green Cellars—made us understand that if there is a movement to define the food and wine of this region, then it is clearest in the vineyard.

What has put this region on the map are the diverse grape-growing practices that have evolved through trial and error in this climate, with these soils, as well as an understanding by the winemakers of the importance of working with the rhythms of nature and their commitment to doing so. The sum of their experiences has given Oregon a true identity as a wine region. Though young, it undeniably equates with quality.

At our restaurant I am rigorous about having our staff taste everything. Every bottle the servers open, they test. I encourage them to have an opinion and learn to identify a flaw before the customer encounters it. Over time, they too sense what wines are lacking in some way because they have learned what they should be. You can read and talk all you want, but the magnificent thing about wine education is that in the end it's all about taste.

Vitaly and I don't always sit down together at the restaurant to devise wine and food pairings—we have developed over time an unspoken, shared understanding of how wine should be paired with food. There are, however, times we collaborate to tailor wines to specific dishes—when Vitaly is asked to do an event for a particular winery, for example. It's not out of the question for us to open our refrigerator at home and try everything we find in it—pickles, mustard, hot sauce—to see what works. "There are no rules" is our motto when we create dishes to accompany a given wine, although we work hard to maintain our point of view about food—driven by season and locale, supported by a similar attitude toward wine. When the results of our collaborations express themselves with a certain audacity, that is my reward for focusing on wine in a more creative way.

At the restaurant, we have put together a wine list that reflects Oregon, Washington, and France because they are close to home and to our hearts. The wine suggestions in this book are those that at one time or another found their way onto our list. I encourage you to taste and drink wines from all over the world. If a wine from anywhere on earth makes you pause, gasp, or laugh—and you like it—drink it and take note. Follow no rules; obey no guidelines. This practice will keep you, as it does me, in a constant state of hunger.

Chapter 1
Appetizers

Roman-Style Chopped Chicken Liver

Makes 1 1/2 cups

My mother and I left Russia in 1976, when I was 12, setting out through Eastern Europe by train and by bus, feeling like gypsies and happy to be free at last. Eventually we got to Rome, home to centuries-old Jewish traditions and, in the 1970s, the Italian version of Ellis Island.

The food there made my head spin—I tasted my very first bite of pizza, my first gelato. The smell of coffee would reel me into a café from a block away. My mother got creative with what little means we had and made sure we ate well, in a way that would pay huge dividends in my adult life. She reinvented her cooking, incorporating the brave new flavors of our temporary home. And as the foods around me evolved, my palate evolved with them. Noodles bored me before, but when made with lots of garlic, olive oil, and cheese, they sparked my interest. Before Rome, I could hardly swallow chopped liver, but when my mother infused it with the flavors of anchovies, sage, and capers, I found it irresistible.

This recipe, then, is like an heirloom, a blend of my family traditions with the flavors of Rome. When I want an authentic Jewish touch, I serve this chopped liver with matzo. When I want to recall Rome, I slather it on Grilled Flatbreads (page 17). While a great appetizer, it is equally good spread on rye bread as a sandwich, which I garnish with sliced red onion and pickles.

1/4 cup extra-virgin olive oil

1/2 pound chicken livers, lobes halved

Kosher salt and freshly ground black pepper

1 large shallot, finely minced

3 cloves garlic, finely minced

2 anchovy fillets, drained and chopped

5 large fresh sage leaves, finely chopped

2 tablespoons drained capers

1/4 cup cream sherry

2 tablespoons balsamic vinegar

2 tablespoons brandy

1 hard-boiled egg, peeled and coarsely grated on the largest holes of a box grater

In a large skillet, heat the olive oil over medium heat until it shimmers. Add the livers, season with salt and pepper, and sear until lightly colored on the bottom, about 1 minute.

Turn the livers over. Add the shallot, garlic, anchovies, sage, and capers. Cook, stirring, until the shallots have softened (it's fine if they take on a little color), about 3 minutes. Pour in the sherry and balsamic vinegar, decrease heat to medium-low, and simmer for about 1 minute. Transfer the liver mixture to the work bowl of a food processor fitted with the metal blade. Add the brandy and pulse a few times until coarsely chopped.

Transfer the chopped liver to a small bowl, fold in the egg, and season with salt and pepper. Allow to come to room temperature, cover, and refrigerate until completely cold. Chopped liver can be made up to a day in advance.

Stuffed Eggs

Serves 4 to 6

My contribution to the culinary world's vast repertoire of deviled eggs includes this Mediterranean filling of tuna, anchovies, and capers. The addition of mustard and paprika grounds the egg in tradition.

    I'm often asked if there is a trick to peeling eggs. There isn't. I will share a few tips, though: Avoid using very fresh eggs. As eggs age, air fills the space between the outer shell and the inner membrane. The longer eggs sit, the more air gets in and the easier the eggs are to peel when cooked. It is that simple. Also, the night before cooking the eggs, rest them on their sides. This will help center the yolks.

6 large eggs	2 anchovy fillets, drained
1/3 cup good-quality tuna packed in olive oil, well drained	1 tablespoon drained capers, plus caper juice
1 clove garlic, finely chopped	2 tablespoons Aioli (page 203)
1 tablespoon finely chopped fresh Italian parsley	Freshly ground black pepper
1 tablespoon Dijon mustard	Paprika, for garnish

Arrange the eggs in a pot just big enough to contain them in a single layer. Add enough cold water to cover the eggs by 1 inch. Bring to a boil over high heat and cook for exactly 7 minutes. Transfer the eggs to a small bowl and cool them under cold running water.

    When the eggs are cool, peel them and halve them lengthwise. Carefully scoop out the yolks and transfer to the work bowl of a food processor fitted with the metal blade; reserve the whites.

    To prepare the filling, add the tuna, garlic, parsley, mustard, anchovies, capers, and aioli to the yolks. Puree until smooth, scraping down the sides of the work bowl with a spatula as necessary. If needed, thin the mixture with a little caper juice. Once mixed to a smooth puree, season with pepper.

    You can cook the eggs and prepare the yolk mixture up to 2 hours ahead of serving. Store them separately in covered containers in the refrigerator, and assemble right before you're ready to serve.

    When ready to serve, transfer the filling to a pastry bag fitted with a large star tip. Pipe the egg yolk mixture into the whites. Sprinkle the tops with paprika and serve. Or, drop a spoonful of yolk mixture into each egg white half, then sprinkle with paprika.

Crispy Oysters with Massaman Curry Bisque and Minted Cucumber Salad

Serves 4 to 6

Martha Hubbard, our former sous-chef, spent several years living and working in Thailand, where she learned to make this sweet curry paste.

You can find kaffir lime leaves, mirin (Japanese rice wine), and lemongrass at Asian grocery stores. If you have your fishmonger shuck the oysters, ask to save the shells as well as the oyster liquor because you're going to use both. The recipe for Massaman curry makes more than is called for in this dish. The leftover curry, covered tightly and refrigerated, will keep for a week or so.

24 large oysters

1 English cucumber, peeled, halved lengthwise, seeded, and cut into 1/4-inch dice

1/4 cup loosely packed fresh mint leaves, coarsely chopped

1/4 cup mirin

1/4 cup rice vinegar

Kosher salt and freshly ground black pepper

1 cup crème fraîche or coconut milk

1/4 cup Massaman Curry Paste (recipe follows)

Juice of 1/2 lime

1 cup all-purpose flour

1 tablespoon cayenne pepper

Rock salt, for serving

Canola or grapeseed oil, for pan-frying

Scrub the oysters under cold running water to clean them. Set a strainer over a small bowl. Shuck the oysters over the strainer, letting the oyster liquor drain into the bowl. Save the bottom oyster shells for serving and discard the top shells. Refrigerate the oysters and oyster liquor until ready to use.

To prepare the cucumber salad, combine the cucumber, mint, mirin, and rice vinegar in a small bowl. Season with salt and pepper, stir, and set aside.

To prepare the curry bisque, in a small saucepan, combine the oyster liquor, crème fraîche, curry paste, and lime juice. Cook over low heat until the flavors come together and the bisque thickens slightly, about 5 minutes. Season with salt and pepper. Set aside and keep warm.

To prepare the oysters, sift the flour with cayenne into a small bowl. Line a plate with paper towels and have ready.

In a large skillet, heat 1/4 cup of the oil over medium-high heat until it shimmers. Lightly dredge 6 of the oysters in the seasoned flour. Shake off excess flour, then carefully drop them into the skillet. Cook until they are crispy and golden brown all over, about 1 minute per side. Drain on the towel-lined plate and season with salt. To retain crispness, fry and serve the oysters in batches, adding and heating fresh oil as needed.

Make a generous bed of rock salt on a large serving platter or several smaller plates. Arrange the reserved oyster shells on the bed of salt. Place a spoonful of cucumber salad in each shell and top with a hot cooked oyster. Pour a generous spoonful of heated curry bisque over each oyster and serve.

Massaman Curry Paste

Makes about 3/4 cup

1 cinnamon stick, broken up into smaller pieces	2 ounces fresh ginger, peeled and finely grated
1 star anise	1/4 cup packed brown sugar
1/2 teaspoon cumin seed	4 anchovy fillets, drained
1 teaspoon coriander seed	2 cloves garlic, coarsely chopped
1 teaspoon cardamom pods	2 fresh or frozen kaffir lime leaves
1 stalk lemongrass	Juice of 1 lime
2 large red bell peppers, peeled, cored, seeded, and chopped	

In a small dry skillet, combine the cinnamon stick, star anise, cumin, coriander, and cardamom. Toast the spices over low heat until their fragrance fills your kitchen, about 2 minutes. Cool slightly, transfer to a spice mill or coffee grinder, and grind to a fine powder.

Trim the woody root and the very top of the lemongrass stalk. Remove and discard the outer leaves, and slice the remaining stalk very thinly. In the work bowl of a food processor fitted with the metal blade, combine the bell peppers, lemongrass, ginger, brown sugar, anchovy fillets, and garlic. Add the ground spice mixture and puree until smooth.

With a spatula, scrape the bell pepper–spice mixture into a small saucepan and add the kaffir lime leaves and lime juice. Cook over low heat, stirring occasionally, until the mixture becomes a thick paste, about 30 minutes. Transfer to a small container and set aside to cool.

To Drink

For this dish, I look for a wine that will hold up nicely to the exotic flavors of Southeast Asia. Oregon's Sineann Gewürztraminer has the right bite of acid, spice, and coconut to harmonize with the pungent curry and refreshing mint. Or go with an Alsatian Gewürztraminer from Rolly Gassmann—rich with spice, juicy pineapple, and enough residual sugar to balance out the briny flavor of the oysters. **–K.P.**

Vegetable-Stuffed Morels, Green Garlic Confit, and Parmesan Cream

Serves 4

As the snow recedes, morels begin to appear in the Pacific Northwest. When the first basket of these crinkly conical wonders shows up in our kitchen, we all gather to inhale their woodsy perfume. Giant morels are rare, so when we get them, we save them for stuffing.

Another herald of spring is green garlic. Though any garlic that hasn't been cured can be referred to as green, we use the tender shoots farmers harvest when they thin their garlic patches. One of the farmers I work with, George Weppler, dedicates separate patches of land to it and calls it garlic scallions. When cooked, it is mild and very sweet. Along with wine and cream, it sets a nice stage for meaty mushrooms. Look for it at farmer's markets.

Stuffing the mushrooms with a spoon or by hand is almost impossible. Instead I suggest using a pastry bag outfitted with a small straight metal tip.

1/2 cup (1 stick) unsalted butter

12 stalks green garlic, trimmed and thinly sliced into 1/8-inch rounds

Kosher salt and freshly ground black pepper

1/3 cup red wine

2/3 cup port wine

1/2 cup plus 2 tablespoons heavy cream

1/4 cup grated Parmesan cheese

12 large morels

1 carrot, peeled and finely diced

1 onion, finely minced

2 tablespoons fine bread crumbs

1 large egg yolk

2 tablespoons Persillade (page 198)

2 tablespoons chopped fresh chives, for garnish

Chive blossoms, for garnish

To prepare the green garlic, in a large skillet, melt 4 tablespoons of the butter over low heat. Add the green garlic, season with salt and pepper, and stir to coat. Cover and simmer until it is meltingly tender but not colored, about 15 minutes. If the pan seems dry, add a touch of water to prevent the garlic from burning. Set aside.

To prepare the cream sauce, in a small saucepan, combine the red wine and 1/3 cup of the port. Bring it to a boil over high heat. Decrease the heat to low and reduce the liquid by half, about 10 minutes. Add the 1/2 cup of cream and bring it to a simmer. Remove from the heat, season with salt and pepper, and add the grated Parmesan, stirring until it melts, about 2 minutes. Set aside and let cool, then refrigerate until ready to serve.

Line a large plate or baking sheet with paper towels and have ready. To cook the mushrooms, place the morels in a large pot and add enough water so they float freely. Toss in a generous pinch of salt and bring to a boil over high heat. When at a boil, remove the mushrooms from the liquid with a slotted spoon. Discard the cooking liquid. Rinse the mushrooms well under cold running water. Give each a gentle squeeze to get rid of excess water. Trim off the stems and let the mushrooms dry on paper towels. When dry, dice the stems finely.

To prepare the stuffing, melt 2 tablespoons of the butter in a skillet over low heat. Add the diced mushroom stems, carrot, and onion. Season with salt and pepper and cook, stirring, until the vegetables have softened, about 10 minutes. Pour in the rest of the port and cook until the pan is dry, another 5 minutes. Remove from the heat, stir in the remaining 2 tablespoons cream, bread crumbs, egg yolk, and persillade. Set aside to cool.

To assemble, fit a pastry bag with a round tip big enough to fit the opening of the smallest morel. Fill the bag with stuffing and pipe the mixture into each mushroom. Use your forefinger to compact the stuffing as you pipe it.

Line a large plate or baking sheet with paper towels and have ready. To finish, in a large skillet, melt the remaining 2 tablespoons of butter over medium heat. Season the stuffed morels with salt and pepper, and very carefully sauté them on all sides until browned and crispy, about 5 minutes. Transfer to paper towels to absorb any excess butter. Combine the sautéed mushrooms and cream sauce in a large skillet over low heat and bring it to a simmer. Warm the green garlic over low heat as well, if needed.

To serve, place a generous spoonful of green garlic confit in the center of 4 dinner plates. Divide the mushrooms evenly between them. Spoon the cream sauce over and sprinkle with chopped chives and chive blossoms. Serve immediately.

Chef's Tip

With their hollow centers and multitude of pleats, morels collect a lot of dirt, debris, and, occasionally, unwanted creatures. Simply washing them is not enough to fully clean them. So I first briefly blanch them in salted water, which doesn't kill the flavor as you might think, but merely renders the mushrooms civilized enough to eat.

To Drink

This dish is made with port and red wine but works best with a rich, creamy white wine to match its Parmesan, cream, and earthy morels. Penner-Ash Viognier, with grapes harvested in the hot climate of Oregon's Rogue Valley, is big and complex enough to suit. Alternatively, try a Meursault from Guy Bocard in France—toasty, nutty, with hints of oak and minerality, and a long finish. **–K.P.**

Minute-Cured King Salmon, Salade Russe, and Caviar Crème Fraîche

Serves 4 to 6

What is known as Salade Russe (Russian Salad) in France is called Salade Olivier in Russia. Both are cold salads of diced vegetables and other ingredients dressed in a mayonnaise-type sauce—the luxe original, Salade Olivier, was created in Moscow by a French chef and included both lobster and caviar. I grew up eating Salade Olivier on special occasions, and learned an all-vegetable version called *macedoine de legumes* at the French Culinary Institute. So this dish is part of my own history, and my version, with caviar and crème fraîche, restores some of its original opulence. I serve it alongside silky salmon lightly cured with lemon juice and olive oil.

1 large Yukon gold potato

1/2 pound green beans, stemmed

1 large carrot, peeled and cut into 1/3-inch dice

1 large beet, roasted, peeled, and cut into 1/3-inch dice

1 large hard-boiled egg, peeled and coarsely grated on the largest holes of a box grater

2 tablespoons drained capers, coarsely chopped

1 medium dill pickle, cut into 1/3-inch dice

1 large sprig of dill, leaves stripped and coarsely chopped

1 bunch chives, finely chopped

1/2 cup Aioli (page 203)

Kosher salt and freshly ground black pepper

1/4 cup crème fraîche

1 ounce American sturgeon caviar

Juice of 1 lemon

3 tablespoons extra-virgin olive oil

1 pound wild King salmon fillet, pin bones removed (see Chef's Tip), skinned, and very thinly sliced

In a small saucepan, cover the potato with cold water and season it with salt. Bring to a boil over high heat and cook until tender when pierced with a knife (don't overcook), about 20 minutes. Cool the potato, peel, and cut into 1/3-inch dice.

Have a bowl of ice water ready. Bring another pot of water to a boil and season with salt. Add the green beans all at once and cook until tender, yet still bright green, about 5 minutes. With a slotted spoon, transfer the beans to the ice water to stop the cooking (don't discard the cooking water). Drain them and dry on paper towels. Cut into 1/3-inch lengths and set aside in a bowl.

Have a bowl of ice water ready. Cook the diced carrot until tender in the same boiling water as the green beans, about 5 minutes. Drain and refresh them in the ice water to stop the cooking. Drain them and dry on paper towels as well. Set aside in a bowl.

To make the salad, in a large bowl, combine the potato, green beans, carrot, beet, grated egg, capers, and pickle. Add the dill, chives, and aioli. Season with salt and pepper, then mix gently with a spoon to incorporate all the ingredients. Cover and set aside.

In a small bowl, combine the crème fraîche with the caviar and half of the lemon juice. Set aside. In another small bowl, whisk the rest of the lemon juice with the olive oil.

Lay all the salmon slices side by side. Brush them liberally with lemon oil, then season generously with salt and pepper. Turn the salmon slices over, brush with lemon oil, and season again. Divide the slices among individual serving plates. Spoon some caviar-crème fraîche mixture over the salmon. Place a healthy spoonful of salad next to the salmon and serve.

Leftover salad keeps well in the refrigerator and makes a perfect lunch the next day.

Chef's Tip

You can either remove the slender pin bones one by one with a pair of needle-nose pliers, or have your fishmonger do it.

Mushroom Omelet Soufflé

Makes one 8-inch omelet; serves 2

In France, they take their eggs very seriously—I remember we spent a whole week on them at the French Culinary Institute. But they don't typically eat them at breakfast, as we do. Cut in two and served with salad, this omelet makes lunch for two, or try it as an unexpected plated appetizer.

In the French tradition, I like my omelet slightly under-cooked. The trick of beating the eggs for a long time yields an omelet with a fluffy texture. This recipe calls for morels, but it is equally good if made with chanterelles, porcini, or, if the seasons align just right, a mixture of all three. Use fresh farm eggs when making this omelet for the most vibrant color and outstanding flavor. Find them at a farmer's market or at an upscale grocery store.

4 tablespoons unsalted butter

3 ounces fresh morels, cleaned (see page 13)

1 small shallot, finely minced

Kosher salt and freshly ground black pepper

3 large eggs

1/3 cup coarsely grated Gruyère or sharp cheddar cheese

1 tablespoon chopped fresh chives, for garnish

Preheat the oven to 375°F. Melt 2 tablespoons of the butter in a large skillet over medium heat. Add the mushrooms and shallot, season with salt and pepper, and cook, stirring, until the mushrooms crisp and shallots soften, about 3 minutes. Set aside and keep warm.

In a large bowl, combine the eggs and a large pinch of salt. Whisk the eggs until doubled in volume. Melt the remaining 2 tablespoons of butter in an 8-inch nonstick ovenproof skillet over low-to-medium heat. Pour in the eggs and cook, without stirring, until the bottom sets and forms a lightly colored skin, about 2 minutes.

Place the omelet in the oven and bake until it is mostly cooked, yet still retains some liquid on the surface, about 3 minutes. Remove from the oven, place the mushrooms in the center, and scatter with grated cheese to cover.

Tilt the pan slightly to the side, and fold over one third of the omelet. Tilt the pan onto a cutting board while encouraging the omelet to form a roll. Cut in two and gently transfer each half to a plate. Sprinkle with chives and serve as a first course.

Grilled Flatbreads

Makes 12 flatbreads or 1 sheet of focaccia

This versatile recipe produces delicious homemade bread two ways. As grilled flatbread, it would make a crispy, toasty, chewy, and slightly charred addition to an elegant al fresco summer feast. Baked in the oven, it's a light and tender focaccia that's perfect in any season. Serve it with Tapenade, Fava Bean Puree, or Grilled Goat Cheese Wrapped in Chestnut Leaves (recipes follow).

1 1/4 cups warm (110°F) water	1 tablespoon extra-virgin olive oil, plus more for brushing
1 1/4 teaspoons active dry yeast	1 1/2 cups all-purpose flour
1 1/2 teaspoons kosher salt	1 1/2 cups bread flour
	Sea salt, for sprinkling

In the bowl of a heavy-duty stand mixer fitted with the dough hook, combine the warm water and yeast and let rest until the top surface has a thin layer of foam, about 5 minutes.

Add the salt, the 1 tablespoon of olive oil, and both flours. Mix on low speed until the dough begins to come together, about 2 minutes. Scrape down the sides of the bowl and the dough hook and increase the speed to medium-high. Continue to mix until the dough is slightly moist, smooth, and elastic, about 6 minutes.

Form the dough into a ball (lightly oil your hands if the dough seems sticky). Place in a large oiled bowl, turning to coat with oil, and cover tightly with plastic wrap. Let the dough rise in a warm place (about 75°F) until it has doubled in size, 1 1/2 to 2 hours.

For flatbreads, have a lightly oiled baking sheet ready. Punch down the dough and divide into 12 equal portions. Form the pieces into balls and place on the prepared baking sheet. Cover with a clean, dry kitchen towel and let rise for 30 minutes.

Preheat an outdoor grill to high, letting it get extremely hot. It's ready when you can't hold your hand 5 inches from the grate for more than 2 seconds.

Generously oil a baking sheet. Flatten 1 ball of dough into a disk and place on the baking sheet (the oil will allow the dough to crisp and keep it from sticking as it's stretched into shape). Using the fingers and palms of your hands and gentle pressure, stretch the dough to an oval about 8 inches long and 1/4 inch thick. A few small tears are fine—they add to the bread's rustic charm.

Using both hands, lift the dough from the baking sheet and drape it on the grill over the hottest part of the fire. Watch it carefully: within a minute, the underside of the dough will get crispy, dark, and firm, and the top will puff slightly. Lightly brush the surface with oil and turn the dough over with tongs. Cook until the underside is slightly charred, another minute or so. Remove from the grill and repeat with the remaining dough balls. Sprinkle the flatbreads with sea salt, slice crosswise, and serve.

To make focaccia, punch the dough down after the first rise and roll it out on a well-oiled rimmed baking sheet or pan that measures anywhere from 9 by 13 inches to 12 by 16 inches. The larger pan will give you a thin, crispy focaccia not unlike a pizza crust, while the smaller will produce one that is thicker and more breadlike that could be split to make a sandwich. Cover the pan with plastic wrap, and let the dough rise in a warm spot (about 75°F) for 30 minutes.

Preheat the oven to 350°F. Gently coax the dough into the corners of the baking sheet, trying to keep the dough evenly thick all over. Lightly dimple the dough with your fingers, drizzle with more olive oil, and sprinkle with salt. Bake until pale golden and crispy, about 30 minutes.

Focaccia tastes best if baked and served the same day, although it can be baked and frozen for about a week. To serve, thaw and reheat in a 350°F oven.

Fava Bean Puree

Makes about 1³/4 cups

Fresh fava beans, to my mind the perfect culinary expression of early summer, are doubly concealed. They nest inside thick and furry pods and are cloaked by a thin skin. To enjoy, they must first be shucked, then cooked and the skin peeled away to reveal the bright green and tender beans. We call this dish "favanade" for its similiarities to tapenade. I find fava beans even more perfect when pureed. If you prefer them whole, just toss all the ingredients together and enjoy a lively salad.

Kosher salt

3 pounds fresh fava beans, shucked

1/4 cup grated Parmesan cheese

1/2 cup extra-virgin olive oil

Juice of 1 lemon

5 large fresh mint leaves

3 cloves garlic, finely chopped

Freshly ground black pepper

Have a bowl of ice water ready. Fill a saucepan with salted water and bring to a boil over medium-high heat. Add the shucked beans all at once and cook for 2 minutes. Refresh them in the ice-water bath to stop the cooking. Break open the outer membrane with your fingernails and gently squeeze to pop the bean out.

In the work bowl of a food processor fitted with the metal blade, combine the beans, Parmesan cheese, olive oil, lemon juice, mint leaves, and garlic. Puree until smooth, scraping down the sides of the bowl as needed. Generously season with salt and pepper. Cover and refrigerate until ready to serve. The puree is best when served within a couple of hours of being made.

Tapenade

Makes 1¹/4 cups

This recipe was taught to me by a cook from Nice, and I have prepared it for years. He told me that in Provence it is referred to as "black butter." In Nice, this delicious appetizer is made with the addition of tuna.

4 anchovy fillets, drained

3 tablespoons drained capers

2 cloves garlic

1/3 cup good-quality tuna packed in olive oil, well drained

3 sprigs of thyme, leaves only, chopped

1 large sprig of summer savory, leaves only, chopped

Juice of 1/2 lemon

1/4 cup plus 3 tablespoons extra-virgin olive oil

1/2 pound niçoise or kalamata olives, pitted

Kosher salt and freshly ground black pepper

In the work bowl of a food processor fitted with the metal blade, add the anchovies, capers, garlic, tuna, thyme, savory, lemon juice, and the 1/4 cup of olive oil. Puree to a smooth paste. Scrape down the sides of the bowl as needed. Add the olives, and pulse until coarsely textured and incorporated into the mixture. Transfer the mixture to a small bowl; drizzle in the remaining olive oil and stir to incorporate. Season with salt and pepper. Transfer to a small serving bowl, cover, and refrigerate up to a day ahead of serving. Bring to room temperature before serving as the oil congeals when cold.

Grilled Goat Cheese Wrapped in Chestnut Leaves

Serves 4

I discovered a wonderful-looking goat cheese at a local market. It was marinated in plum brandy, sprinkled lightly with cracked black pepper, and wrapped in chestnut leaves. At home, I warmed it on the grill, then unwrapped it and served it with flatbread. The texture was creamy and the taste divine.

The next day I went back to the store for more, but sadly all were gone. I decided to try to replicate it, using a small log of fresh goat cheese, leaves from a chestnut tree in my front yard, and good Kirschwasser and black peppercorns from my pantry. It's not quite the same, but it made its way onto the restaurant's menu and stayed on as long as the chestnut tree supplied the leaves. Fresh grape leaves are an alternative, or you may simply place the marinated cheese unwrapped under a hot broiler for about 15 seconds, or in a 350°F oven for 5 minutes. Wrap the cheese a day or two in advance of grilling to allow all the flavors to come together nicely. If grilling is not an option, warm the wrapped cheese briefly in an oven to melt the center.

3-ounce log fresh goat cheese, halved crosswise	2 mature chestnut or grape leaves, stems snipped, washed, and dried
Large dash of Kirshwasser or your favorite fruit brandy	Extra-virgin olive oil, for drizzling
1 teaspoon whole black peppercorns, cracked	Large pinch of coarse sea salt, for sprinkling

Prepare the cheese for grilling 1 or 2 days before you want to serve it. Place the 2 rounds of goat cheese side by side on a small plate. Drizzle both with Kirschwasser, then sprinkle with cracked pepper. Turn the rounds over and repeat. Place 1 of the leaves on a work surface, then criss-cross it with another. Lay 1 round of cheese in the center, sprinkle with some of the marinade drained off the plate the cheese rounds sat on and fold the leaves over the cheese to enclose it. Secure with a toothpick. Repeat with the other piece of cheese and the remaining leaves. Refrigerate if not grilling right away.

When ready to serve, preheat an outdoor grill. Lightly brush the goat cheese packets with olive oil. Place them over a cooler part of the grill just to warm them, about 1 minute per side. Unwrap carefully, drizzle with olive oil, sprinkle with sea salt, and serve.

Chef's Tip

If you can't find a three-ounce log of goat cheese, buy one that is tasty and firm and cut it to the size you need. You can wrap the leftover cheese with fresh chestnut leaves and save for another day. The wrapped goat cheese only improves with age.

To Drink

Grassy fava beans, salty olives, and tangy goat cheese all call out for a sparkler. I like Oregon's Argyle Brut or a St. Innocent Sparkling (both creamy and citrusy), or the Crémant de Loire, Brut NV from Domaine des Baumard (our sparkling house wine at the restaurant)—clean, with uncomplicated green citrus aromas. Alternatively, my beloved Bandol Rosé from Domaine Tempier in Provence is versatile enough for any of these appetizers. **–K.P.**

Grilled Figs Wrapped in Prosciutto

Serves 4

Toward the end of August we get a burst of late-summer figs. They can be eaten straight from the tree, made into preserves, or baked in a tart. But I like them as the star of this simple, elegant grilled appetizer that I finish with a drizzle of fruity olive oil.

4 firm, ripe black or green figs, halved lengthwise

Extra-virgin olive oil

Kosher salt and freshly ground pepper

4 slices prosciutto, halved lengthwise

4 large fresh mint leaves, coarsely chopped, for garnish

Preheat an outdoor grill. Lightly brush the figs with olive oil and season with salt and pepper. Grill briefly over hot coals on both sides to warm them and caramelize their sugars, about 1 minute per side.

Wrap the grilled figs with prosciutto. Drizzle with a bit of olive oil and top with a few more grindings of pepper. Sprinkle with mint and serve right away.

Walla Walla Onion Tart with Fresh Goat Cheese and Summer Herb Pesto

Makes one 10-inch tart; serves 8

One story has it that over 100 years ago, a French soldier brought an onion bulb from Corsica to Washington State and planted it in the Walla Walla Valley. It took, grew, and blossomed into the state's official vegetable, prized for its remarkably high sugar content and incomparable flavor. Since the Walla Walla Valley extends into Oregon, this onion is as much at home here as across the border. This tart helps realize the onion's sweet potential. The pesto replaces the usual pine nuts with a prized Oregon crop—hazelnuts.

1 1/4 cups all-purpose flour, plus more for dusting	Kosher salt and freshly ground black pepper
1/2 teaspoon salt	3 large eggs
1/2 cup (1 stick) plus 2 tablespoons cold unsalted butter, diced	1/2 cup heavy cream
4 to 5 tablespoons cold water	1/3 cup grated Parmesan cheese
1/4 cup plus 2 tablespoons extra-virgin olive oil	3 tablespoons balsamic vinegar
2 pounds Walla Walla onions, halved and thinly sliced	4 ounces fresh goat cheese, crumbled
1 bay leaf	Summer Herb Pesto (recipe follows), for accompaniment

To prepare the dough, in a bowl, sift together the 1 1/4 cups flour and the 1/2 teaspoon salt, then place in the work bowl of a food processor fitted with the metal blade. Add the butter and pulse until the mixture resembles coarse cornmeal. Add the water 1 tablespoon at a time and pulse just until mixture comes together. Turn out the dough onto a work surface, gather into a ball, wrap in plastic wrap, and refrigerate for at least 1 hour. The dough can also be made 1 day in advance and kept refrigerated. Bring it to room temperature before rolling it out.

To prepare the onions, in a large skillet, heat 5 tablespoons of the olive oil over medium heat. Add the sliced onions and bay leaf, and season generously with salt and pepper. Stir frequently until the onions soften, pick up color, and the liquid they release has evaporated, about 30 minutes. Set aside to cool.

Preheat the oven to 375°F. Spray a 10-inch tart pan with removable bottom with nonstick vegetable spray.

To form the tart shell, roll out the pastry on a flour-dusted work surface to form a 1/4-inch-thick disk that is slightly larger in diameter than the tart pan. Carefully arrange the pastry in the tart pan. Roll a rolling pin across the rim of the tart pan to trim off any overhanging pastry. Prick the bottom of the pastry several times with a fork.

Carefully lay waxed paper on the pastry and weight it with dried beans or raw rice. Bake the unfilled shell until the pastry is golden around the edges and set, about 45 minutes.

While the tart shell bakes, assemble the custard. In a large bowl, combine the eggs, cream, balsamic vinegar, Parmesan, and the remaining 1 tablespoon of olive oil. Season generously with salt and pepper and whisk all ingredients together. Reserve.

Let the blind-baked tart shell cool partially on a wire rack. Carefully remove the paper and weights from the tart pan. Return the tart shell to the oven and bake again until the crust is uniformly golden in color, another 10 minutes.

Remove the baked tart shell from the oven and set on a baking sheet. Fill the crust with the cooked onions, distributing them evenly. Pour in the custard and top evenly with crumbled goat cheese. Return it to the oven and bake until the top is lightly browned and the custard is set, about 45 minutes. Cool the tart in the pan on a wire rack for 15 minutes.

Carefully remove the pan sides. Serve the tart sliced into wedges and topped with a dollop of pesto. Leftover tart and pesto can be stored, covered and refrigerated, for another day or so.

Summer Herb Pesto

Makes 1¹/₂ cups

1 bunch basil, picked and washed

1 bunch dill, picked

1 bunch mint, picked and washed

1 bunch chives, coarsely chopped

2 cloves garlic, peeled and finely minced

¹/₄ cup grated Parmesan cheese

¹/₄ cup roasted hazelnuts

³/₄ cup extra-virgin olive oil

Juice of 1 lemon

Kosher salt and freshly ground pepper

Place all ingredients except salt and pepper into the work bowl of a food processor fitted with the metal blade. Puree until smooth. Season with salt and pepper. Refrigerate until needed (it is best used within an hour of serving).

To Drink

A crisp Alsatian-style white wine with a slice of this Walla Walla onion tart spells summer. Marcel Deiss's Pinot Blanc from Alsace has a subtle note of pear that is delightful with the crust's baked-bread aromas. Alternatively, the easy-drinking Ayres Pinot Blanc from Oregon's northern Willamette Valley has crisp acidity with a hint of sweetness to match and temper the sweet caramelized onions, rich buttery crust, and grassy pesto. **–K.P.**

Curried Squash and Goat Cheese Fritters with Green Goddess Dipping Sauce

Serves 4 to 6

We make these fritters in the summer with zucchini and in the winter with butternut squash. Curry gives the dish an exotic spice kick, and the goat cheese moderates the flavor.

Green goddess dressing, named after a 1920s stage play, is an American original now making a comeback. It is loaded with pungent herbs that give the dressing a bright clean flavor and a beautiful pale color. It provides cool contrast to the hot fritters and leaves a fresh, luxurious sensation in your mouth. Chickpea flour brings the dish together; it's available in many ethnic, upscale, and co-op groceries.

1 pound summer squash (such as zucchini), ends trimmed	3 tablespoons Persillade (page 198)
Kosher salt and freshly ground black pepper	2 large eggs, lightly beaten
1 1/2 teaspoons curry powder	1/4 cup chickpea flour or all-purpose flour
2 ounces fresh goat cheese	Canola oil, for deep-frying
1/2 onion, finely diced	Green Goddess Dipping Sauce (recipe follows), for accompaniment

Using a box grater, coarsely grate the squash into a large bowl. Sprinkle with 1 tablespoon of salt and mix and squeeze with your hands. When the squash begins to leach liquid, hold up a handful over the sink and squeeze to remove as much water as you can. Place it into another bowl. Repeat until all the squash has been wrung dry.

In the bowl with the squash, add the curry powder, goat cheese, onion, persillade, and eggs. Mix with a wooden spoon until well incorporated. Sprinkle with the flour and season with a few grindings of pepper. Mix until all the flour has been absorbed.

Use a heavy-bottomed soup pot large enough to accommodate a batch of fritters without crowding. Fill the pot with about 3 inches of oil. Heat the oil over high heat until it reaches 325°F on a deep-fat thermometer. Decrease the heat to maintain the oil at that temperature.

Fry the fritters in batches of 5 or 6 and serve them hot from the pot. For each fritter, scoop up a heaping soupspoon of batter and carefully drop it into the hot oil. Fry until golden brown all over, flipping them once or twice to ensure even cooking, about 7 minutes. With a slotted spoon, remove them from the fat to paper towels to drain. Continue deep-frying until all the batter has been used. If the oil cools below 325°F, return it to 325°F before continuing. Sprinkle with salt and serve immediately after frying with a bowl of green goddess sauce for dipping.

Green Goddess Dipping Sauce

Makes about 1 1/2 cups

1/4 cup fresh basil leaves	1/2 cup sour cream
1/4 cup dill fronds	4 anchovy fillets, drained
1/4 cup fresh tarragon leaves	3 tablespoons cider vinegar or white wine vinegar
1/4 cup fresh Italian parsley leaves	1/4 cup buttermilk
1/4 cup fresh mint leaves	Kosher salt and freshly ground black pepper
1/2 cup Aioli (page 203)	

Combine all ingredients except salt and pepper in a blender and liquefy. Season with salt and pepper. Transfer to a small container, cover, and refrigerate until ready to use. Green goddess tastes best when freshly made, but will keep overnight, tightly covered and refrigerated. Any leftover dressing is delicious on a salad or as a sauce for fish or chicken.

Speaking in Tongues

There are a million ways a chef's memory, training, experience, and inspiration can coalesce into the creation of a new dish. This is the story of Crisp Pan-fried Lamb's Tongue with Spicy Saffron Aioli (page 27).

Once, while Kimberly and I were dining at Union restaurant in Seattle, chef Ethan Stowell joined us at the table. Ethan shares my love of obscure cuts of meat and told me that night about the butcher who sells lamb's tongue at Seattle's famous Pike Place Market. My mind filled with memories: the tongue sandwiches on rye with mustard that I'd eaten at the Second Avenue Deli in New York; my father taking me to a deli in Brighton Beach in Brooklyn where I ordered beef tongue with pickles; a Spanish dish of pan-fried tongue with a tantalizing spicy dipping sauce. It occurred to me that lamb's tongue— which I'd never worked with before—might provide the perfect way to introduce tongue at our restaurant and satisfy my own craving. The next morning, Kimberly and I went to Pike Place Market and came away with four pounds (about twenty tongues).

Back in my kitchen, I decide that I will brine the tongues before poaching them in a court bouillon. Brining is a better method than surface seasoning for developing flavor in dense meats like tongue (a technique I first learned from my grandmother). Poaching in a court bouillon—a very gentle way of cooking—will ensure tenderness.

Once the tongues are poached, I'll bread and fry them and serve them with a spicy aioli, using eggs from Golden Gait farm, one of our regular suppliers.

I prepare the brine by boiling water with salt, sugar, cinnamon, bay leaves, and black peppercorns. Once the sugar and salt dissolve, the pot comes off the heat to cool. The tongues are immersed in the brine; I will refrigerate them for twenty-four hours.

The next day, I make a court bouillon. I mix white wine and water in a pot large enough to hold the tongues, then add a carrot, an onion stuck with a clove, salt, and peppercorns. As a rule, bringing the liquid to a boil prior to adding the meat helps enrich the flavor of the meat; after the bouillon boils, I decrease the heat to low and simmer it for thirty minutes to develop its flavors. Then I submerge the tongues, cooking them gently for about two hours. I know they are done when the paring knife I insert into a tongue meets with no resistance. I remove the tongues from the cooking liquid and place them on a cutting board to cool slightly. They will be much easier to peel when cool enough to handle but still warm.

Tongue consists of an outer membrane and inner meat. The heat of cooking causes the outer membrane to separate from the meat. I begin peeling where I see separation, using a small, sharp paring knife to clean away all the membrane. I also remove all traces of bone, cartilage, and fat from the thicker, root end of each tongue.

The tongues could be eaten at this stage, simply sliced and served with pickles and mustard. I have other plans for them, so I set them aside while I make the aioli.

Aioli made by hand has a dramatically different texture than one made by machine. I opt for the motion of the pestle, which allows me to achieve an aioli with a custard-like texture. (A whip or machine would yield the airy texture of a mousse.) The flavor of olive oil is also altered by high-speed emulsions, which create an aggressive taste that tends toward bitterness.

Patience and care are the keys to successfully building an aioli, because the egg used in the sauce requires time to absorb the oil. I find it very pleasing to experience how the saffron lends its color, and the lemon broadens the taste of the sauce while lightening the oil, how the garlic adds its spicy kick, and cayenne its stimulating warmth. The results I get from the mortar and pestle always feel worth the effort. The oil maintains a flavor quality that old French cooks might have identified as *plus agréable*, and the final sauce is sunshine yellow and silken.

I select a straight-sided skillet large enough to hold all the tongues. As I pour oil into the skillet for frying I have two things in mind: I want the meat to develop a uniform golden color, yet I don't want the bread crumbs to burn. Once the tongues go into the pan, I don't fuss or poke them while they fry, but leave them to cook for about 45 seconds to a minute per side before turning them over. If they need more color, I turn and cook them until the crumbs are the color I want. I remove the tongues from the pan, set them on a bed of paper towels to absorb some of the oil, and sprinkle them generously with salt. I place them on the cutting board and cut them into thick, diagonal slices. I arrange the slices on a plate and nestle a bowl of aioli sauce beside them. I taste. The spicy Spanish flavors electrify the rich tastes of aioli and tongue, the sauce velvety and smooth from my patient work with the pestle, the pan-fried tongue crisp to the bite with a soft center. It is just as I had imagined, and will make a satisfying addition to our menu.

Crisp Pan-Fried Lamb's Tongue with Spicy Saffron Aioli

Serves 6

Lamb tongue may not be available at your supermarket. You'll have better luck at a meat market staffed with butchers (not meat vendors), or an ethnic market such as Basque, Italian, Middle Eastern, kosher, or Hispanic. Note that the tongue must sit in brine overnight before you use it.

Brine

1 cup kosher salt

1/4 cup sugar

4 quarts cold water

1 2-inch cinnamon stick

5 bay leaves

1/4 cup whole black peppercorns

6 whole lamb tongues (about 1 1/2 pounds total)

Court Bouillon

1/2 (750-ml) bottle dry white wine

4 cups cold water

1 large carrot, peeled and coarsely chopped

1 onion

1 whole clove

1 teaspoon kosher salt

1/4 cup whole black peppercorns

Spicy Saffron Aioli

Aioli (page 203)

Large pinch of cayenne pepper

Large pinch of saffron threads

1 cup all-purpose flour

2 tablespoons pimentón (smoky Spanish paprika)

Pinch of cayenne pepper

1 teaspoon sea salt

1 teaspoon freshly ground black pepper

3 large eggs

1 cup fine bread crumbs (see page 138)

Grapeseed oil, for pan-frying

Sea salt, for sprinkling

In a large pot, combine all the brine ingredients and bring to a rolling boil over high heat. Remove from the heat and let the mixture cool to room temperature. Place the tongues in a storage container, pour over the brine, cover, and refrigerate for 24 hours.

When ready to cook, remove the tongues from the brine, drain, and reserve, discarding the brine.

To prepare the court bouillon, in a 3-quart pot, combine the wine, the 4 cups water, carrot, onion, clove, salt, and peppercorns, and bring the liquid to a boil over high heat. Reduce temperature to low and simmer, uncovered, until the broth develops flavor, about 30 minutes.

To poach the tongues, slip them into the broth and simmer gently, uncovered, until they are tender enough that a knife inserts easily into the meat, about 2 hours. Remove them to a cutting board. To reuse the poaching liquid, strain it into a heatproof container, cool it in an ice-water bath, and refrigerate; it will keep for about a week.

While the tongues are still warm, place them on a cutting board and trim away any gristle, fat, and bone. Use a small paring knife to separate the outer membrane to reveal the inner meat. Reserve.

To prepare the Spicy Saffron Aioli, follow the recipe for Aioli (page 203), adding the cayenne and saffron to the garlic paste in the mortar and continue to mash the paste until the saffron turns the mixture bright orange, about 1 more minute. Continue with the recipe as written.

To bread the tongues, arrange 3 small bowls side by side. Sift together the flour, pimentón, cayenne, sea salt, and black pepper into the first bowl. Add the eggs to the second bowl and beat them with a fork until frothy. Place the crumbs in the third bowl.

Have a wire rack ready. Dredge 1 tongue evenly in the flour mixture, shaking off any excess. Drop the flour-coated tongue into the egg bowl. With your other hand (I work with one hand for dry ingredients, the other for wet to keep the flour and crumbs from clumping), transfer it from the egg bowl to the crumb bowl, turning to coat evenly. Transfer to the wire rack. Repeat with the remaining pieces of meat.

Line a plate with paper towels and have ready. To cook the tongues, in a large heavy-bottomed skillet (of a size to hold all 6 pieces without crowding), heat 1/2 inch of grapeseed oil over high heat until it reaches 350°F on a deep-fat thermometer.

Crisp Pan-Fried Lamb's Tongue with Spicy Saffron Aioli, *continued*

Decrease the heat to medium-high, place all the breaded tongues in the oil at the same time, and fry, turning once, until they are uniformly golden, 45 seconds to 1 minute per side. Watch that the crumbs don't burn. When done, transfer them to the prepared plate and season with a light sprinkling of sea salt.

For each serving, on a cutting board, slice 1 tongue diagonally into finger-thick slices. Arrange the slices on a plate, and serve without delay, accompanied by a small bowl of aioli.

To Drink

With this dish, try a Soter North Valley Oregon Rosé from the Yamhill-Carlton growing area of the Willamette Valley. Hints of raspberry and cranberry play off the rich, gamy flavor of the tongue, while low acid and a subtle sweetness complement the smoky-spicy aioli. Easy drinking.   **–K.P.**

Escargots Bordelaise with Roast Marrow Bones

Serves 4

This dish combines marrow with earthy snails in a rich red wine sauce. It has become such a popular appetizer that I do not dare take it off the menu.

Marrow bones should be available at any quality butcher shop. When you place your order, ask the butcher to cut them to size for you. Start this recipe a day ahead as you will need to soak the bones in water for at least twenty-four hours before cooking to get rid of residual blood.

Outside of France there are literally no fresh snails available. After years of searching I finally found snails worthy enough for use at the restaurant. And without shame, I admit the best part—they are canned! Just open the can, and they are ready to use. They are available by mail order (see Resources, page 222).

8 marrow bones, cut into 2- to 3-inch lengths	24 snails, drained
12 cloves garlic	1 cup Sauce Bordelaise, My Way (page 215)
1 cup extra-virgin olive oil	Kosher salt and freshly ground black pepper
1 small onion, thinly sliced	
5 sprigs of thyme	1/4 cup Persillade (page 198), for garnish
4 thick slices Brioche (page 216), crusts removed	Sea salt, for garnish

A day ahead of cooking, place the marrow bones in a large bowl and add enough cold water to cover them by 1 or 2 inches. Seal the bowl with plastic wrap and refrigerate at least 24 hours. Drain the bones and pat them dry. With a sturdy knife, scrape the membrane from around the marrow bones. Set aside.

Line a plate with paper towels and have ready. In a small saucepan, cover the garlic cloves with olive oil and cook them over low heat until soft, about 20 minutes. Transfer the cloves to the prepared plate and let them cool. Reserve the oil for another use.

Preheat the oven to 400°F. Arrange the onion slices evenly on a rimmed baking sheet, and scatter with the thyme branches. Set the marrow bones upright on the onion-herb layer. Roast until the tops of the bones brown and bubble, about 20 minutes. Remove from the oven, cover loosely with aluminum foil to keep warm, and reserve.

Arrange the brioche slices on another baking sheet and toast in the oven until golden brown, about 10 minutes. Alternatively, grill them on a hot grill for 30 seconds per side, until distinct grill marks are visible and the brioche is warmed through.

To make the sauce, in a 12-inch skillet, add the snails and garlic, then the bordelaise sauce. Season with salt and pepper. Warm over low heat for about 10 minutes, stirring occasionally, to concentrate the flavors.

To serve, place an equal amount of cooked bones in the center of 4 small soup bowls. Spoon the snails, garlic, and their sauce evenly around the bones. Arrange the toast, persillade, and sea salt on the side, and serve immediately.

To Drink

Vitaly prepares his escargots Bordeaux-style, with a rich sauce grounded by sweet roasted garlic. It pairs beautifully with Bordeaux grape varietals, such as Cabernet Sauvignon, Cabernet Franc, and Merlot. Columbia Valley and Yakima Valley in Washington produce red wines that have the heft to stand up to this sauce. I recommend Zanzibar Cellars or Andrew Will, Sheridan Vineyard. I would also recommend a French Bordeaux, such as a Cru Bourgeois from Saint-Estèphe or Saint-Émilion, whose flavor profiles have a softer fruit structure than their Washington counterparts. **–K.P.**

Chapter 2
Soups, Sandwiches, and Salads

Dungeness Crab and Corn Chowder

Makes about 8 cups; serves 6 to 8

Crab and corn is one of my favorite combinations. I remember making lobster and corn chowder when I worked at Union Square Café in Manhattan. With this recipe, which uses Dungeness crab caught along the Oregon coast, I aim to capture the spirit of the Pacific Northwest and give a nod to my East Coast roots. I serve this chowder with Cheddar Cheese Biscuits (page 218).

Crab Broth

1/4 cup extra-virgin olive oil

Shells from 2 Dungeness crabs (see page 214)

1 yellow onion, coarsely diced

1 large carrot, peeled and coarsely diced

1 leek, green part only (reserve white part for chowder)

2 large corn cobs (reserve corn kernels for chowder)

4 sprigs of thyme

1/4 teaspoon cumin seed, toasted and ground

1/4 teaspoon coriander seed, toasted and ground

Pinch of cayenne pepper

2 tablespoons tomato paste

2 cups dry white wine

8 cups Corn Broth (page 206) or water

Kosher salt and freshly ground black pepper

2 tablespoons extra-virgin olive oil

6 ounces Smoked Bacon (page 204), cut into 1/2-inch dice

2 leeks, white parts only, quartered lengthwise and cut into small dice

1 carrot, peeled and cut into small dice

2 tablespoons all-purpose flour

6 small yellow fleshed potatoes, peeled and cut into 1/2-inch dice

Corn kernels from 2 ears of corn

1 cup heavy cream

Dungeness crab meat from 2 cooked crabs (see page 214), for garnish

2 tablespoons Persillade (page 198), for garnish

To prepare the crab broth, in an 8-quart soup pot, cook the olive oil and crab shells over high heat, stirring to thoroughly coat the shells with oil, about 5 minutes. Add the onion, carrot, leek greens, and corn cobs and cook until the vegetables brown slightly, about 5 minutes. Sprinkle with thyme, cumin, coriander, and cayenne. Cook, stirring, to bloom the spices, about 3 minutes. Stir in the tomato paste. Add the wine, decrease the heat to medium, and cook until the liquid reduces by half, about 10 minutes.

Add the 8 cups of corn broth and simmer until the flavor of crab is pronounced, about 1 hour. Season to taste with salt and freshly ground black pepper.

Strain everything through a colander set over a large bowl, pressing the solids to extract the maximum amount of liquid. Measure 8 cups for the base of the chowder, and set aside. If any broth remains, store it for another use.

To make the chowder, in a 6-quart soup pot, heat the olive oil over medium heat. Add the bacon and cook, stirring occasionally, until slightly browned, about 5 minutes. Add the diced leek whites and the carrot and cook, stirring, until the carrot pieces have softened slightly, another 5 minutes. Sprinkle with flour and stir until well mixed. Add the 8 cups reserved crab broth, then the potatoes and corn kernels. Bring to a simmer over medium heat. Add cream, reduce the heat to low and simmer gently until the potatoes are tender, about 15 minutes.

When ready to serve, divide between soup bowls, top with the reserved crab meat, garnish with persillade, and serve at once.

Curried Butternut Squash and Pear Bisque

Makes about 6 cups; serves 4 to 6

This soup is so easy to make, as it uses water instead of stock. Water lets the squash realize its full potential here. Pears, winter squash, and apple cider all appear on farm stands at about the same time, and their varying degrees of sweetness have a natural affinity for one another. Curry powder adds an exotic kick and helps balance the sweetness of the other ingredients.

1/4 cup extra-virgin olive oil

1 large onion, halved and thinly sliced

1 1/2 pounds butternut squash, peeled, seeds and strings scooped out, and cut in 1-inch cubes

1 large pear, preferably Bosc, peeled, halved, cored, and coarsely chopped

Kosher salt and freshly ground black pepper

4 1/2 teaspoons mild curry powder

1 cup apple cider

3 cups water

1 cup heavy cream

Crème fraîche, for garnish

Dill sprigs, for garnish

In a 6-quart soup pot, heat the olive oil over medium heat. Sauté the onion, stirring frequently, until soft, about 5 minutes. Add the squash and pear and season with salt and pepper. Decrease the heat to low and cook, stirring occasionally, until the squash softens and slightly caramelizes, about 15 minutes.

Add the curry powder and continue stirring for 1 minute to let the curry flavors bloom. Pour in the apple cider. Increase the heat to medium, add the 3 cups water, and simmer until the squash is completely cooked through, about 30 minutes.

Stir in the cream and return the soup to a simmer. Season with salt and pepper. In batches, carefully liquefy the hot soup in a blender.

To serve, pour the soup into bowls and garnish with a dollop of crème fraîche and dill sprigs.

This soup can be made a day in advance, cooked in an ice-water bath, and refrigerated overnight.

Chef's Tip

I always season long preparations like soups or stews at the beginning of the cooking and adjust to taste at the end. Seasoning early means the salt and pepper get absorbed more evenly for a more balanced and uniform flavor.

Consommé, the Culinary Miracle

Consommé strikes me as the model of classic French refinement—its very name derives from *consommer*, French for "to complete." It is a dish whose final, pure, and perfect form makes every deliberate, precise step required for success a pleasure.

Given how much work goes into the preparation of this aromatic liquid, I always feature it prominently on a menu. Winter menus present consommé with shaved truffles and roasted root vegetables. In spring, consommé accompanies the first seasonal vegetables, such as asparagus and morel mushrooms. Personally, I prefer the flavor of consommé made with game meats like venison or rabbit, but I also like it with birds such as pheasant, duck, or chicken. When preparing crab or lobster dishes, I favor a consommé conjured from their shells.

Oxtail consommé, perhaps the best known of them all, is made from beef tails. Tail meat imparts rich flavor, and the gelatin from the bones produces an elegant texture. However, I would not recommend that home cooks try an oxtail consommé on their first attempt, because it can be temperamental. If the liquid boils during the preparation, the gelatin can bond with solids and fat molecules, causing the stock to become irreparably cloudy. Instead, begin with a rich, golden Chicken Consommé (page 39).

To make chicken consommé, the first step is to make Chicken Stock (page 213). I select a heavy-bottomed pot large enough to hold the meats, bones, and vegetables without crowding. For the vegetables, I choose celery root rather than stalk celery because it provides a more pronounced flavor. I bone a four-pound chicken, separating leg and breast meat (see page 208). The leg meat will be dedicated to making the "raft"—a mixture of egg white, vegetables, and meat used to clarify the stock. The breast could be poached in the finished consommé or used in another recipe.

The bones, neck, and giblets go into the pot along with the peeled, coarsely chopped vegetables; fresh thyme, parsley, and bay leaf; and salt and a handful of peppercorns. I add white wine for flavor and just enough cold water to cover the ingredients in the pot. Too much water dilutes the finished product; with the proper amount of water, the finished consommé will jell when cold. Once the liquid comes to a boil, I lower the temperature so the mixture barely simmers and let it cook for 1$^1/_2$ hours—slow cooking extracts more flavor into the stock.

What never changes is the need to skim the stock religiously. If left untouched, the foam and solid particles can cloud the stock. When the stock has cooked sufficiently and developed the flavor I want, it comes off the stove and is strained. The bones are discarded, and the liquid is made to cool quickly in an ice-water bath before chilling overnight in the refrigerator.

The next day, I scoop off the hardened fat that has formed on the surface of the chilled stock. To clarify the stock, choose a pot that is tall and narrow. It should be large enough to hold twice the amount of stock you will put in it and to give the raft room to float. It should also have a thick bottom, which will heat more evenly and will help prevent the egg whites from sticking.

The defatted stock is then poured into the pot and warmed gently, just until it melts. Meanwhile, I prepare the raft by grinding leg meat and vegetables and mixing them with egg whites that have been whipped until frothy. Broken bits of eggshells can also be mixed with the whites to provide the extra bonding protein needed to clarify the stock. The finished mix of meat, vegetables, and egg whites constitutes the raft. Adding seasoning to it—salt and pepper—helps flavor the clarifying liquid.

Before adding the raft to the warm stock, it must be brought to the same temperature as the stock (a technique called tempering) because otherwise the egg whites would coagulate and harden if subjected to rapid heating. To accomplish this, I slowly whisk in a ladleful of warm stock to the egg white mixture. Then I slip the mixture into the stockpot and let the stock slowly come up to a simmer, whisking occasionally to prevent the egg whites from sticking to the bottom of the pot. (If the egg whites sink and stick, they would not efficiently gather all the bits into the raft and the liquid would not be as clear.)

After a while, a solid mass—the raft—will begin to form on the surface of the liquid. As the egg whites warm, they rise, gathering and trapping solids and impurities with them. I look for a tiny stream of foamy liquid seeping through the top of the raft, like a geyser ready to burst. I allow that action to continue for a few minutes, then poke a bigger hole to encourage a percolating action. As the liquid passes over the raft, it leaches flavor back into the liquid. The foaming subsides as the raft hardens. When the liquid goes clear, the stock has been transformed into consommé.

Always taste the consommé before straining to confirm a rich level of flavor. Don't hesitate to cook it longer if the flavor is weak. Ladle the liquid carefully through a fine-mesh strainer lined with cheesecloth. At this point, it is ready to assume its role as the star attraction.

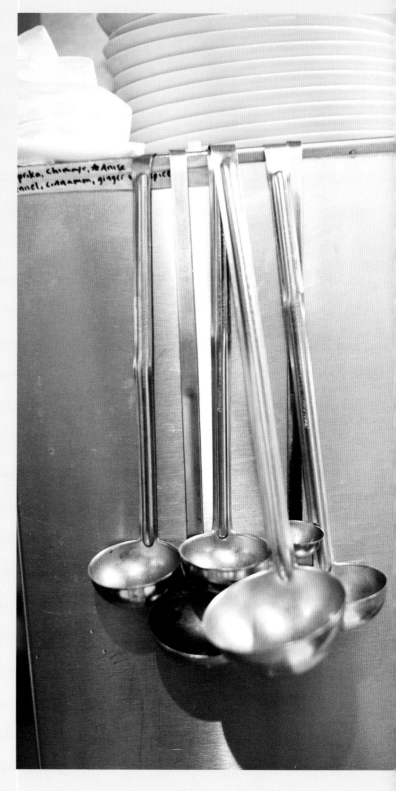

Chicken Consommé

Makes about 8 cups

12 cups Chicken Stock (page 213)

2 chicken legs, boned and skinned (see page 208), or 1 pound lean ground chicken meat (ground without fat or skin)

1 small onion, cut into large dice

1 small carrot, peeled and sliced into rounds

5 sprigs of Italian parsley, leaves only

10 sprigs of thyme, leaves only

1 tablespoon kosher salt, plus more for seasoning

1 tablespoon freshly ground black pepper

Whites and crushed shells from 8 large eggs

In a heavy-bottomed 6-quart soup pot, gently warm the stock over low heat. Maintain its warmth, testing the temperature of the stock with an instant-read thermometer to ensure it doesn't rise above 120°F.

While the stock warms, prepare the chicken and vegetables. In the work bowl of a food processor fitted with the metal blade, place the chicken, onion, carrot, parsley, thyme, salt, and pepper. Pulse until the vegetables are the size of a lentil. Do not puree.

In a large bowl, whisk together the egg whites and crushed eggshells until frothy. Add the chopped chicken and vegetables and whisk to combine. Whisk in 1 cup of warm stock to the eggs; repeat 2 or 3 times.

Slide the egg white–stock mixture into the remaining warm stock. Let simmer, whisking frequently (so the whites don't separate and sink to the bottom of the pot where they can stick), until a solid mass (the "raft") begins to form on the surface of the stock, about 30 minutes. Stop whisking and simmer for about 15 minutes more.

At this point, small amounts of steam will try to break through the raft, creating little holes. To facilitate the release of steam, insert the handle of a wooden spoon into an opening, and gently widen one of the holes. As the liquid percolates through the opening, it flavors the stock. The raft in turn gathers any solids and clarifies the liquid. It can take another 30 minutes for the foam to subside and the liquid to become clear.

Taste the clear liquid coming off the top of the raft to ensure the flavor is rich enough for your taste. Don't hesitate to cook the consommé longer or to season it more if its flavor is not what you think it can be.

Line a strainer with cheesecloth and set it over the container in which you will store the consommé. Have a bowl of ice water ready. When the consommé is done to your liking, ladle the liquid gently into the strainer, letting it flow through without pressing. Discard the solids that are left in the pot.

Cool the consommé quickly by setting the storage container in the ice-water bath. If you don't plan on using the consommé within 1 or 2 days, transfer it to smaller containers and freeze for up to 3 months.

Chef's Tip

An egg mixture will curdle if combined with a hot liquid unless it is done in stages, a technique called tempering. The usual way is to add small amounts of the hot liquid to the eggs to gently equalize the temperatures of both eggs and liquid. Then the eggs and remaining hot liquid can be safely combined.

Spiced Chickpea and Vegetable Soup with Charmoula

Makes 8 cups; serves 6 to 8

This vegan soup proves that a dish doesn't require meat or even cream to taste great. I use spices to achieve a complexity of flavors, and seasonally ripe ingredients for freshness. Charmoula is a staple marinade in North African cooking—I think of it as Moroccan pesto. The cooking of southern France can reflect Moroccan influences, so I feel the soup complements the style of food we do at the restaurant. Charmoula is also good as a condiment for grilled fish, vegetables, or meat, and as a garnish for soups. Although the marinade can be prepared a day ahead, I find it tastes best right after it is made.

1 cup dried chickpeas

12 cups cold water

Large pinch of saffron

1 cinnamon stick

2 star anise

2 bay leaves

1 tablespoon kosher salt

1/4 cup extra-virgin olive oil

2 leeks, white parts only, halved lengthwise, washed, and sliced into 1/4-inch half moons

1 large carrot, peeled and cut into 1/2-inch dice

1 bulb fennel, white part only, trimmed and cut into 1/2-inch dice

Kosher salt and freshly ground black pepper

1 teaspoon fennel seed, toasted and ground

1 teaspoon cumin seed, toasted and ground

Pinch of red pepper flakes

6 ounces kale, stemmed and coarsely chopped

4 large ripe tomatoes, grated

1/2 cup Charmoula (recipe follows)

In a bowl, cover the chickpeas with 4 cups of the cold water and soak overnight in the refrigerator. (Do not use canned chickpeas, as you need the cooking liquid from the dried chickpeas for the recipe.)

Drain the chickpeas and transfer to a 3-quart soup pot, adding the remaining 8 cups of cold water. Add the saffron, cinnamon stick, star anise, bay leaves, and salt. Cook over medium-high heat until the chickpeas have softened, about 30 minutes. Discard the star anise, cinnamon stick, and bay leaves. Set the chickpeas aside in their cooking liquid.

In a 6-quart soup pot, heat the olive oil over medium heat. Add the leeks, carrot, and fennel. Season generously with salt and pepper. Cook, stirring, until the vegetables have softened, about 10 minutes. Add the ground fennel, cumin seed, and red pepper flakes and continue stirring to let the spices bloom, about 1 minute. Add the kale and cook until wilted, about 3 minutes. Stir in the tomatoes and cook another 3 minutes. Pour in the chickpeas and their cooking liquid. Bring the soup to a simmer. Taste and season with salt and pepper.

To serve, divide among soup bowls, garnish each with a generous tablespoon of charmoula, and serve immediately.

Charmoula

Makes about 1/2 cup

1/2 bunch Italian parsley, leaves only, finely chopped

1/2 bunch mint, leaves only, finely chopped

1/2 bunch cilantro, leaves only, finely chopped

1 teaspoon cumin seed, toasted and ground

1 teaspoon fennel seed, toasted and ground

3 cloves garlic, finely chopped

Juice of 1 lemon

Kosher salt and freshly ground black pepper

1/3 cup extra-virgin olive oil

In a small bowl, combine the parsley, mint, cilantro, cumin, fennel, and garlic. Stir in the lemon juice and season with salt and pepper. Mix in the olive oil. Transfer to a small container, cover tightly, and refrigerate until needed.

Chef's Tip

When preparing charmoula, or any vinaigrette for that matter, remember to add salt before the olive oil so it has a chance to dissolve and uniformly season the vinegar.

Tomato-Bread Soup

Makes about 4 cups; serves 2 to 4

The arrival of the first tomatoes in our kitchen signals the beginning of summer. We all get so excited because the moment opens up a world of new possibilities. This soup, which recalls Tuscan panzanella and combines ripe tomatoes with day-old bread, is one. At the restaurant, we generate a fair amount of leftover bread, prosciutto ends, and Parmesan rinds. This recipe is a delicious attempt at being sustainable, frugal, and creative. Any leftover soup makes a great pasta sauce.

1/2 cup extra-virgin olive oil, plus more for drizzling

1 bulb garlic, separated into cloves, peeled, and thinly sliced

1 large onion, halved and cut into 1/4-inch dice

2 pounds ripe tomatoes, peeled, seeded, and grated (see page 44)

Kosher salt and freshly ground black pepper

4-ounce piece prosciutto end (optional)

4-ounce piece Parmesan-cheese rind (optional)

2 1-inch-thick slices day-old bread (about 4 ounces), crusts removed, cut into 1/4-inch dice

1/2 cup coarsely chopped fresh basil

3 cups water

4 teaspoons grated Parmesan cheese, for garnish

In a 6-quart soup pot, heat the olive oil over medium-low heat. Add the garlic and onion and cook, stirring frequently, until the onion is translucent with no coloration, 7 to 10 minutes. Add the grated tomatoes and season generously with salt and pepper. Add the prosciutto end and Parmesan rind and cook for another 10 minutes. The tomatoes will release their liquid at this stage.

Add the water, then the diced bread, and cook for another 15 minutes. Taste to make sure the flavors are well developed. If the soup still seems a bit watery, season again and cook a bit longer.

When the soup is to your liking, remove the prosciutto and the Parmesan rind and stir in the chopped basil.

At this point the soup is ready to serve, though you may want to pass it through a food mill for a smoother texture. I prefer it rustic-style straight out of the pot. Divide between soup bowls, garnish with grated Parmesan, and drizzle with olive oil. Serve with crusty bread.

Chilled English Pea Soup with Dungeness Crab

Makes about 4 cups; serves 2 to 4

Peas are as sweet as sugar at their peak of ripeness. This very simple, colorful, and elegant summer soup captures that moment of perfection. The addition of a savory infusion of herbs refreshes the palate while letting the peas shine with flavor. Prepare it the day you serve it, because after that moment of perfection, the brightness fades.

Whole leaves from 1 bunch basil (reserve the stems)	4 cups shucked English peas
Whole leaves from 1 bunch mint (reserve the stems)	4 ounces Dungeness crab-meat, picked and squeezed dry (see page 214)
4 cups water	Juice of 1/2 lime
Kosher salt and freshly ground black pepper	Dash of Tabasco
	1/4 cup crème fraîche

Reserve 4 leaves each of mint and basil to garnish the finished soup. Add the remaining basil and mint, stems included, to a soup pot. Add the 4 cups water, along with a scant tablespoon of salt, and bring to a boil over medium-high heat. Remove from the heat and let the herbs steep in the water until it is cool. Strain and reserve the herb-infused liquid, and discard the cooked herbs.

Have a bowl of ice water ready. Season a pot of water with enough salt that you can taste it, bring to boil over medium-high heat, then add the peas. Cook the peas until they are soft yet still retain bright green color, about 5 minutes. Drain the peas and refresh them immediately in the ice water.

In a blender, liquefy the peas along with 2 cups of the herbal infusion. Thin the soup with more infusion if the mixture seems too thick. (If any infusion remains, store it in the refrigerator for another use.) Pass the soup through a coarse strainer and adjust the seasoning. Set aside and keep cold.

In a small bowl, combine the crabmeat, lime juice, and Tabasco. Season with salt and pepper and stir to mix well.

To serve, ladle the soup into bowls. Gently swirl a spoonful of crème fraîche into each bowl, then garnish with crabmeat. Tear the remaining mint and basil leaves, arrange on top of each soup, and serve at once.

Pairing Wine with Soup

The role of a soup is to warm or cool, depending on the time of year. For heartier and cream-based soups, I suggest a slightly oaky Chardonnay with a creamy texture and a flash of acid that shows itself well with food that is both savory and sweet. Woodward Canyon Chardonnay from Washington or Black Cap Chardonnay from Oregon fit the bill. On the other hand, a Viognier, like Penner-Ash Viognier from Oregon, would highlight the sweetness in a soup made with corn or chickpeas, and round out the flavors of the dish. A nice shot of chilled dry sherry accents the tomato and the aromatic Parmesan rind in Tuscan bread soup. **–K.P.**

Gazpacho

Makes about 4 cups; serves 2 to 4

When standing by the stove is not an option on a hot summer day, enjoy this well-chilled celebration of vegetables. It seems to capture the distinctive flavors of the season in one delicious gulp. The tomatoes in the recipe are grated instead of chopped, a very easy, all-in-one step for peeling and chopping a tomato.

2 large red bell peppers

3 large ripe tomatoes, halved across their midsection

1 medium English cucumber, peeled and sliced into $1/4$-inch rounds

1 small sweet yellow onion, coarsely chopped

2 cloves garlic, crushed with the back of a knife

$1/4$ cup extra-virgin olive oil, plus more for drizzling

$1/4$ cup sherry vinegar

Generous dash of Tabasco

Kosher salt and freshly ground black pepper

1 hard-boiled egg, peeled and grated on the largest holes of a box grater, for garnish

To peel the bell peppers on a gas burner, place them on a burner set on high heat. Using tongs, rotate them on all sides until they become uniformly blackened. To roast and peel the peppers in the oven, roast them in a 350°F oven until the skins brown and loosen, about 30 minutes.

For either method, place the cooked peppers in a bowl, cover with plastic wrap, and let sit until cool enough to handle, approximately 10 minutes. Peel off the skins, remove the seeds and stems, and set the peppers aside.

Squeeze out the seeds from the tomato halves and discard. Holding the rounded portion of the tomato against your palm over a large bowl, grate the tomato on the largest holes of a box grater. Add the bell peppers, cucumber, onion, and garlic, and then pour in $1/4$ cup of the olive oil, the sherry vinegar, and Tabasco. Season with salt and pepper. Cover and refrigerate the mixture for about an hour to marry the flavors.

In a blender, puree the mixture in several batches. Divide between soup bowls and drizzle with olive oil. Garnish with grated egg and serve.

Chilled Borscht with Cucumber Salad

Makes about 12 cups; serves 10 to 12

If Eastern Europe had soul food, it would probably involve beets. Nothing better expresses their core than borscht—cold or hot, with beets chopped or coarsely grated, with meat or vegetarian, with potatoes or cabbage (or neither!). There are a world of borscht possibilities.

I love this version, served cold with crème fraîche instead of the customary sour cream, and garnished with a savory summer salad of cucumber, green onion, and dill. I use only red beets for this borscht as they retain their color during cooking for a vivid presentation. As an alternative to dicing the vegetables, feel free to grate them on the largest holes of a grater before cooking. You can also puree them in a food mill after cooking. Either a blender or a food processor will dramatically change the texture and the color of borscht, so don't use either. This recipe will make quite a bit. Keep it covered in the refrigerator and share with your friends and family for several days to come. It only gets better.

3 pounds red beets, peeled and cut into 1/4-inch dice

1 large bulb garlic, separated into cloves, peeled, and finely chopped

Kosher salt and freshly ground black pepper

1 large russet potato, peeled and cut into 1/4-inch dice

1 onion, finely minced

2 bay leaves

12 cups cold water

1 English cucumber, peeled, seeded, and finely diced

1/4 cup coarsely chopped fresh dill

1 bunch green onions, trimmed, and thinly sliced

1 cup crème fraîche or sour cream

Juice of 1 lemon

Dill fronds, for garnish

1 radish (such as French Breakfast), thinly sliced, for garnish

In a large bowl, mix the beets with the garlic and 3 tablespoons of salt. Let the mixture sit while assembling the other ingredients, about 15 minutes.

In a soup pot, combine the potato, onion, bay leaves, and beet mixture. Cover with the 12 cups of cold water and cook over low-to-medium heat until the vegetables are tender and the resulting broth is sweet and flavorful, about 45 minutes. Season with salt and pepper. Have a bowl of ice water ready. Transfer the soup to a container and cool down in the ice water until completely cold. Refrigerate until ready to serve.

To prepare the salad, in a bowl, mix the cucumber, chopped dill, and green onion with crème fraîche and lemon juice. Season with salt and pepper and set aside.

To serve, ladle the soup into bowls, swirl a healthy spoonful of cucumber salad into each one, and garnish with a couple of dill fronds as well as a few rounds of radish. Serve right away.

Paley's Burger

Serves 4

Here is our idea of the classic burger, meant to spoil you forever for any lesser version. Kobe beef is available to us in Oregon because it is raised in neighboring Idaho. I look for good quality, hormone- and antibiotic-free chuck or top sirloin. Using a stand mixer with a grinder attachment, I grind the meat just before cooking so it doesn't oxidize, which robs it of its juices and rich color.

This burger is always on the bar menu at the restaurant. We serve it with fries (see page 50), George's Gathered Greens (page 60), and Bread-and-Butter Pickles (page 220).

4 (1/4-inch-thick) slices Smoked Bacon (page 204)	Kosher salt and freshly ground black pepper
2 pounds American Kobe beef chuck or top sirloin, trimmed of excess fat and sinew	4 slices cheddar cheese
	4 Brioche burger buns (page 216)
1/4 cup plus 2 tablespoons extra-virgin olive oil	1/4 cup Ketchup (page 201)
1 medium onion, sliced into 4 (1/2-inch-thick) rounds	1/4 cup whole-grain mustard aioli (see page 50)

Preheat the oven to 400°F. Preheat an outdoor grill. If using charcoal, once it's glowing hot, distribute the coals evenly throughout the bottom of the grill.

Place a small wire rack on a baking sheet. Lay the bacon slices on the rack and bake in the oven until browned and crispy, about 10 minutes. Decrease the oven temperature to 200°F. Transfer the slices to an ovenproof dish and keep warm in the oven. Drain the bacon fat from the baking sheet (reserve it for another use), and return the empty rack-topped sheet to the oven.

Cut the beef into small enough strips to fit into the meat grinder and grind the beef. On a clean work surface, divide the meat into 4 equal-sized mounds. Hold 1 portion between the palms of your hands and work in a circular motion to form a firm round ball.

Place 1 beef round on a dinner plate and flatten into a 3/4-inch-thick patty. Repeat with the remaining beef portions. Cover and refrigerate while assembling the other ingredients.

Drizzle 2 tablespoons of the olive oil over the onion slices and season with salt and pepper. Place them on the grill and cook on both sides until they get distinct grill marks, about 5 minutes per side. Transfer to the rack-topped baking sheet already in the oven and keep warm.

Remove the beef patties from the refrigerator. Season them on both sides with salt and pepper, and brush both sides with the remaining 1/4 cup of olive oil. Place the burgers on the grill and cook until the meat turns opaque, about 5 minutes. Turn the burger over carefully, mindful that freshly ground beef can be crumbly and fragile. Place 1 piece of cheese on each patty and cook until the internal temperature is 130°F for medium-rare, another 5 minutes or so.

Halve the buns and warm them, cut side down, on the grill, about 2 minutes. Assemble the burgers in the order we follow at the restaurant: I start with a spoonful of ketchup on half of the bun and aioli on the other. The burger goes onto the bottom, followed by an onion slice, a slice of bacon, then the bun top. I carefully slice it in half and—it's yours!

To Drink

One of the most requested duos at the bar is this burger and a chilled Tanqueray No. Ten martini served up with a twist (it's also chef's favorite). With hints of spice, ripe dark fruit, and bacon fat, Tyrus Evan Del Rio Vineyard Claret also makes good company for the rich beef and mustardy aioli. We take our burger seriously, and Dusky Goose Pinot Noir is a serious wine, with penetrating layers of lush fruit that makes for a winning combination. **–K.P.**

Why French Fries Are American

Every year my mother and I celebrate the date of our arrival in this country. It became a tradition to mark our anniversary over burgers and fries at Café America in Manhattan. Even during lean times we found the means to live it up on this important day. Now we live three thousand miles apart—me in Portland, she in New York—so mostly we send each other red, white, and, blue flowers with a "God Bless America" greeting attached.

For our thirtieth anniversary, she asked that I fly home to go out for burger and fries. Sadly, Café America had closed, so rather than look for a new place worthy of our celebration, I offered to make our traditional fare at her New York studio apartment. It seemed easy enough, until I learned that she had invited twenty of our relatives and friends to join in. The proud mother wanted to show off her son's accomplishments.

I started planning a month ahead, approaching this meal with utmost seriousness, as I do when I take my culinary "show" on the road. I read the menu to my mother over the phone:

Chilled Dungeness crab and freshly shucked oysters with lemon and cocktail sauce

Crudités of raw vegetables with stone-ground mustard aioli

American Kobe beef burger on a homemade brioche bun with ketchup, cheddar cheese, and bacon

Our own spiced potato chips

Bread-and-butter pickles

Carrot cake with cream cheese frosting

After a brief silence, she exclaimed, "Vitalinka, no French fries? We have to have French fries. You make such good ones. Besides, aren't French fries American?"

She was fixated on those damn spuds as if nothing else mattered. I had purposely tried to omit them from the menu—I knew how hard they would be to make in a tiny New York City kitchen. I would have no such luck, though. It was my duty as a son—and an American citizen—to make French fries for my mother in my new Motherland.

On the day of my flight, I carefully packed a very large cooler with pickles, ketchup, cocktail sauce, mustard aioli, bacon, and brioche burger buns, all homemade; twenty pounds of Kobe beef chuck; and Oregon cheddar cheese, local wine, and Oregon Dungeness crabmeat. Our pastry chef, Wednesday Wild-Wilson, made a great carrot cake that I carefully wrapped, packing the frosting separately. I'd buy the rest of the ingredients in New York.

At Citarella in Greenwich Village, my mother and I ordered five dozen Fisher Island oysters at the seafood counter. We picked out russet potatoes (the best for frying), lemons, and enough vegetables for our crudités. We chose bottled water, and found grapeseed oil (a good, if expensive, choice for frying), and the deep-fat thermometer I needed to measure the temperature of the oil.

Back in my mother's apartment, the refrigerator seemed to expand as if made of rubber to accommodate all the food. A glance at the clock reminded us time was short, so we got right to work. The meat grinder she had borrowed made sounds like a racecar, but worked at the speed of an old jalopy. Elbow-to-elbow, my sous chef mother and I reminisced and talked about music, art, and food. The time flew and the temperature rose, but we did not care. My mother's friend David arrived early to help, and in a final flurry of work, we finished almost everything by the time the first guest rang the doorbell.

One last task was left—cutting and cooking the French fries. With everything else out of the way, it was easier than I had feared. I poured grapeseed oil into the largest pot I could find, attached the thermometer to its rim, and set it over medium heat. While the oil was slowly coming to temperature, I washed the potatoes under cold running water. I remembered that I had bought a Japanese mandoline on a previous trip to New York and—miraculously—found it in the same spot in the kitchen drawer where I'd left it. I filled the sink with cold water and cut the fries directly into it.

As the oil reached 300°F, I drained and dried the potato batons. I slipped a batch into the oil and, instantly, a familiar smell and a crackling sound filled the tiny kitchen and a smile broke out on my mother's face. She had been right. How could we not have fries on such a day?

As the foam subsided on the surface of the oil, I fished out the fries with a sturdy pair of tongs, dropped them on a baking sheet, and slipped the sheet into a

warm oven while I fried the rest. After all the potatoes got their first dunking, I let the oil come up to 320°F, then plunged all the fries at once into the oil. When they all turned a uniform golden color, I lifted them out, shook off the excess oil and transferred them to a bowl my mother had bought especially for the occasion. I hardly had time to sprinkle the fries with salt before my mother whisked them off to the table, where sounds of pleasure and approval greeted them—these perfect American French fries, crunchy on the outside and fluffy inside.

Twenty of us, all immigrants, gathered in that tiny room that evening. Incredibly, the view from my mother's window includes the Statue of Liberty and Ellis Island. We ate truly American food, the harvest and craft of producers from coast to coast. It gives me chills whenever I think about it.

American French Fries

Be prepared to fry the potatoes twice: once to cook them so they fluff inside and again to get them crispy on the outside. When I use an electric fryer, I always follow the manufacturer's instructions. To make good fries in a pot on the stove, a deep-fat thermometer is essential. It ensures that the oil is at the proper temperature for deep-frying and lets you check that the oil isn't overheating, a potentially danger-ous situation. A mandoline is a very useful slicing tool for cutting the potatoes (and other vegetables) quickly and to a uniform size. Both the deep-fat thermometer (also called a candy thermometer) and the mandoline are available at most cookware stores. The third essential is a pot that is large and tall enough to contain the oil without overflowing when the potatoes are slipped in. With fries, I prefer mustard aioli over ketchup, reserving the latter for burgers.

3 tablespoons whole-grain mustard	12 cups grapeseed or canola oil
1 cup Aioli (page 203)	3 large russet potatoes
	Kosher salt

In a small bowl, mix together the mustard and aioli and transfer to a serving bowl. Cover and refrigerate until needed.

In a tall 8-quart soup pot, heat the oil over high heat until it reaches 300°F on a deep-fat thermom-eter. Keep the thermometer attached to the side of the pot at all times.

Have a bowl of cold water ready. Scrub the potatoes under cold running water. Cut the potatoes lengthwise into long ½-inch-thick batons (sticks) using a sharp knife or a mandoline set on the widest setting. Immediately place them in the bowl of cold water to prevent discoloration.

When the oil is at temperature, increase the heat to high. Drain the potatoes well, pat them dry, and carefully drop a third of them into the hot oil. This is the moment when the oil could overflow. If it looks like it might, pull a few potatoes out quickly, using a slotted spoon or tongs, until the oil subsides.

Have a baking sheet ready. Keep an eye on the temperature of the oil. It will drop to about 260°F after the potatoes are added. Continue cooking the potatoes without disturbing them until the oil heats back to 300°F, about 5 minutes. Remove the cooked potatoes carefully with a slotted spoon or tongs. Shake them lightly over the pot to drain excess oil. Place them on the prepared baking sheet. Repeat with the rest of the potatoes. Occasionally, between batches, the temperature of the oil can get too high. If that happens, turn off the heat and wait until the oil cools to 300°F before proceeding.

Once all the potatoes have been fried, fry them all together a second time, this time at 320°F. They will crisp in about 5 minutes. Shake off excess oil, transfer them to a large serving bowl, and sprinkle generously with salt. Serve them immediately with whole-grain mustard aioli on the side.

Truffled Crab Melt

Serves 4

I've served this decadent variation of that diner favorite the tuna melt as part of an elegant lunch or cut in bite-sized pieces as an hors d'oeuvre. It is definitely fun, not at all fussy or difficult. A good-quality purchased mayonnaise will do nicely here, but if you like, try homemade aioli (page 203).

We use an Italian sheep's milk cheese, Boschetto al Tartufo, for its intense truffle taste and good melting qualities. Swiss Gruyère, which is easy to find, works as well. If fresh truffles are not in season, subsitute frozen ones. Truffle butter is available at specialty food stores or online (see Resources, page 222).

4 thick slices Brioche (page 216) or challah

4 teaspoons truffle butter, melted

1/2 pound Oregon Dungeness crabmeat, squeezed dry and picked over (see page 214)

2 ounces fresh Oregon black truffle, brushed clean and coarsely chopped

1 apple, peeled, cored, and thinly sliced

Generous dash of Tabasco

2 tablespoons finely minced sweet red onion

2 tablespoons finely chopped Italian parsley

Juice of 1/2 lime

1/4 cup Aioli (page 203)

Kosher salt and freshly ground black pepper

4 ounces truffle cheese, such as Boschetto al Tartufo, shredded (about 1 cup shredded)

Preheat the broiler. Brush one side of the brioche slices with the truffle butter and set on a baking sheet, buttered side up. Toast the bread until golden, about 3 minutes. Remove the toasts and turn the oven temperature to 400°F.

In a bowl, mix the crabmeat with the chopped truffle, sliced apple, Tabasco, onion, parsley, and lime juice. Fold in the aioli to incorporate. Season with salt and pepper.

Top the toasts, buttered side down, with the crab salad and sprinkle with the cheese. Bake in the upper third of the oven until the crab salad has warmed through and the cheese has melted, about 5 minutes. Serve immediately.

To Drink

The lovely berry flavor of a Cabernet Franc, fruity with a dry finish, shines through in Olga Raffault's Chinon Rosé from France, forming a perfect bond with the buttery brioche, sweet crabmeat, and decadent truffles. The locally produced Soter Beacon Hill Sparkling Brut Rosé, made from Pinot Noir grapes, offers similar flavor profiles with an added note of elegant sparkle. It complements the sandwich nicely. **–K.P.**

Paley's Reuben

Serves 4

My take on the Reuben sandwich calls for braised red cabbage instead of the traditional sauerkraut. I didn't make the switch to improve this classic, but merely to put my own splash of paint on an already colorful canvas. Julia Child ate every morsel when she had it at the restaurant.

You could buy the ingredients for a Reuben already prepared, but the taste difference is obvious when you put extra effort into making everything from scratch. I slowly roast the corned beef because it concentrates the flavors imparted by curing. It strikes me that the customary method of boiling the meat washes those flavors away. Note that you need to cure the meat four days ahead of cooking. The Russian dressing can be made up to three days in advance.

Your local butcher is a great source for curing salt. If he does not have it he will direct you to a place that will. Local grocery store may also have it. Look for "quick-tender" or "tenderizing salt" on the label.

2/3 cup Russian Dressing (recipe follows)	8 ounces Braised Red Cabbage (page 150)
8 slices dark rye bread	4 slices Swiss Gruyère cheese
8 ounces thinly sliced Corned Beef (recipe follows)	4 tablespoons unsalted butter

Preheat the oven to 400°F.

Generously spread Russian dressing on all the bread slices. On 4 slices, layer corned beef, cabbage, and Gruyère in that order. Cover each sandwich with the remaining bread.

In a 12-inch skillet, melt 2 tablespoons of the butter over medium heat. Brown 2 of the sandwiches, about 3 minutes per side. Transfer to a baking sheet. Wipe the skillet, add the remaining 2 tablespoons of butter and brown the other 2 sandwiches. Place them on the baking sheet as well.

Warm the 4 sandwiches in the oven until the cheese has melted, about 10 minutes. Remove to a cutting board, slice each in half, and serve immediately.

Russian Dressing

Makes 1 cup

1/3 cup Ketchup (page 201)	3 tablespoons finely chopped fresh chives
1/3 cup Aioli (page 203)	3 tablespoons drained capers, coarsely chopped
2 tablespoons Prepared Horseradish, well drained (page 202)	

Combine all the ingredients well. Transfer to a container and refrigerate, tightly covered, until ready to use.

Corned Beef

3 1/2 pounds beef brisket, trimmed of silver skin	1/4 cup kosher salt
1 teaspoon curing salt (sodium nitrite), optional	1/4 cup plus 2 tablespoons whole-grain mustard
1/4 cup ground coriander	1/4 cup plus 2 tablespoons packed brown sugar
1/4 cup ground bay leaves	1/2 cup white wine
2 tablespoons freshly ground black pepper	

To cure the meat, place the brisket in a shallow 8 by 12-inch glass dish. Thoroughly massage the curing salt into the meat on all sides, making sure to get the edges and corners as well.

Rub the surface of the brisket with half the coriander, half the ground bay leaf, half the black pepper, and half the salt, in that order. Remember you are curing, not just seasoning, so keep going even if it seems like too much spice.

Turn the brisket over and rub in the remaining spices and salt, including all the edges and corners. Cover tightly with plastic wrap and refrigerate. Turn the meat after 2 days, cover, and refrigerate for 2 more days.

Preheat the oven to 300°F.

To roast the meat, mix the mustard and sugar in a small bowl. Remove the brisket from the cure. Pat it dry with paper towels and place it in a roasting pan. Slather the mustard mixture over the top, and pour in the wine. Cover tightly with aluminum foil and bake in the oven until fork tender, about 4 hours.

Let the meat cool, then wrap and refrigerate until ready to use. Discard the cooking liquid.

Corned beef made with curing salt keeps at least 1 week in the refrigerator. Beyond a week, freeze any leftovers.

To Drink

Most any beverage works with a Reuben. My preference is for a local handcrafted microbrew such as Rogue Mocha Porter with its hints of hops and cocoa, a good match for the dark rye and Russian dressing. In another direction, a Riesling with crisp acidity and opulent fruit flavors like Brooks Ara from Oregon or Domaine Weinbach's Riesling from Alsace will cut through the meaty richness of the sandwich. **–K.P.**

Warm Spot-Prawn, Tomato, and Feta Salad

Serves 4

Spot prawn season in the Pacific Northwest starts in early October. If the timing is right, late summer tomatoes are still around—a crossover of seasons that I love.

There is something particularly satisfying about salads that have both warm and cold tastes. In this recipe, while the prawns cool, the lettuce wilts and the cheese melts, all tastes and sensations blending into a wonderfully rich and complex combination.

I prefer an Israeli sheep's milk feta, Pastures of Eden (see Resources, page 222), because it is rich and melts nicely. If you can't find it, use any good-quality feta. Although "spots" (as we locals call spot prawns) are the sweetest, any wild prawn will work.

1 large onion, sliced into rounds $1/2$ inch thick

Kosher salt and freshly ground black pepper

$1/4$ cup extra-virgin olive oil, plus more for roasting

1 medium head lettuce, like butter lettuce or red oak lettuce, separated into whole leaves

2 vine-ripened tomatoes, cut in $1/2$-inch-thick slices

Pinch of red pepper flakes

4 cloves garlic, thinly sliced

16 spot prawns, shelled and deveined

$1/2$ cup dry white wine

Juice of 1 lemon

2 tablespoons drained capers

$1/4$ cup anise-flavored liqueur, such as Pernod, Ricard, or ouzo

6 ounces feta cheese

2 tablespoons Persillade (page 198)

Preheat the oven to 400°F.

Place the onion slices on a baking sheet, season with salt and black pepper, and drizzle with some of the olive oil. Roast until the edges turn slightly golden, about 30 minutes. Keep warm.

Line 4 plates with whole lettuce leaves. Place 2 tomato slices in the center of the plate. Separate the onions into individual rings and arrange randomly on the plates.

In a skillet large enough to hold all the prawns, warm the $1/4$ cup of olive oil on medium heat. Add the red pepper flakes and sliced garlic and cook at a sizzle for 30 seconds. Season with salt and black pepper. Add the prawns and cook until they begin to lose their translucency, about 2 minutes. Add the white wine, lemon juice, and capers, increase the heat to high, and cook for 2 more minutes. Remove from the heat and stir in the Pernod, feta, and persillade.

Spoon over the prepared salads and serve immediately.

Pairing Wine with Salad

All of the salad recipes in this chapter vary in their proportions of salty, vinegary, sweet, and creamy flavors. A floral and herbaceous Sauvignon Blanc, like J. Christopher's Sauvignon Blanc from Croft Vineyard in Oregon, would complement them all. It has sweet green apple flavors and a minerality that will love any vinaigrette. Or, try a Sancerre from the Loire, such as Gérard Boulay Clos de Beaujeu, with aromas of fragrant wildflowers and subtle smokiness. This French Sauvignon Blanc especially complements the Oregon blue cheese used in Spinach Salad with Smoky Bacon and Blue Cheese Dressing (page 56). —K.P.

Spinach Salad with Smoky Bacon and Blue Cheese Dressing

Serves 4

When I was a teenager in New York, my mother would treat my piano recitals as special occasions and take me out to eat afterward. We would always go to one particular restaurant (now long closed) and sit by the big window facing Broadway, where we could see the Juilliard School across the street. I particularly enjoyed the chef's salad with its tangy, salty blue cheese dressing. As an adult, I still love blue cheese. The one I prefer for this recipe is Oregon Blue, made in the southern part of the state by the Rogue Creamery (see Resources, page 222). With local cheese, spinach and eggs from nearby farms, and house-cured bacon, this salad has come to represent a blending of fond memories with a strong sense of place.

1/4 cup buttermilk

1/4 cup sour cream

1 small shallot, finely minced

4 teaspoons cider vinegar

6 ounces Oregon Blue or other blue cheese (such as Maytag, Point Reyes, or Roquefort), crumbled

Kosher salt and freshly ground black pepper

8 ounces Smoked Bacon (page 204), sliced into 1/2-inch-thick by 1-inch long pieces (lardons)

1 small Walla Walla sweet onion (or any local sweet onion), halved, and thinly sliced

8 ounces fresh spinach, stemmed, washed, and spun dry

2 large hard-boiled eggs, peeled and quartered

In a bowl, whisk the buttermilk with the sour cream, shallot, and cider vinegar. Stir in half the blue cheese. Season the dressing with salt and pepper.

Heat a large nonstick skillet over medium heat and cook the bacon until crisp, about 8 minutes. Using a slotted spoon, transfer the bacon to paper towels to drain.

To serve family-style in a large salad bowl, scatter the onion slices over the spinach, toss, and season with salt and pepper. Add the dressing and toss again. Arrange the eggs on top of the salad. Sprinkle over the bacon and the remaining blue cheese and serve.

Spicy Greens with Fresh Cherries, Prosciutto, and Goat Cheese

Serves 4 to 6

As kids, my friends and I used to jump my neighbor's fence to steal cherries from his tree. One day, we found a ladder propped against the cherry tree and a large bowl next to it. Our neighbor's message was loud and clear: we were to fill his bowl, then our own—a convenient arrangement, we decided. We served as his private picking crew for years. Eating a bowl of cherries delights me still, as does an occasional childish match of pit-spitting.

When the first cherries appear, I use them every chance I get. This early summer salad is a light, refreshing, seasonal marvel, making use of sweet, tangy, salty, and spicy flavors.

1 1/2 cups fresh cherries, pitted

1/3 cup balsamic vinegar

8 ounces mixed spicy greens, such as rocket, cress, and mizuna

1 spring onion, with green part, thinly sliced

Kosher salt and freshly ground black pepper

1/4 cup extra-virgin olive oil

4 to 6 slices prosciutto, halved lengthwise

5 ounces fresh goat cheese, crumbled

In a small saucepan, combine the cherries with the balsamic vinegar and bring to a boil over high heat. Remove from the heat and let the cherries cool completely in the vinegar, about 15 minutes.

Put the combined greens and the sliced spring onion in a large bowl. Season with salt and pepper. Add the cherries and the balsamic vinegar. Pour in the olive oil and toss to dress the salad.

Divide evenly among the salad plates, top with prosciutto, and garnish with goat cheese. Serve immediately.

The Magic of George and the Soil

I t's late January and I am paying George Weppler and his wife, Fran, a visit. George produces absolutely mythic vegetables on sixteen acres situated between a hillock and a river in Brownsville, a couple of hours drive south of Portland. When I park and get out of the car, I can see my breath. As I take in the scene I feel like the earth around me is giving off its own breath, softening everything with a damp mist, like an image from a Chinese scroll painting.

George appears from around the corner of the house; he has been working on one of his water gardens. At five feet nine inches tall, he is physically solid—when he was young and played football, his nickname was Raw Meat. Now nearly seventy years old, he is clearly still a force to contend with.

Talking to George about food always inspires me. He claims to be a total amateur in the kitchen, but I don't agree—I still use a technique for preparing salmon on a cedar plank that he shared with me a long time ago (Cedar-Planked Salmon, page 92). We have worked together for twelve years.

Because of George's natural curiosity, intelligence, and sheer wealth of knowledge about what's in, on, and under the dirt, I sometimes sense that he himself grew from the soil. He has not just adapted to the drawbacks of his small acreage and the toughness of the seasons in Oregon, he's learned to use them to his advantage.

We head behind the house to a cluster of rough old buildings, one of which is used for packing and shipping. It's a comfortable place to linger and talk, and the intoxicating aroma of truffles fills the air. We stand by a table on which boxes are stacked with my order for today. Their contents are handwritten on the side (greens, truffles). I can smell the earth in which they grew.

George explains that in 1964, a five-hundred-year flood inundated this property. When the waters receded, the dark, rich soil that the rains carried down from the mountains blanketed the fields. Where the floodwaters didn't reach, the soil remains heavier, clumped with clay. Because George's soil is deep and loose and easily turned, he beds plants even in January, even in a heavy rain. The land was a potato patch before he started to farm here in 1978. Before that, it was used to grow hops. A century ago, the same soil was pasture for milk cows. Knowing the history of this dirt allows him to say with pride, "This land has never had poison deliberately put on it." To control weeds, he scorches them with a propane torch, allowing them to decay back into the soil.

Walking with the river to the left and the house to the right, we meander out into the winter fields. "We can grow eight crops a year in the same piece of ground," George says, and recites the inventory of plants as we pass: kale, cress, tatsoi, red spinach, and mâche (which he claims is practically indestructible). The plant varieties he has established will make it through bad weather. "We've just had two weeks of cold weather, below fifteen degrees," he says. "But a lot more things make it than you would think."

He plucks some arugula leaves for us to taste. They are marvelous, their spicy flavor heightened by their perfect freshness. As George talks, he reveals how a truly gifted farmer thinks. He combines deep understanding of the complex relationships among his plants, his soil, and his farm's microclimate with a nimble mind that thrives on experimentation and problem solving.

The soil under our feet—river-bottom loam that has had dairy manure plowed into it four times a year for twenty-five years—feels like carpeting. It's unbelievably lush. The shape of the land, though, settles cold air right on top of George's farm. The magic of George's soil needs the magic of George's skill and ingenuity to keep his farm in balance.

Inside one of the plastic greenhouses engineered on the farm, you would think it was another season. Later in the year, George will plant tomatoes here. "You know the secret I found for making veggies taste very good? You give them enough water to stay alive, barely enough to stay healthy, and nothing extra." For example, making tomatoes fight for their life produces fruit with concentrated flavor that isn't diluted by too much water.

George confides more about the techniques he uses to increase the yield and quality of his produce, such as interplanting tomato plants with other crops and getting one hundred potatoes out of one potato.

"Want to know how?" he grins.

We're standing beside one of the planting beds inside the greenhouse. He shows me how he plants a single potato in the middle of the bed. When the green shoots of that plant break ground, he puts a worn car tire around the plant and fills it with dirt. He extends a strong arm to indicate the height and depth of the plant, and remarks, "By the time it grows this tall, it's this deep, and solid with potatoes." Any part of a potato that remains beneath the soil forms a tuber. By containing their growth in a small space, he gets the plants to form tubers over and over and over.

"You get these old mature potatoes on the bottom and by the time you get to the top, you get new potatoes." The new ones are buttery, the bottom ones more starchy, perfect for producing snowy purees. All of them have the amazing taste his soil encourages, and he is able to offer me potatoes for the restaurant long after other growers have run out.

As he holds the plastic covering open for us to exit the greenhouse, he says, "All the tricks make a difference."

George's Gathered Greens

Serves 4

My idea of a beautiful salad is one composed of the freshest greens, simply served with a squeeze of lemon and a drizzle of excellent olive oil. I seldom venture further. George Weppler, whose farm is near Portland, harvests a constantly evolving variety of seasonal greens for us. Butter lettuce, red oak, and Lollo Rosso go into summer salads. Arugula, lambs lettuce, and a variety of cresses give distinction to winter salads. No matter what time of year or the variety, they are always crisp and delicious.

8 ounces mixed greens, root ends trimmed, and separated into leaves

1 lemon, halved

^{1}/4 cup extra-virgin olive oil

Kosher salt and freshly ground black pepper

Fill a large bowl (or the sink) with cold water. Float the greens in the water, letting the dirt sink to the bottom. Gently remove the leaves and spin them dry in a salad spinner, a few at a time. Don't crowd them or the fragile leaves may get damaged.

Put all the greens in a large salad bowl. Season with salt and pepper. Squeeze the lemon juice directly over the greens, then drizzle in the olive oil. Mix with your hands until the salad is glistening with dressing, and serve.

Grilled Romaine with Anchovy-Caper Vinaigrette and Parmesan

Serves 4

This salad is for anchovy lovers. There is something about the intense, briny flavor of this tiny fish that I can't resist, so I use them liberally in my cooking. Warmed romaine pleasantly amplifies the fragrance of the vinaigrette while remaining crispy. Capers and thinly shaved Parmesan complete the salty package, while lemon and olive oil keep the saltiness in check. When selecting romaine, make sure the lettuce is tight, heavy, and bright green. Choose a green, grassy tasting olive oil.

8 anchovy fillets (see Chef's Tip)	Kosher salt and freshly ground black pepper
Juice of 1 lemon	$1/2$ cup extra-virgin olive oil
$1/4$ cup Persillade (page 198)	1 large head romaine lettuce, quartered lengthwise
$1/4$ cup drained capers, coarsely chopped	3-ounce chunk good-quality Parmesan cheese

If the anchovies are packed in oil, drain and chop them finely. If they are salt cured and packed, rinse, skin, and bone them, and chop them finely.

To make the vinaigrette, in a small bowl, stir together the anchovies, lemon juice, persillade, capers, and 6 tablespoons of the olive oil. Set aside.

Preheat a grill. Fill a large bowl with cold water. Float the lettuce quarters in the water, shaking them to encourage the release of dirt and sand, particularly at the root end. Remove from the bowl and dry with paper towels.

Place the lettuce into another large bowl. Drizzle with the remaining 2 tablespoons of olive oil, season with salt and pepper, and toss the lettuce to coat. Grill the lettuce wedges briefly, 30 seconds per side, to develop grill marks that lend smoky flavor.

To serve, divide the grilled lettuce among 4 plates and spoon the vinaigrette over. Using a vegetable peeler, shave thin Parmesan ribbons over the lettuce wedges, and serve immediately.

Chef's Tip

We buy fresh anchovies when we can and prepare them by twisting the head to pull the guts out all at once. We then wash them in cold water, toss with salt, and refrigerate, covered, for 1 day, to drain. As the final step, we pack alternating layers of salt and fish and let sit covered in the refrigerator for another 24 hours. When we are ready to use them, the fish are rinsed of salt, boned, and skinned.

The best canned anchovies, whether salt or oil cured, come from the Mediterranean, so I look for brands from Spain, Italy, or Morocco.

Summer Green Bean and Grilled Peach Salad

Serves 4 to 6

Who says a salad must have greens? Here, snappy green beans lap up the flavor of a thick peach dressing that would surely cause lettuce to go limp. The warmth of the grilled peaches, combined with the tang of cheese and the crunch of nuts, create a quintessential summer experience.

We use freestone peaches like Canadian Harmony, Suncrest, or Veteran when they are available. They are easier to cut into uniform wedges that are easier to grill. For a colorful presentation, take advantage of the many green bean varieties that the season has to offer.

1 1/2 pounds fresh green beans, stems trimmed

Kosher salt and freshly ground black pepper

3 large ripe peaches, pitted and quartered

1 tablespoon Dijon mustard

1/4 cup balsamic vinegar

1/2 cup extra-virgin olive oil

1/4 cup toasted hazelnuts, coarsely chopped

2 ounces hard, aged goat cheese (such as crottin), coarsely grated

Have a bowl of ice water ready. Bring a large pot of well salted water to a boil over high heat. Cook the beans until just slightly tender, about 5 minutes. Drain and plunge in the ice-water bath to stop the cooking. Drain, dry on paper towels, and set aside.

To make the peach vinaigrette, in a blender, liquefy 4 peach quarters, the mustard, balsamic vinegar, salt, and pepper. Transfer to a small bowl and slowly whisk in 1/3 cup of the olive oil. Set aside.

Preheat an outdoor grill to high. Line up the remaining 8 peach quarters in 2 rows of 4. Insert 2 skewers, side by side, through each row of 4 peaches (using 2 skewers prevents the wedges from spinning when turned over).

Brush the skewered fruit with the remaining olive oil. Season with salt and pepper and grill on both sides, about 1 minute per side.

To assemble the salad, slide the peaches off the skewers into a large bowl. Combine with the green beans and gently toss with the vinaigrette. Transfer to a large serving platter, sprinkle with hazelnuts and goat cheese, and serve.

Chef's Tip

When making vinaigrette, I whisk in the oil by hand because I find that the whirling, high-speed action of a blender alters the taste and makes the sauce bitter.

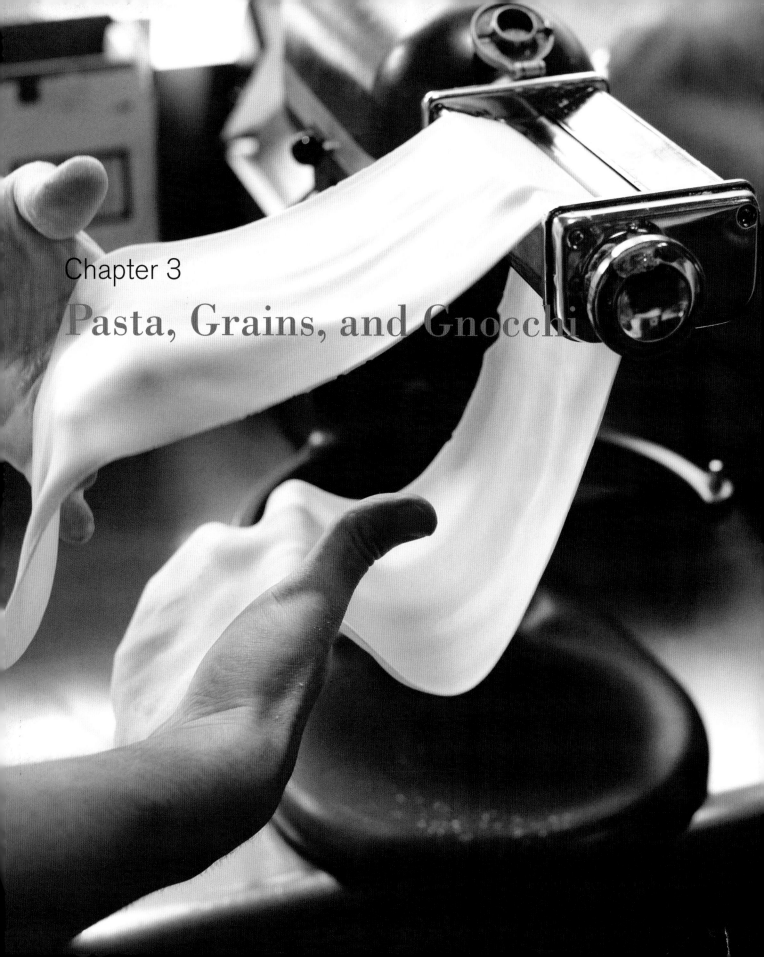

Chapter 3

Pasta, Grains, and Gnocchi

Basic Pasta Dough

Makes about 1 pound

For a richer taste and more tender texture, we now only use yolks from duck eggs when we make pasta. Cindy, our duck egg lady, arrived one day with a bigger-than-usual harvest of duck eggs, so we tried them with pasta. We never used chicken yolks again. Duck eggs may be more difficult to find, but they are worth searching out. However, finding a good egg, duck or chicken, is of paramount importance.

2 cups all-purpose flour, plus more for kneading and dusting

Pinch of kosher salt

3 duck egg yolks or 5 large chicken egg yolks

2 tablespoons extra-virgin olive oil

6 to 7 tablespoons white wine

To make pasta by hand, sift the flour and salt together onto a wooden board. Make a well in the center. Place the yolks in the center of the well along with a drizzle of the olive oil. Using a fork or your fingers, slowly incorporate the flour into the yolks. When the mixture starts clumping, add the white wine, 1 tablespoon at a time, until the mixture comes together in a ball.

Gather up the ball of dough and set it aside. Scrape and discard all the flour that stuck to the board. Dust the board with more flour and knead the dough for about 5 minutes to incorporate all the ingredients. Cover the dough with a kitchen towel and let rest for 30 minutes before rolling.

To make pasta in a stand mixer, sift the flour and salt together into the bowl of a heavy-duty stand mixer fitted with the paddle attachment. Add the yolks and the olive oil. Mix on lowest speed until the mixture resembles coarse meal, about 2 minutes. While the mixer is running, add the white wine, 1 tablespoon at a time, until the mixture gathers into a ball.

Sprinkle a wooden board with a light dusting of flour. Transfer the pasta dough onto the board and knead 6 or 7 times. Let the dough rest for 30 minutes, covered with a kitchen towel, before rolling.

Pasta dough can be made in advance, wrapped tightly in plastic wrap, and frozen for up to 1 week. I do not recommend refrigerating the dough for more than 1 day, as it tends to oxidize and discolor with time. Bring to room temperature before using.

To roll the pasta dough, divide the dough into 4 pieces. Have some flour on hand to dust the dough if it ever seems moist or sticky while you are rolling it. With a pasta machine fixed at the widest setting, feed one piece of dough through the rollers. Fold the dough in half and pass it through again. Continue to feed the dough through the rollers (folding it in half before each pass) until it feels smooth and satiny, about 10 to 15 passes. Remember to dust the dough lightly with flour if it seems moist or sticky.

Narrowing the setting after each pass, roll the sheet of dough until the pasta is the thickness you like. Because I like pasta thicker and with a little chew, I stop rolling at setting number 6, about $1/16$ inch thick. Roll the remaining 3 pieces of dough in the same manner.

Dry and shape the fresh pasta sheets as directed in the recipe you are using.

Hand-Torn Pasta with Clams, Bacon, and Tender Spicy Greens

Serves 4 to 6

This is our version of that very popular pasta dish—spaghetti with clam sauce. Bacon adds a complementary layer of flavor to the clams, while the greens enliven the color. We deliberately make the shape of the pasta wider and uneven in order to capture more sauce in every bite.

When you buy clams, make sure they are tightly closed. When you bring them home they may open to breathe. In that case, tap them gently with your finger. If they close, use them; if they do not close, discard them.

1 pound Basic Pasta Dough (page 66), at room temperature, or prepared fresh pasta sheets

All-purpose flour, for dusting

Kosher salt and freshly ground black pepper

3 tablespoons extra-virgin olive oil

5 ounces unsmoked bacon, cut into 1/4-inch dice

Pinch of red pepper flakes

3 cloves garlic, finely chopped

2 pounds manila clams, scrubbed clean

1 cup white wine

2 tablespoons Persillade (page 198)

3 tablespoons unsalted butter

1 cup tightly packed greens, such as arugula or watercress

1/4 cup fine bread crumbs

To shape the pasta, lightly dust a wooden cutting board with flour. Divide the ball of pasta dough into 4 equal pieces. Lightly coat each with flour and flatten each enough to feed easily into the pasta roller. Roll each piece out on a pasta machine, ending at setting number 6.

Place the 4 sheets of pasta on a work surface lightly dusted with flour, keep uncovered, and let sit for about 10 minutes to dry. If the pasta is too wet it will stretch instead of tearing. Have a baking sheet lightly dusted with flour ready.

Tear the sheets into irregular pieces about 2 inches wide. (Odd-shaped pieces add to the rustic appearance of the dish.) Transfer the pieces to the prepared baking sheet, cover loosely with parchment paper, and refrigerate while preparing the other ingredients.

To make the clam sauce, in a 6-quart pot, heat the olive oil over medium heat. Add the bacon and cook until brown and crispy on all sides, about 5 minutes. Pour off half the bacon fat and discard. Add the red pepper flakes and the garlic and sizzle for 1 more minute, stirring constantly to prevent burning. Add the clams and stir to coat with the bacon fat. Season with salt and pepper. Pour in the wine, cover, and cook until the clams have opened, about 5 minutes. Remove from the heat, stir in the persillade, and cover to keep warm.

To cook the pasta, bring a 6-quart pot of water to a boil over high heat, and add enough salt so you can taste it. Add the torn pasta and cook, stirring to prevent it from sticking, until al dente, about 3 minutes. Drain the pasta in a colander. Transfer to a large, deep serving platter.

To serve, add the butter to the pasta and toss until melted. Pour the clam mixture over the pasta, then add the greens and toss until the pasta is well coated with sauce. Sprinkle with the bread crumbs and serve immediately.

Pasta alla Chitarra with Pork Sugo and Porcini

Serves 4 to 6

One of my favorite pasta shapes is chitarra, cut on an instrument called a chitarra from the Abruzzo region of Italy. It looks like a slide guitar with strings on both sides and a well to catch the cut pasta ribbons (see page 70). I make sheets of fresh pasta, place them on top of the strings, and use a rolling pin to cut the sheets into uniform strands that resemble fettuccini or a square-shaped spaghetti, depending which side of the chitarra I use. For a similar result use dry pasta alla chitarra, which is available at selected stores. Fresh or dry spaghetti or fettuccini would make a suitable substitute as well. If using dry pasta, follow the cooking instructions on the package. Here, I pair it with sugo, an Italian ground-pork sauce with added porcini mushrooms.

Fresh porcini are available in late spring and early fall. If you can't find them, substitute a cultivated variety like crimini or portabella. You can also get fresh or frozen porcini by mail (see Resources, page 222).

1 pound Basic Pasta Dough (page 66), at room temperature, or prepared fresh pasta sheets

All-purpose flour, for rolling out the pasta

1 1/2 pounds ground pork shoulder

1 teaspoon paprika

1 teaspoon ground fennel seed

2 star anise, ground (optional)

1/2 teaspoon ground cinnamon

1/2 teaspoon ground ginger

1/2 teaspoon ground allspice

1/2 teaspoon red pepper flakes

1 teaspoon kosher salt

1 teaspoon freshly ground black pepper

1/4 cup extra-virgin olive oil

1 pound fresh or frozen porcini mushrooms, cleaned (see page 70) and cut into large chunks

1 onion, finely diced

6 cloves garlic, finely minced

1 cup red wine

1 (14-ounce) can good-quality crushed tomatoes, with the juice

2 cups Chicken Stock (page 213)

2 tablespoons unsalted butter

1/4 cup grated Parmesan cheese, plus more for garnish

2 tablespoons Persillade (page 198), for garnish

To shape the pasta, lightly dust a wooden cutting board with flour. Divide the ball of pasta dough into 4 equal pieces. Lightly coat each with flour and flatten enough to feed easily into the pasta roller. Roll each piece out on a pasta machine, ending at setting number 6. Remember to dust the dough with flour if it ever seems sticky while you roll it.

Place the 4 sheets of pasta on a work surface lightly dusted with flour, keep uncovered, and let sit about 10 minutes to dry a bit. Lightly flour a baking sheet and have ready.

To cut fresh pasta with a chitarra, square off the pasta sheets and trim both narrow ends to fit the chitarra. Flour the strings, cover them with 1 pasta sheet, and roll across the pasta with a rolling pin to cut it into strands. To keep the pasta from clumping, dust it lightly with flour after it drops into the well of the chitarra. Repeat with remaining pasta sheets. Transfer the strands to the prepared baking sheet, cover loosely with parchment paper, and refrigerate while preparing the other ingredients.

To cut fresh pasta sheets with another pasta cutter, follow the manufacturer's instructions. You could also cut the pasta sheets by hand. Simply fold the pasta into thirds and cut across to desired thickness.

To make the sauce, in a large bowl, add the pork, paprika, fennel seed, star anise, cinnamon, ginger, allspice, red pepper flakes, salt, and pepper. Mix well until evenly combined. Set aside.

In a 6-quart soup pot, heat the olive oil over medium heat. Add the mushrooms and cook, stirring, until soft, about 5 minutes. Add the onion and garlic and cook until translucent, another 5 minutes. With your hands, break up the pork mixture into uneven, bite-sized pieces and stir into the pot. Sauté, stirring, until the pork develops some golden color, about 10 minutes.

Add the wine and reduce until it has all been absorbed, about 10 minutes. Stir in the tomatoes and

continue to simmer for another 10 minutes. Add the stock, bring the mixture to a simmer, and cook, stirring frequently, for an additional 10 minutes.

If serving right away, keep the sauce hot while the pasta cooks. If not, cool down immediately in an ice-water bath and refrigerate up to 1 day.

To serve, bring a large pot of salted water to a boil over high heat. Gently shake off excess flour from the pasta and slip it into the water. Cook until al dente, 3 to 4 minutes. When done to your liking, drain the pasta well in a colander and transfer to a large serving bowl. Add the sauce to the pasta, then the butter and Parmesan. Toss to coat, sprinkle with persillade, and serve.

To Drink

This combination of substantial porcini and pork with hints of heat and spice pairs well with many of our local Pinots. I suggest Provocateur Pinot Noir from Jim Prosser of J. K. Carriere, with penetrating, dark fruit overtones that bring out the sugo's fennel, anise, cinnamon, and ginger. Along different lines but still in harmony with this dish's spices are blends of Syrah and Grenache from Paul Jaboulet Aîné from the Rhône region, particularly his juicy, fruity Crozes-Hermitage Les Jalets. **–K.P.**

About Porcini Mushrooms

Like any mushrooms that grow in the wild, porcini require a more thorough cleaning than their cultivated counterparts. There is a common misconception that mushrooms should be brushed, never washed. If they are dirty, I wash them. Nothing will spoil a diner's appetite quicker than biting into dirt.

The pickers we buy from usually cut the mushrooms in half to check for worms. When they spot tiny pinholes on the side of a mushroom, indicating the presence of worms, they discard it, letting the little creatures finish what they've started.

The best-quality porcini mushrooms, referred to by locals as boletes, are small, tight, heavy, and very firm to the touch. They get big, soft, and spongy with age. The gills underneath the cap will also darken, changing from light gray when young to dark green as they get older. The darkened gills should be removed and discarded.

Clean the mushrooms one at a time. Brush them while rinsing under cold running water to get rid of dirt and twigs. Trim the root end if dirty, and remove the gills if they are dark green. Pat the mushrooms dry and slice and cook them right away.

Pappardelle with Fava Beans and Mint

Serves 4 to 6

Fava beans arrive in late spring. Their preparation demands persistence, but the reward is well worth the effort. A gentle blanching will separate the bean from its skin, revealing the vibrant green, intensely flavored morsel. For extra brightness, I pair favas with lemon, mint, and Parmesan, simply tossed with the wide pasta ribbons, pappardelle. I go the extra mile and make my own pasta, but the fava beans still taste delicious paired with an excellent dried pasta.

1 pound Basic Pasta Dough (page 66), at room temperature

All-purpose flour, for dusting

Kosher salt

$1/4$ cup extra-virgin olive oil, plus more for drizzling

4 cloves garlic, finely minced

Large pinch of red pepper flakes

2 pounds fresh fava beans, shucked, blanched, and peeled (see page 19)

$1/4$ cup grated Parmesan cheese, plus more for garnish

$1/2$ cup loosely packed fresh mint leaves

2 tablespoons Preserved Lemon Peel (page 219)

To shape the pasta, lightly dust a wooden cutting board with flour. Divide the ball of pasta dough into 4 equal pieces. Lightly coat each with flour and flatten enough to feed easily into the pasta roller. Roll each piece out on a pasta machine, ending at setting number 6. Remember to dust the dough with flour if it ever seems moist or sticky while you are rolling it.

Flour a baking sheet and have ready. Cut each pasta sheet crosswise into thirds, then fold each third in half. Cut each folded half lengthwise into $1/2$-inch-wide strips. Place the strips on the prepared baking sheet, lightly sprinkle with more flour, and cover with a clean kitchen towel.

To cook the fava beans, in a large skillet, heat the olive oil over medium heat. Add the garlic and red pepper flakes and sizzle for 30 seconds. Add the fava beans and cook, stirring, until warmed through, about 1 minute. Remove from the heat and keep warm.

Bring a large pot of well-salted water to a boil. Cook the fresh pasta until al dente, about 2 minutes. Drain, saving $1/2$ cup of the cooking water. Add the pasta to the fava bean mixture in the skillet and pour in the reserved $1/2$ cup pasta cooking water. Place the skillet with the fava bean mixture over medium heat until heated through. Stir in the $1/4$ cup Parmesan and mint leaves.

To serve, divide the pasta and sauce among the bowls, garnish with more Parmesan and the preserved lemon.

To Drink

In late spring and early summer when favas appear on our menu, I love to feature food-friendly white wines from local winemakers. Good examples are the straightforward Pinot Blanc–based Giuliano and Chardonnay-based Giovanni from Cameron Winery, or their perfectly balanced, golden-hued Clos Electrique Blanc that especially highlights the mint, garlic, and Parmesan in this dish. A French alternative, Savennières Clos du Papillon from Domaine des Baumard, with muted flavors of fruit, fig, and caramel, is herbaceous like the mint and slightly nutty, a good foil to the starchy broth that finishes the pasta. **–K.P.**

Shopping for Mushrooms

I'm driving west from Portland toward Vernonia with Lars, whom I refer to as The Mushroom Guy. He is a broker who forages and sells mushrooms and truffles directly to our restaurant. Lars has been foraging for mushrooms in Oregon for twenty-five years. His expertise is deep and his opinions are strong, and in a day of hunting mushrooms with him, I will get lessons in practical geology, forestry, political economy, ecology, history, and mushrooming culture, along with a precious small harvest of morels.

Mushrooms are the aboveground fruiting bodies of fungi that live largely in and around trees, or, in the case of saprophytes (decomposers) like morels, in dead organic matter. The fungi whose fruits we call chanterelles, truffles, and porcini are symbiotic with trees, diverting some of the carbohydrates from a tree as it begins to move those carbohydrates from the canopy down to the roots for the winter. Lars explains that forest conditions and forestry practices have a profound impact on mushroom yield. For example, clear-cutting (harvesting all trees at once) won't yield a harvest of symbiotic chanterelles for twenty years; morels (which are saprophytic) will appear the year following a clear-cut.

"On abandoned pasture land that was planted with timber, you have great truffles twenty years later," Lars tells me. "Grasslands in temperate areas near coniferous forests—which you find in Oregon—give you morels."

Today, we're looking for morels an hour's drive from Portland on the east side of the Coast Range, about eight hundred feet above sea level. We arrive at the clear-cut opening in the forest. I've never seen a clear-cut up close before, and from a distance, one always seemed a little sinister. But here in the midst of it, despite the fact that there are no trees, you can see that the clear-cut still lives. New trees have been planted. All sorts of things are growing among the stumps and brush.

We walk mostly in silence. From time to time, Lars shares his perceptions of the landscape. He can see the clear-cut was replanted last winter.

"This area was surface logged—you can see the Cat tracks." He points at the cross-hatch marks in the ground left by a bulldozer. "That's a good indicator for morels. The more the ground is torn up, the more likely you'll get morels."

A little later: "See that thistle? When you find thistles the size of a dinner plate, you are in a clear-cut that is the right age for morels."

We wander and scan. Footprints and cut morel stems show us someone's been here before us. Suddenly Lars stops. "See if you can find morels. Can't you find them?" Lars can see a perfect, pristine morel, but I can't even though I'm looking right at it. The midday light isn't providing enough contrast. "If you were a professional picker," he tells me, "this would be the right time to take a nap." Finally the treasure takes shape in my vision. "There it is!" I exclaim as I bend down to pick it.

As we walk, Lars continues to coach me, moving from topic to topic, trying to shape my ability to observe. He points out, "I see another weathered morel going black in the sunlight right under your nose. It's turning black because it's been aboveground longer than the others. When you have extended cloudy cold weather, the morels never do turn black." I don't care if it was weathered: I see it, so I have to pick it.

We find more morels already dry on the stem. "These started growing long ago," he tells me. "Really new mushrooms will have small stems that are smooth and white. As the morel grows the stem gets rough and dark. The cap will stop growing, but not the stem. In a mature morel, the stem is bigger than the cap."

He picks and hands me the morels, and watches me place them carefully into my little wooden basket. I am proud of our finds, and that gives him pleasure. We walk on and fall back into silence, feeling the warm sun on our faces.

I listen to the sound of my shoes crunching wood chips and watch for mushrooms. When Lars points out the hills to the east of us and traces the horizon with his finger to Forest Park, an area near where I live, I feel like he is domesticating this vast space for me, allowing me to understand where I am.

"A fresh one dead ahead," he says. "It has a slight olive cast." And another—"the biggest of the day," he says appreciatively. "It's in the shadow of my head." I search and search and search. "I'm giving you a discrete square foot of ground to look at," he teases until I exclaim, "Oh, yeah!" "Look at it," he directs. "It's in great shape." He continues, "Hydration in fresh mushrooms indicates how much shelf life to expect. As soon as they start dehydrating, you've got to dehydrate them all the way. You can't just pack them in a box and expect them to hold up."

I regard my tiny harvest. "It will make a nice omelet," I say. Then I tell him how my grandmother cooked mushrooms: "They call chanterelles 'little foxes' in Russian. She cooked hers for a long time and they developed an amazing nutty taste. First-of-the-season mushrooms retain a texture that seems squeaky. They crunch and have deep, rich flavor." My cook's mind has taken over. I can't wait to get back to my stove.

Soft-Egg Raviolo, Morels, and Asparagus

Serves 6

"It's like getting a surprise package!" exclaimed one diner after tasting this dish. As you cut into the raviolo, the egg yolk bursts, oozing over herbed goat cheese, earthy morels, and woodsy asparagus, creating a different sensation every time you take a bite.

This Italian specialty, usually reserved only for special occasions when truffles are in season, gets a Pacific Northwest redo with the substitution of spring morels for the truffles. If morels are not in season, use any wild or exotic mushroom. For added drama, I look for cage-free, organic eggs as they have the brightest yolks. In any case, be sure of the quality and provenance of your eggs, since the yolks will not be fully cooked.

6 1/2 ounces fresh goat cheese

1/4 cup Fresh Ricotta Cheese (page 219)

1/2 cup good-quality grated Parmesan cheese, plus more for garnish

10 sprigs of thyme, leaves only, finely chopped

10 chives, finely chopped

6 tablespoons Persillade (page 198)

All-purpose flour, for dusting

1 pound Basic Pasta Dough (page 66), at room temperature, or prepared fresh pasta sheets

6 large egg yolks, kept separate, plus 1 whole large egg, beaten, for egg wash

1/4 pound fresh morel mushrooms

4 cups cold water

Kosher salt and freshly ground black pepper

6 tablespoons unsalted butter

12 spears asparagus, woody ends snapped off, cut into 1-inch pieces

1/4 cup white wine

3 tablespoons aged balsamic vinegar, for drizzling

In a large bowl, thoroughly combine the goat cheese, ricotta, Parmesan, thyme, chives, and 3 tablespoons of the persillade. Cover and refrigerate until ready to use.

To shape the pasta, lightly dust a wooden cutting board with flour. Divide the ball of pasta dough into 4 equal pieces. Lightly coat each with flour and flatten enough to feed easily into the pasta roller. Roll each piece out on a pasta machine, ending at setting number 6. Remember to dust the dough with flour if it ever seems moist or sticky while you are rolling it.

Each sheet should be about 6 inches wide by 15 inches long; cut them to size if necessary.

Place the 4 sheets of pasta on a work surface lightly dusted with flour. Using a soupspoon, center a generous spoonful of the goat cheese mixture about 3 inches in from the left edge of one sheet. Flatten the filling while making a well in the center. Place the next spoonful 3 inches to the right of the first, and then a third spoonful another 3 inches away. Flatten and make a well in the center of each mound. Prepare a second sheet of pasta in the same manner. Carefully place an egg yolk in the center of each well.

On one of the filled pasta sheets, brush egg wash around each mound of filling. Completely brush a plain sheet of pasta with egg wash and place it, egg-wash-side down, over the prepared, filled pasta sheet, stretching it over the filling. Working from the center of the sheet out, press gently around each mound of filling (try not to trap air bubbles). This will seal in the fillings and "glue" the two sheets of pasta together. Prepare the remaining filled and plain sheets the same way.

Have a platter lightly dusted with flour ready. With a rolling cutter or knife, cut between the raviolis, leaving a 1-inch margin of unfilled pasta all around each one. Trim off the corners of each raviolo for a more uniform look. Transfer the ravioli to the prepared platter. Dust with a little more flour and refrigerate, loosely covered with parchment paper, while preparing the other ingredients.

To prepare the sauce, trim off the stems of the morels and reserve them for another use. Halve the mushrooms lengthwise and place them in a small saucepan. Cover with 4 cups of cold water, sprinkle with 1 tablespoon of salt, and bring to a boil over high heat. Remove from the heat. Drain the mushrooms in a colander, reserving 1 cup of mushroom cooking liquid and discarding the rest. Rinse the mushrooms in cold water, gently press dry with your hands, and arrange on paper towels.

In a 12-inch skillet over medium heat, melt 3 tablespoons of the butter. Add the morels and cook to warm through, about 3 minutes. Add the asparagus and stir until glistening with butter. Add the 1 cup reserved mushroom cooking liquid and the wine. Cook until almost dry, about 10 minutes. Add the remaining 3 tablespoons butter and persillade and cook, stirring, until melted. Season with salt and pepper. Keep warm.

When ready to cook the pasta, bring a large pot of well-salted water to a boil over high heat. Gently brush off the flour from the ravioli and drop them in the boiling water. After the ravioli float to the surface, cook for 5 minutes to warm the filling through. The egg yolk will still be fairly runny.

To serve, carefully remove the ravioli, one at a time, with a slotted spoon and place in individual pasta bowls. Top each with a spoonful of the morel-asparagus mixture. Liberally sprinkle with more Parmesan and drizzle with balsamic vinegar. Serve immediately.

To Drink

Pairing wine with intensely grassy asparagus is always a challenge. Adelsheim Vineyard, one of Oregon's pioneer wineries, produces an unusual Auxerrois that partners well with the "leaky" eggs of this dish and also draws out the flavor of the goat cheese. From Alsace, Domaine Zind Humbrecht Riesling Heimbourg has a whisper of sweetness that complements the goat cheese and completes the dish elegantly. **–K.P.**

Dungeness Crab and Corn Risotto

Serves 4 to 6

I learned to prepare risotto from chef Francesco Antonucci of New York's Remi restaurant. His technique is unorthodox: rather than adding the broth throughout cooking, he incorporates most of it right away, reserving a small amount to adjust the final texture. While the risotto cooks, he stirs it only enough to prevent the grains from sticking to the pan. However, he stirs vigorously when finishing the risotto with butter and cheese to bruise the grains and release starch.

I follow his lead and am never disappointed. The technique allows sufficient release of starch with little damage to the grains of rice and always finishes with a beautiful appearance that makes me think of caviar.

3 to 4 cups Corn Broth (page 206)	2 small ears of corn, shucked
1/4 cup extra-virgin olive oil	1 cup Dungeness crabmeat, drained and picked clean (see page 214)
1 small onion, finely diced	
Kosher salt and freshly ground black pepper	3/4 cup grated Parmesan cheese
1 1/3 cups Carnaroli rice	1/4 cup loosely packed basil leaves, cut in chiffonade (thin strips)
1 cup dry white wine	
6 tablespoons unsalted butter	1/4 cup Basil Pesto (page 200)

To make the risotto, in a saucepan, bring the broth to a boil over high heat, decrease the heat to low, and keep hot.

In a 3-quart saucepan, warm the olive oil over medium heat. Add the diced onion, season with salt and pepper, and cook without letting the onion color until the pieces are translucent, about 3 minutes. Add the rice all at once, stir to coat with oil, and cook, stirring frequently, about 2 minutes.

Increase the heat to high, add the wine, and continue to cook, stirring gently, until all the wine has been absorbed, about 3 minutes.

Pour in 3 cups of the hot broth and boil for about 10 minutes. Stir occasionally to prevent the rice from sticking to the bottom of the pan. (Don't leave the spoon in the pan between stirrings or the rice will not cook evenly.)

In a small skillet, melt 4 tablespoons of the butter over low heat. Add the shucked corn and the crab and warm gently for about 5 minutes.

After the rice has cooked for 10 minutes, test for doneness by biting into a few grains. When ready, the center of the grain should still have a little resistance, and the risotto should still be fairly liquid. If the rice seems too chewy, cook for another minute. Mix the corn-crab mixture into the rice, stirring gently to distribute, and cook another 2 minutes. When ready to serve, the risotto should be the consistency of porridge. If it seems too dry, thin as needed with more broth.

Remove the pan from the heat. Add the remaining 2 tablespoons of butter along with 1/2 cup of the grated cheese and stir the risotto vigorously with one hand while shaking the pot with the other for about 1 minute. The texture will become creamy, and the butter and cheese completely incorporated. Stir in the pesto.

Serve in individual bowls, garnished with basil and the remaining 1/4 cup of Parmesan.

To Drink

Ideal partners for rich Parmesan cheese and sweet creamy corn are Chehalem Ian's Reserve Chardonnay or Westrey Chardonnay, both from Oregon. Your choice: the former is full-bodied, with a buttery, caramel-like finish, while the latter offers a softer finish with citrus notes. A number of French white Burgundies would also do, but a personal favorite of mine is the Puligny-Montrachet produced by Etienne Sauzet. Well-balanced and straightforward, it perfectly complements this delicate combination of crab and corn. **–K.P.**

Chef's Tip

Of the three types of rice most commonly used for making risotto—Arborio, Vialone Nano, and Carnaroli—we prefer Carnaroli in our kitchen. While it is more expensive than the others, I consider it worth the higher price because its rich starches create a risotto with the most velvety texture and silky finish. When making risotto, keep the following in mind:

- Cut the onions the size of a grain of rice so they melt and disappear.
- Don't brown the onions. The finished risotto should look white and luxurious.
- Many Italians use an espresso cup to calculate how much rice to use. One espresso cup ($1/3$ standard measuring cup) of rice per person works for me. In the absence of an espresso cup, a closed handful of rice per person does the trick.
- Stir with a wooden spoon, not metal; wood is gentler on the rice.

Farro with Wild Mushrooms, Beef Marrow, and Truffles

Serves 4 to 6

Bluebird Grain Farms, located in north-central Washington, is the family farm of Brooke and Sam Lucy, who grow a number of heirloom grain crops, including emmer, an ancient wheat known also as farro. The fabulously rich flavor of their farro is the best I've ever tasted (see Resources, page 222). It keeps a very pleasant, chewy texture even after prolonged cooking.

Beef marrow accentuates the nutty flavor of the farro in this recipe, but you may substitute 2 tablespoons of olive oil to cook the onion and toast the farro. This dish is good on its own or paired with a main course of game, fowl, or beef.

2 tablespoons extra-virgin olive oil	1 small onion, finely diced
6 ounces wild mushrooms (such as chanterelles or porcini), cleaned and cut into bite-sized pieces	2 cups emmer farro, soaked overnight
	1 cup dry red wine
Kosher salt and freshly ground black pepper	2 tablespoons cold unsalted butter
6 cups Chicken Stock, plus more if needed	1/3 cup grated Parmesan cheese, plus more for garnish
3 ounces beef marrow (optional), soaked overnight, cut into small pieces, and kept cold (see page 31)	3 tablespoons Persillade (page 198)
	1 medium (about 1 ounce) fresh Oregon black or white truffle, optional

Line a plate with paper towels and have ready. In a large skillet, heat the olive oil over medium heat. Add the mushrooms, season with salt and pepper, and cook until tender, about 5 minutes. Transfer the mushrooms to the prepared plate to drain and cool.

In a saucepan, bring the stock to a boil over high heat, decrease the heat to low, and keep hot for cooking the farro.

In a saucepan, melt the marrow over medium heat. Add the onion, season generously with salt and pepper, and cook until the onion is translucent, about 3 minutes. Add the farro and toast, stirring with the onions, until well coated, about 1 minute. Pour in the wine and cook, stirring, until all the wine has been absorbed. Pour in half the hot stock, decrease the heat to low, and cook, stirring often, until the farro grains are plump and tender and the cooking liquid absorbed, about 1 hour. Add stock as needed so the farro is always submerged in liquid. After 1 hour, test a few grains for doneness. If they still seem crunchy, continue to cook, adding more stock as needed, until they have a pleasant chew (this could take another 30 minutes).

When the farro is cooked and no liquid remains, add the mushrooms and stir until heated through, about 1 minute. Remove from the heat and add the butter, Parmesan, and persillade. Stir vigorously to melt the butter.

To serve, transfer the farro mixture to a deep serving bowl and sprinkle with more grated Parmesan. Thinly shave the truffle over the farro and serve immediately.

Chef's Tip

Cooking emmer farro takes up to twice as long as the more commonly used farro made from spelt. Soaking the emmer overnight substantially reduces its cooking time.

To Drink

An Oregon Pinot Noir is an obvious companion for a dish made with wild mushrooms, marrow, and locally harvested truffles and grain. Ken Wright, one of the most generous-spirited and meticulous winemakers we know, makes a wine that is a perfect match for this dish. His Ken Wright Cellars Pinot Noir Abbott Claim Vineyard draws out the mushrooms and marrow with black cherry fruit and floral aromas, and cuts through emmer's toothiness with delicate, lingering tannins. Not a French red Burgundy, but another Oregon Pinot Noir, made by Mike Etzel of Beaux Frères, is my alternate recommendation. Beaux Frères Willamette Valley Pinot Noir hints of forest and mushrooms, and its satisfying balance makes you pause and savor this dish to the last bite. **–K.P.**

Herbed Ricotta Gnocchi with Dungeness Crab

Serves 4

Every now and then I break free of the culinary taboo against mixing cheese and fish. The combination of ricotta, crab, and lemon may seem a bit unorthodox, but they have a wonderful affinity for one another.

Making ricotta gnocchi is less involved than preparing their potato counterpart. This is essentially a filling for ravioli without the pasta, using our own house-made ricotta cheese. Be sure the cheese is well drained. Too much whey will make the batter too loose to hold its shape during cooking.

Kosher salt

9 ounces Fresh Ricotta Cheese (page 219), well drained

$1/4$ cup plus 3 tablespoons all-purpose flour, sifted

1 large egg

6 tablespoons extra-virgin olive oil

$1/3$ cup grated Parmesan cheese

1 tablespoon chopped fresh Italian parsley

1 tablespoon chopped fresh savory

1 tablespoon chopped fresh tarragon

1 tablespoon chopped fresh chives

4 tablespoons unsalted butter

1 cup Dungeness crabmeat, drained and picked clean (see page 214)

Juice of $1/2$ lemon

2 tablespoons Persillade (page 198), for garnish

Preserved Lemon Peel (page 219), for garnish

Fill a 3-quart pot three-fourths full with water, bring to a boil over high heat, and salt well. Decrease the heat to medium.

To make the batter, in the work bowl of a food processor fitted with the metal blade, add the ricotta, flour, egg, 2 tablespoons of the olive oil, $1/2$ teaspoon salt, half the Parmesan, parsley, savory, tarragon, and chives, and process until smooth.

Have a large platter ready. To make the gnocchi, transfer one third of the batter to a pastry bag fitted with a large straight tip, or a self-sealing plastic bag with one corner snipped $1/2$ inch wide. Working over the simmering water, squeeze out the batter, cutting it into 1-inch lengths with a small knife to form the gnocchi, working in batches so as not to crowd the gnocchi. Poach the pieces until firm, about 3 minutes. With a slotted spoon, gently transfer the cooked gnocchi to the platter. Drizzle with olive oil. Repeat with the remaining batter. Reserve $1/4$ cup of gnocchi cooking water.

To make the sauce, in a large skillet, melt the butter over medium heat; add $1/4$ cup of gnocchi cooking water. Gently transfer the poached gnocchi to the pan. Stir in the crab and lemon juice and cook, stirring carefully, until the mixture is warm through, about 3 minutes.

To serve, spoon the gnocchi into individual pasta bowls, and garnish with the remaining Parmesan cheese, persillade, and lemon peel.

To Drink

The herb-infused ricotta gnocchi pairs nicely with a fruity Pinot Gris with tropical overtones. Two Oregon wines come to mind. Soléna Cellars Oregon Pinot Gris is viscous and fleshy and tastes of white stone fruit. Sineann Pinot Gris Oregon reflects tropical fruit and zesty minerals. The citrus present in both wines finds its complement in the preserved lemon that finishes the dish, and reflects both winemakers' personalities, friendly and engaging. **–K.P.**

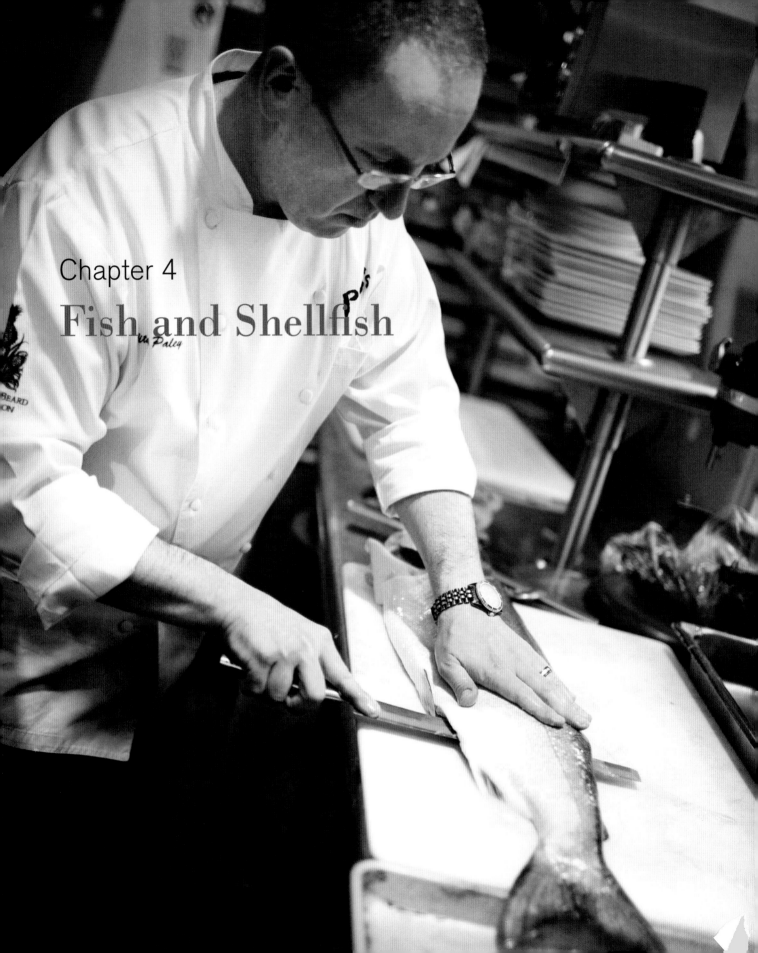

Chapter 4

Fish and Shellfish

Poached Escalopes of Halibut with Dungeness Crab Broth

Serves 6

In the dead of winter, offshore storms affect fishing and limit what we can get. I love having fish on the menu, so I know the seas have calmed when Alaskan halibut becomes available in late March. It is then that the cold northern waters begin to yield halibut with pearly white, beautifully translucent flesh that is very lean and requires little cooking. My technique relies on a hot soup bowl and hot broth to render the fish barely warm—the best way to enjoy it, I think. Any vegetables in season will make a compatible side dish.

Kosher salt and freshly ground black pepper

12 baby carrots, peeled and trimmed

12 asparagus spears, peeled, trimmed, and cut in 2-inch pieces

12 sugar snap peas, stem and string removed

1 small head purple, cheddar, or white cauliflower, separated into small florets

3 small fingerling potatoes

1/2 cup (1 stick) unsalted butter, softened

3 tablespoons Persillade (page 198)

Grated zest of 1 lemon

Juice of 1/2 lemon

3 tablespoons chopped fresh chives

3 cups Crab Broth (page 34)

4 ounces cooked Dungeness crabmeat (see page 214)

1 pound fresh halibut, sliced paper-thin

3 radishes (such as French Breakfast), thinly sliced

Sprigs of chervil or Italian parsley, for garnish

Have a large bowl of ice water ready. Bring a large pot of water to a boil over high heat. Add enough salt so you can taste it. Blanch the carrots, asparagus, sugar snap peas, and cauliflower separately until just tender, about 5 minutes each. If using purple cauliflower, blanch it last, as it will turn the water purple and the color will bleed onto the other vegetables. Refresh all the vegetables in an ice-water bath. Dry well on paper towels and reserve until needed.

Preheat the oven to 350°F.

In a small saucepan, place the potatoes and enough salted water to cover. Cook over high heat until cooked through, about 20 minutes. When cool enough to handle, peel and slice into 1/4-inch-thick rounds. Set aside.

In a small bowl, prepare herb butter by mixing the softened butter with the persillade, lemon zest, lemon juice, and chives; reserve.

Place heatproof soup bowls in the oven and heat until hot to the touch, about 5 minutes. In a small saucepan, bring the broth to a boil over high heat and keep warm.

In a 12-inch skillet, melt 6 tablespoons of the herb butter over low heat. Add the carrots, asparagus, sugar snap peas, cauliflower, and potatoes and stir for about 3 minutes to warm them through. Add the crabmeat and continue stirring until hot, another 3 minutes.

Carefully remove the soup bowls from the oven and brush the bowls with the remaining herb butter. Season the bottoms of the bowls with salt and pepper. Divide the halibut among the bowls, laying the slices on the seasoned bottoms. Pour the hot broth over the halibut, dividing it evenly. Spoon the vegetable-crab mixture into the broth. Garnish with sliced radish and herb sprigs and serve immediately.

To Drink

David Autrey and Amy Wesselman, a husband-and-wife team of Oregon winemakers, are quite successful at creating food-friendly wines. Their straightforward Westrey Chardonnay delivers the floral purity of citrus, clean unoaked flavor, and a minerality that leads the delicate sweetness of the crab to the flavors of the tender seasonal vegetables. This is a wine that is right on.

Still on a floral note, François Chidaine, Vouvray, Montlouis Sur Loire Les Tuffeaux is a French white wine from the Loire Valley made from the Chenin Blanc grape. This grape varietal is expressed beautifully here with honeylike sweetness. The wine's golden hues and wildflower aromas pair beautifully with the tender young vegetables and sweet crab. **–K.P.**

Olive Oil–Poached Halibut Cheeks with Salsa Verde

Serves 4 to 6

Poaching fish in fat may seem like an anomaly. Wine or broth is the usual poaching liquid, and common knowledge says that fat is only used for frying. But when halibut cheeks, prized for their unique and meaty texture, are poached in olive oil, their flesh turns incredibly flaky and completely luxurious.

Halibut cheeks are extracted by fishermen right as the fish are caught. They are hard to come by. When you find them, buy as many as you can afford—they freeze well. If they aren't available from your fishmonger, substitute halibut fillets.

Salsa verde works well with all manner of fish. It's very simple to prepare and offers bright and vibrant flavor. It has an ephemeral quality that is best captured if eaten soon after it's made.

Salsa Verde

3 tablespoons chopped fresh Italian parsley

3 tablespoons chopped fresh tarragon

3 tablespoons chopped fresh basil

4 anchovy fillets, drained and finely chopped

2 large cloves garlic, finely minced

1 tablespoon drained capers

3 tablespoons coarsely chopped pitted green olives

1 hard-boiled egg, peeled and finely grated on the smallest holes of a box grater

Juice of 1 lemon

Kosher salt and freshly ground black pepper

3/4 cup extra-virgin olive oil

Halibut

Extra-virgin olive oil, for poaching

2 pounds halibut cheeks, trimmed, or halibut fillet, skinned and trimmed

Kosher salt and freshly ground black pepper

Sea salt, for finishing

To make the salsa verde, in a large bowl, mix together the parsley, tarragon, basil, anchovies, garlic, capers, olives, egg, and lemon juice. Season with salt and pepper and stir in olive oil. Refrigerate, covered, until ready to use.

In a 6-quart soup pot, add $1^1/2$ inches of olive oil. Heat over medium heat until it reaches 160°F on a deep-fat thermometer. Decrease the heat to the lowest setting.

Divide the fish equally into 4 to 6 pieces and season with salt and pepper on all sides. Submerge the halibut in the oil and poach until a wooden skewer slips easily into the fish, about 15 minutes. Make sure the fish remains completely submerged; do not hesitate to add more oil if needed.

To serve, working with 1 piece of fish at a time, remove from the oil with a slotted spatula and gently shake off any excess oil. Arrange on a dinner plate, sprinkle with sea salt, and serve at once with salsa verde.

To Drink

Two Oregon Chardonnays offer enough acidity to complement the union of warm, flaky halibut and sweet green herbs. Bethel Heights Chardonnay surrounds the fish with a rich and creamy finish. The fruit in Lange Chardonnay cools the sweet and briny salsa. Or try a crisp French Chardonnay like Fougeray de Beauclair, Marsannay Blanc. It has a bite of acid and subtle, tropical character that also brings out the sweetness of the herbs. **–K.P.**

Poppy Seed–Crusted Albacore Tuna with Chickpea Puree and Fennel Salad

Serves 4 to 6

This is my idea of a perfect dish for a hot summer evening. All the cooking is done ahead so I can enjoy the company of friends. I keep it light, relying only on healthy olive oil for fat.

For results that will yield tuna with a perfect, raw center when cooked, select a loin that after cleaning is approximately twelve inches long and three to four inches wide. Note that the chickpeas must soak overnight before cooking. I prefer to use olives with pits for this dish, and just warn my guests to watch out for them.

1 1/2 cups dried chickpeas, soaked overnight in cold water

Kosher salt and freshly ground black pepper

Large pinch of saffron

3 large cloves garlic, coarsely chopped

3/4 cup extra-virgin olive oil, plus more for drizzling

2 tablespoons poppy seeds, plus more if needed

12-inch-long albacore tuna loin (about 1 1/2 pounds), skin and blood line removed

1 small bulb fennel, greens trimmed

Juice of 1 lemon

3/4 cup ripe cherry tomatoes, halved

1/3 cup niçoise olives with pits

1/4 cup Preserved Lemon Peel (page 219)

1/4 cup loosely packed fresh mint leaves

Sea salt, for finishing

To cook the chickpeas, drain them and transfer to a soup pot. Add enough cold water to cover by 1 inch. Add 1 tablespoon of salt and then the saffron. Cook the chickpeas over medium heat until very tender, about 60 minutes. (If I have forgotten to soak the chickpeas, I usually double their cooking time.) Always keep the chickpeas completely submerged during cooking, adding more water as needed. When done, drain and cool completely. Save the cooking water for another use. It will make a great, intensely flavored vegetarian soup stock.

To make the puree, in the work bowl of a food processor fitted with the metal blade, process the cooled chickpeas, garlic, and 1/2 cup of the olive oil until very smooth. Season to taste with salt and pepper, and set aside.

To cook the tuna, divide the tuna loin into 3 equal pieces, season on all sides with salt and pepper, then roll in poppy seeds to coat uniformly. Tightly wrap each piece of fish in 1 piece of aluminum foil, keeping the foil smooth and without crimps.

Heat a large, dry skillet over high heat until very hot, about 5 minutes. Sear the tuna, still wrapped in

foil, on all sides, about 5 minutes altogether. (This technique ensures that poppy seeds stick easily to the outside of the fish and the inside remains raw.)

Unwrap each piece of fish right after cooking so it does not cook further. Set aside at room temperature.

To make the fennel salad, slice the fennel paper-thin, using a mandoline if possible. Put the slices in a bowl, add the lemon juice, and mix gently. Add the tomatoes, olives, lemon peel, and mint. Add the remaining 1/4 cup olive oil. Season with salt and pepper and gently toss all ingredients to coat.

To serve, slice the tuna into 1/2-inch-thick pieces. Place a dollop of chickpea puree in the center of each plate. Set slices of tuna on the plates next to the chickpea puree and sprinkle the fish with sea salt. Top each plate with fennel salad and drizzle with more olive oil. Serve immediately.

To Drink

The Sauvignon Blanc wines from Didier Dagueneau brilliantly express the soul of his vineyards and the heart of his grapes. The combined acid and fruit in both his Blanc Fume de Pouilly and Pouilly Fume, Pur Sang plow through the complex flavors of saffron, fennel, chickpea, mint, and garlic. I recommend them both.

In Oregon, Andrew Rich makes Sauvignon Blanc with younger vines that addresses the exotic flavors of saffron and highlights the creamy chickpea puree and preserved lemon. **–K.P.**

Blackened Black Cod with Sauce Gribiche

Serves 4

Black cod is a buttery fish prized for its very high fat content. It can be caught any time of year, weather permitting, which makes it a very attractive main course when halibut and salmon seasons are closed. French in origin, *sauce gribiche* is actually a close cousin to American tartar sauce, but with a more complex taste and a broader range of uses. You should find it familiar and easy to make. It is equally at home with many fish and shellfish preparations, or with poached artichokes or grilled asparagus. *Sauce gribiche* is best served the day you make it because the fresh herbs deteriorate quite rapidly.

Serve this dish with Crispy Potatoes with Romesco (page 148) or grilled Asparagus with Smoked Salmon–Dill Butter (page 133).

Sauce
Aioli (page 203)

2 tablespoons chopped cornichons

2 tablespoons drained capers

2 tablespoons chopped fresh tarragon, finely chopped

2 tablespoons chopped fresh Italian parsley

2 tablespoons chopped fresh chives

1 hard-boiled egg, peeled and coarsely grated on the largest holes of a box grater

Pinch of freshly ground black pepper

Cod
1 1/2 teaspoons kosher salt

1 teaspoon freshly ground black pepper

2 teaspoons chopped fresh thyme

2 teaspoons chopped fresh oregano

1/2 teaspoon cayenne pepper

2 teaspoons sweet Hungarian paprika

1/2 teaspoon ground cumin

1 teaspoon ground fennel seed

2 pounds black cod fillet, skinned

1 tablespoon canola or grapeseed oil

1/2 lemon, seeded, for finishing

2 tablespoons Persillade (page 198), for garnish

To make the sauce, in a small bowl, mix all ingredients together. The resulting sauce should be pretty thick, but if you think it needs thinning, stir in a bit of cold water. Refrigerate, tightly covered, until ready to use.

To make the cod, in a small bowl, mix the salt, pepper, thyme, oregano, cayenne, paprika, cumin, and fennel. Generously coat the fish on both sides with the spice mixture. Heat a large cast-iron skillet over high heat until very hot. Brush the bottom of the pan with 1 tablespoon of oil (the pan should be hot enough so the oil smokes). Carefully add the fish fillets and cook until blackened on both sides, about 2 minutes per side.

To serve, transfer the fillets to a platter, squeeze the lemon over the fish, and sprinkle with persillade. Serve hot with the sauce on the side.

To Drink

The buttery, high-fat content of black cod coated with spices and the salty, herbaceous flavors of *sauce gribiche* meet their match in Trimbach Cuvée Frédéric Émile Riesling from France. Our connection to the wines of Hubert Trimbach is highly personal, as he makes frequent trips to Oregon, and to our restaurant. This wine shows boldness with aromas redolent of Granny Smith apple and honey. It lingers on the palate, revealing a beautiful oily viscosity typical of Alsatian Rieslings.

In Oregon, Harry Peterson-Nedry, winemaker and owner of Chehalem, has a deep understanding of our region, which is why I love to talk shop with him. Chehalem Dry Riesling Reserve has a fruity intensity and razor-sharp acidity that seems to add weight to the already meaty black cod and highlights the briny sauce. **–K.P.**

Salmon Is Life

In my youth I attended endless weddings and bar mitzvahs where I was fed so much flavorless, over-cooked salmon that it fell completely off the list of foods I felt I must have. (Though I did always keep a soft spot for the silky cold smoked salmon known as lox.) When I became a cook and started creating menus, salmon fell into the category of safe foods—popular but boring.

The first time I tasted hook-and-line–caught Oregon wild King salmon, or Chinook, everything changed. It was like no other salmon I'd ever eaten. Now, when spring Chinook are running, usually at the end of March, I can't wait to start cooking them. Their bright red flesh glistens, streaked with fat like well marbled beef. They are delicious no matter how they are prepared (but I recommend cooking them on a cedar plank—see page 92).

I now view having wild salmon on the menu as a precious gift to our customers. Salmon is bound up with the identity of the West Coast, from northern California to Alaska, where the fish's epic migratory routes knit together ocean and river. (Oregon, in fact, refers to itself as Salmon Nation.) There are those who feel the health of all life in this region is measured by the health of the wild fish population.

The story of salmon is breathtakingly dramatic. They push against the powerful flow of currents, climb over rocks, and work to overcome all challenges to get back to their spawning grounds, almost depleting them-selves in the process. They re-form their bodies as they go, so that their flesh changes texture when they have left saltwater for fresh. The effort of the fish to perpetu-ate their life cycle is echoed by the effort of the men and women who build precarious lives around catching them. No fisherman can make a living from catching wild salmon any more. The populations are too depleted, too fragile, the forces arrayed against the salmon (mostly due to human activity from dam building to global warming) too powerful.

We have bought fish from the same source for the past twelve years, and, as it turns out, most of our catch comes from one fisherman, Mark Newell. When I finally had the chance to meet him, it was rather profound to put a face—rugged, with a white mustache—to the guy whose fish I had put on plates night after night.

One quiet day in the off-season, I met Mark on the docks of the old harbor at Newport, which is located about three hours southwest of Portland. The harbor is protected by a jetty extending far out into the water. Mark led me through a maze of weathered fishing vessels, stopping frequently to greet other fishermen making repairs. Everyone seemed eager to tell us a story about his livelihood. When we reached his boat, Mark explained that for these men, "When they can't fish, maybe they're forced to do something entirely different, and wait until they can fish again." Speaking from his own experience, he described how he had to obtain a different license for each fish—an enterprise that turned out to be both expensive and uncertain. He also tried distributing, which involved traveling to a number of ports to buy fish, then reselling them to restaurants or independent markets.

"When you do fish," Mark explained, "first you gotta find 'em." He explained that different species of salmon swim at different depths in the ocean. Then you have to catch them. "When you get a bite, you pull in the line by hand." If the fish he's fighting is a thirty-pound Chinook, it might involve a ten-minute battle. He brings in one fish at a time and even then, he tells me, "What a fisherman can do is regulated to a tenth of a percentage point on individual stock of fish." That means he may be forced to let fifty or even one hundred fish go in an effort to

harvest one. Mark helped me see how regulations confine fishermen, but the timeless hardship of catching wild fish is still determined by the ocean's power, where boats as well as lives are lost every year.

For us as consumers, these factors of power and struggle, of fish and fisherman, are reduced to a vote we make standing in front of the refrigerated case. Whenever it comes to a choice between salmon and business or politics, we as cooks stand on the side of the salmon— wild salmon, that is; we don't ever choose farmed salmon, which is a problematic and inferior product. Wild salmon is a sublime food, and an incredibly moving symbol, on so many levels, of our relationship with the natural world. If we feel we can't afford wild salmon, we think of the fishermen and of the fish and pay the price—and wonder, will the salmon be here tomorrow?

Cedar-Planked Salmon

Serves 4 to 6

I once organized a series of dinners at the restaurant focused on the farmers and growers we work with. One of these dinners featured my long-time friend, farmer George Weppler, who grows some of the most beautiful produce in our state (see page 58). He also is a great cook. During the planning, George mentioned a way he likes to cook salmon. He marinates a piece for a few hours with salt, orange zest, and brown sugar, then rubs it with chopped garlic and places it on a cedar plank, covers it generously with sliced Walla Walla onion and chopped basil, and puts the whole thing on the grill.

This dish tastes as fantastic as it sounds, and it is now a mainstay in our restaurant. If there is a better way to cook salmon, I haven't found it yet. The salmon is best straight from the grill or out of the oven (though it tastes mighty fine cold the next day). It looks very impressive when you place the salmon, plank and all, directly on a serving platter. Sauté of Market Vegetables with Miso Butter (page 137) makes a perfect side dish for the salmon.

When buying salmon always ask if it is wild. If it is not, don't buy it. Try a different recipe. Out of season, wild salmon, available FAS (frozen at sea), is a sustainable substitute to farm raised. (The piece of fish should be cut to fit the plank, leaving 1 to 2 inches all around the cut fish.)

To cook on a grill, preheat a gas grill or get a charcoal grill red-hot. Brush the cedar plank on both sides with 3 tablespoons of the olive oil. Spread the chopped garlic on the plank the length and the width of the salmon fillet. Place the salmon on the

1 (2-pound) piece wild King salmon, scaled (with skin), preferably from the belly of the fish

2 tablespoons kosher salt

1/4 cup packed brown sugar

Grated zest of 2 oranges

1/4 cup plus 2 tablespoons extra-virgin olive oil

1 small bulb garlic, peeled, separated into cloves, and finely chopped

1 Walla Walla onion, halved and thinly sliced

1/2 cup coarsely chopped fresh basil

To marinate the salmon, place the fish in a large glass baking dish. Remove any bones with a tweezer or small pliers. In a bowl, mix the salt, brown sugar, and orange zest and generously rub into both sides of the salmon. Cover the fish and refrigerate for 2 hours.

Cedar-Planked Salmon, *continued*

garlic, and cover evenly with the chopped basil and onion slices. The onion here is not just for flavor; it is meant to protect the fish from burning while it cooks, so pile it on both top and sides of the fish. Drizzle with the remaining 3 tablespoons olive oil.

The grill should be hot enough to ignite the plank when you place the salmon-topped board on the grill grate. If the plank doesn't ignite, very carefully add a few drops of oil onto the burners or coals. Let the plank burn all the way around the fish (the onion will protect the fish from burning). Once most of the exposed plank has burned, cover the grill to smother the fire. Grill the salmon without turning until medium-rare, or 130°F on an instant-read thermometer inserted in the thickest part, about 15 minutes. Serve immediately.

To cook in the oven, preheat the oven to 450°F. Brush 1 side of the cedar plank with 3 tablespoons of the olive oil and place it in the oven for at least 30 minutes to release the wood's aromas. When the kitchen develops a sweet smell reminiscent of a hot sauna, the plank is ready to use.

Spread the chopped garlic on the hot plank the length and the width of the salmon fillet. Place the salmon on the garlic, cover evenly with the chopped basil and onion slices, and drizzle with the remaining 3 tablespoons olive oil. Bake the salmon without turning until medium-rare, or 130°F on an instant-read thermometer inserted in the thickest part, about 15 minutes. Serve immediately.

Chef's Tip

For planks, I find that untreated cedar shingles purchased at a lumber yard work best for me at the restaurant. If you do not want to buy a big stack of shingles, you can buy planks at well-stocked cookware stores.

To Drink

The Pinot Noirs produced by Patricia Green and Jim Anderson of Patricia Green Cellars have always been—and will always be—on our wine list because they stay true to the grape in all its purity. Their Balcombe Vineyard Pinot Noir has balanced red fruit and enticing aromas that play to the brown sugar and orange of the salmon marinade. The sweetness of the Walla Walla onions, the licorice-like basil, and the cedar-plank method of cooking all come together in celebration and give this pairing life.

From France, the red village wines of Givry, Mercurey, and Rully offer easy tannins and a taste of crushed red berries that make a quintessential dinner date with cedar-cooked salmon. The wines' violet aromas harmonize in unison with the sweet and smoky flavors of the dish. **–K.P.**

Bacon-Wrapped Sturgeon Bordelaise

Serves 4 to 6

Sturgeon has long been prized for the merits of its caviar. Because of its meaty flavor and delicate texture, it is also a very good eating fish, delicious smoked or grilled.

Inspired by an old English recipe that treated the sturgeon like meat, frying it before stewing it in veal broth and red wine, I devised a new way to prepare it. To play on the richness of the sturgeon, I wrap it in smoked bacon, pan-fry it, and roast it. The fish is served with my version of the classic French bordelaise sauce. Like the English recipe, it uses red wine and veal stock, but also balsamic vinegar, which balances the richness of the bacon with a soft sweetness and the right amount of acidity. This dish lets me combine the best of French techniques with local and seasonal ingredients.

In a spirit of opulence, I serve Ken's Potato Galette (page 146) as an accompaniment.

2 pounds sturgeon fillet, skinned and divided into 4 equal pieces	1/2 cup Sauce Bordelaise, My Way (page 215)
Kosher salt and freshly ground black pepper	1 teaspoon cold unsalted butter, cut in cubes
16 to 20 (1/16-inch-thick) slices Smoked Bacon (page 204)	1 ounce beef marrow, soaked overnight, cut into small pieces, and kept cold (see page 31)
1/4 cup extra-virgin olive oil	2 tablespoons chopped fresh Italian parsley
All-purpose flour, for dredging	

To prepare the fish, season the pieces all over with salt and pepper. Wrap the sturgeon with bacon tightly and completely (see Chef's Tip), then tightly wrap with plastic wrap. Refrigerate 30 minutes, to help the bacon adhere.

Preheat the oven to 375°F.

In a 12-inch skillet, heat the olive oil over medium heat. Unwrap the fish, dredge in flour, and shake off any excess. Sauté in the hot oil until the bacon is uniformly golden, about 5 minutes per side. Transfer to an ovenproof dish and roast the fish to an internal temperature of 140°F, about 5 minutes. Remove from the oven, set aside, covered loosely with aluminum foil, and finish the sauce.

In a small saucepan, bring the sauce to a boil over medium-high heat. Whisk in the butter and then the marrow until well incorporated, about 1 minute. Remove from the heat and stir in half the parsley.

To serve, slice the pieces of fish into 1-inch-thick slices. Arrange the slices on a large platter. Sprinkle with the remaining parsley and serve with the sauce on the side.

Chef's Tip

To wrap the fish, start at the thinnest end of a sturgeon piece and wrap a piece of bacon in an overlapping spiral as far as it will reach, then start wrapping with another piece where the first ends, and so on until the whole piece of fish is wrapped. You are trying to achieve a continuous band of bacon around the fish, as if you were wrapping tape around a handlebar or around a spliced wire. This method helps keep the bacon from unraveling.

To Drink

Cabernet Franc deserves more recognition. In France's Loire Valley, it is a red grape varietal; in Bordeaux, a blending grape. However in Oregon, Andrew Rich Cabernet Franc stands on its own. This easy-drinking wine with black fruit flavor and soft tannins does more than complement the bordelaise sauce—it completely supports the beauty of drinking a red wine with fish.

In the Loire Valley, I favor any Charles Jouget Chinon from any vineyard site. His Clos de la Cure connects to the bacon fat. Light in style, it carries sufficient weight to treat this fish like meat. **–K.P.**

Bacon-Crusted Razor Clams with Basil Aioli

Serves 4 to 6

Razor clams are dug at low tides on the beaches of the Pacific Northwest. Reaching six inches in length, they get their name from their thin, razor-sharp shells. Luckily, at the restaurant we get them already cleaned from the Quinault Indian Reservation, so we never find out just how sharp they are.

When lightly breaded and fried, their meat is sweet, supple, and pleasantly chewy. Bacon and clams have long been one of my favorite combinations. I find that breading them in the following manner makes it possible for the two flavors to be virtually inseparable in every bite.

1 cup Aioli (page 203)

2 tablespoons Basil Pesto (page 200)

4 ounces Smoked Bacon (page 204), ground in a meat grinder or cut into 1/8-inch dice

1 cup all-purpose flour, sifted

3 large eggs, beaten

2 cups fine bread crumbs (see page 138)

1 pound razor clams, cleaned (about 8 to 10 clams)

Canola oil, for pan-frying

Sea salt

Small basil leaves, for garnish

In a small bowl, make basil aioli by stirring together the aioli and pesto. Cover and refrigerate until needed.

In a 10-inch skillet, cook the ground bacon over low heat, stirring, until the fat has rendered and the bacon bits are golden, about 10 minutes. Transfer the bacon to paper towels to drain. Discard the rendered bacon fat.

Arrange 3 small bowls in a row. In the first bowl, place the sifted flour. In the second, place the beaten eggs. In the third, combine the bacon with the bread crumbs.

Rinse the clams under cold running water and dry them well with paper towels. Place the clams side by side on a work surface and, working with 1 clam at a time, pound it uniformly around the edges with a kitchen mallet to tenderize. Pay particular attention to the square tail end of each clam, as it tends to be the toughest part.

Have a platter lined with paper towels ready. Dredge each clam evenly on both sides to fully coat, first in flour, then egg, and finally in the bread crumb mixture. Lay them in a single layer on the prepared platter.

In a 12-inch skillet, heat 1/2 cup of the oil over high heat until it shimmers, about 3 minutes. Cook 2 to 3 clams at a time, depending on their size. Change the oil and wipe the pan clean between each batch. Carefully drop the clams into the oil, fry for 30 seconds, and turn over. Cook for another 30 seconds and quickly remove. Drain them on paper towels and sprinkle with salt.

To serve, transfer the fried clams to a serving platter, garnish with basil sprigs, and serve immediately with basil aioli on the side.

To Drink

For a dish with razor clams you might expect Pinot Gris, but with basil and aioli I say a light-bodied Pinot Noir. Matello Souris from Oregon's Willamette Valley, made by Marcus Goodfellow, has raspberry-red fruit, perfume, and soft tannins that support the suppleness of the clams. Its delicate berry finish is versatile enough to suit the basil and bacon alike. The bacon crust allows me to take a different direction with a more austere and complex wine from France. A Volnay from Domaine Hubert de Montille—full of delicate fruit and good acidity—has the right personality for this dish. **–K.P.**

Steamed Mussels

Serves 4

Some of the most pristine seafood in the world comes from the coastal waters of northern Washington State, whose islands and peninsulas are famous for their rugged beauty and undisturbed wildlife. For our steamed mussels, we look to farmers on Whidbey Island and elsewhere around Puget Sound and the Olympic Peninsula for sweet, plump, delicious mussels requiring no more than a splash of wine, a little garlic, and butter. We serve them with American French Fries (page 50) in the Belgian tradition. Remember to pass crusty bread to sop up the delicious juices.

4 tablespoons unsalted butter, softened	4 pounds fresh live mussels, scrubbed and debearded
3 tablespoons Persillade (page 198)	1 1/2 cups white wine
3 tablespoons extra-virgin olive oil	Kosher salt and freshly ground black pepper

In a small bowl, make compound butter by mixing the butter and persillade. Set aside.

In a 6-quart soup pot, heat the olive oil over high heat for about 3 minutes.

Add the mussels to the hot oil all at once, stirring to coat with oil. Pour in the wine, add the compound butter, and season with salt and pepper. Cover and cook until the mussels have all opened, about 10 minutes. Discard any that did not open when cooked. Divide the mussels between 4 deep soup bowls. Pour the cooking liquid over them and serve immediately.

Chef's Tip

Follow these instructions when buying and cleaning mussels and you will capture their briny goodness at its best.

- When buying mussels, select ones that are tightly closed and uniform in size.
- Mussels will keep longer if you wait to clean them until just before cooking.
- Clean the mussels under cold running water.
- Use the back of a small paring knife to scrub away all the little barnacles from the outer shell.
- Remove their beards by gently tugging on them.
- Hold mussels in the refrigerator, loosely covered with paper towels or a clean kitchen towel, while assembling the other ingredients.
- Never place live mussels in a plastic bag—they will suffocate.

To Drink

This dish is one of the most popular in our restaurant, and a classic Oregon wine is the obvious partner. Pinot Gris, made by the legendary David Lett of Eyrie Vineyards, is food friendly and delicious. Expressive of local orchards, the wine has a lingering taste of white fruit and pears and a finish that plays to the garlicky broth.

Another good match for this dish is the Leon Beyer Pinot Gris, a classic Alsatian wine—complex with a hint of pear and a bright level of acidity that pulls out the sweetness of the mussels. **–K.P.**

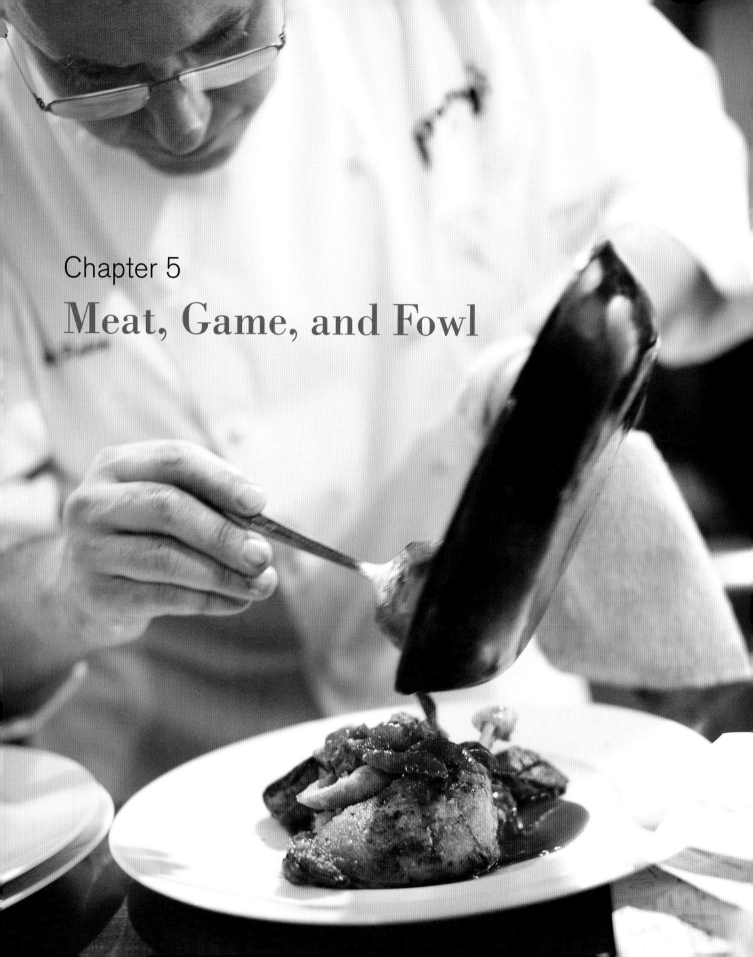

Chapter 5
Meat, Game, and Fowl

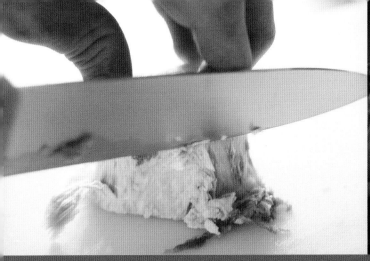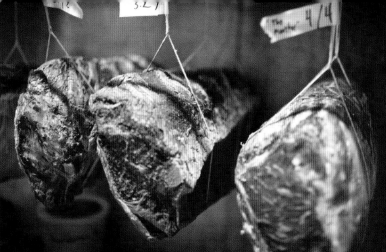

Roast Beef Culotte with Harvest Vegetables and Oxtail Broth

Serves 6

Pot au feu is a simple and hearty mélange of boiled meats and vegetables that is usually served with coarse sea salt, cornichons, and mustard. Inspired by that French classic, I created the following recipe, which roasts the beef, instead of boiling it with the oxtail, to accentuate its beefiness. Oxtail provides potent, soul-satisfying broth and rich, gelatinous meat.

Beef culotte (also known as sirloin cap steak) is a very flavorful cut of meat and a good value, as it is as well-marbled with fat as cuts that cost twice as much. Your best shot to find it (and oxtail) is from a butcher, who will probably need to order it for you.

The oxtail broth subrecipe makes more than you need for this recipe, so freeze what you don't use. It will hold well for up to one month. Count on it to provide flavorful warmth on a cold winter's night. For more about making a clarified broth, see pages 36 and 37.

1 large celery root, peeled, quartered, and cut into 1/2-inch-thick slices

12 baby carrots, peeled and trimmed, or 1 large carrot, peeled, trimmed, and sliced into 1/4-inch rounds

1 red onion, sliced into 1/2-inch rings

6 baby turnips, trimmed, peeled, and quartered, or 1 large turnip, peeled, quartered, and cut into 1/4-inch-thick slices

Kosher salt and freshly ground black pepper

1/2 cup plus 1 tablespoon extra-virgin olive oil

6 ounces fresh porcini or king oyster mushrooms, coarsely chopped

3 pounds beef culotte, excess fat and silver skin trimmed

1 bunch of thyme

Oxtail meat from Oxtail Broth (recipe follows)

4 cups Oxtail Broth (recipe follows)

3 tablespoons Persillade (page 198)

Preheat the oven to 400°F.

In a roasting pan, combine the celery root, carrots, onion, and turnips. Season generously with salt and pepper and add 3 tablespoons of the olive oil. Toss to coat, cover tightly with aluminum foil, and roast for 30 minutes; leave in the oven.

In a skillet, heat another 3 tablespoons of oil and sauté the mushrooms over medium heat until tender, about 5 minutes. Transfer the cooked mushrooms to the roasting pan and continue to cook, covered, until all the vegetables are tender, another 30 minutes or so. Set aside with the foil partially lifted.

Meanwhile, rub the entire culotte generously with salt and pepper. In a large skillet, heat the remaining 3 tablespoons of olive oil and sear the meat on all sides over medium heat until well browned, about 5 minutes per side.

Line a baking sheet with thyme branches. Transfer the meat to the prepared baking sheet and roast until the internal temperature reaches 120°F for rare, about 20 minutes. Loosely cover with foil and let rest for 15 minutes before slicing.

Mix the oxtail meat with the roasted vegetables and reheat, uncovered, in the oven, about 10 minutes. Meanwhile, thinly slice the beef.

To serve, divide the oxtail-vegetable mixture between 6 deep soup bowls and top with beef slices. Sprinkle with persillade, pour over the hot broth, and serve right away. For a more dramatic presentation, pour the broth at the table.

Oxtail Broth

Makes about 7 cups

4 pounds oxtail

Kosher salt and freshly ground black pepper

1/4 cup extra-virgin olive oil, plus more if needed

2 cups port or cream sherry

12 cups Chicken Stock (page 213)

1 small carrot, peeled and coarsely chopped (optional)

1 small onion, coarsely chopped (optional)

Whites and crushed shells from 8 large eggs (optional)

8 ounces lean ground beef (optional)

Slice the oxtail between the vertebrae into 2-inch pieces, or have your butcher do it. Trim and discard as much fat as possible. Season the oxtail generously with salt and pepper.

In a large skillet, heat the 1/4 cup olive oil over medium heat, then sear the oxtail on all sides in the oil until browned, about 5 minutes per side. Transfer to a soup pot.

Pour off and discard the grease from the skillet and deglaze it with port. Cook, stirring and scraping the pan, until the pan drippings have lifted off the bottom, about 1 minute. Pour the resulting liquid into the pot with the oxtail and add the chicken stock. Bring to a boil over high heat, decrease the heat to low, and cook, uncovered, religiously skimming off the fat, until the oxtail is very tender, about 2 hours. If the liquid reduces enough to expose the meat, top off the pot with water so the pieces remain fully submerged throughout cooking.

Have a bowl of ice water ready. Using a slotted spoon or tongs, carefully remove the cooked tail pieces from the liquid and set aside to cool slightly. When cool enough to handle, remove the meat from the bones and set aside. Discard the bones. While the meat is cooling, strain the stock through a fine mesh strainer or cheesecloth into a heatproof container. Cool to room temperature in the ice-water bath without stirring. Once cooled, skim off all the surface fat. If the broth is to your taste and relatively clear, stop here and use the broth. If you want a more intense flavor and a crystal-clear, amber-hued broth, clarify it.

To clarify the broth: In a tall, narrow soup pot, warm the oxtail broth over low heat. Maintain its warmth, testing the temperature of the stock with an instant-read thermometer to ensure it doesn't rise above 120°F. Place the carrot and the onion in the work bowl of a food processor fitted with the metal blade and pulse until finely ground (do not puree); reserve.

In a large bowl, whisk the egg whites and shells together until frothy. Add the ground vegetables, ground beef, and a healthy dose of salt and pepper. Whisk in 1 cup of warm stock until well incorporated, and repeat 2 or 3 times.

Slide the egg white–stock mixture into the remaining warm stock. Simmer over low heat, stirring frequently, until the mixture begins to form a solid mass (the "raft") on the surface of the stock, about 30 minutes. Stop whisking and simmer until the liquid is completely clear and flavorful, about 20 minutes more.

Line a strainer with cheesecloth and set it over a bowl. When the stock is done to your liking, gently ladle the liquid into the strainer, letting it flow through without pressing. Discard the solids. Keep hot if serving right away; cool down in an ice-water bath if making in advance, then refrigerate or freeze.

To Drink

Cabernet Sauvignons from Washington State's Walla Walla Valley are big and robust. Both Leonetti Cabernet Sauvignon and Woodward Canyon Artist Series Cabernet Sauvignon show cedar and dark fruit flavors that perfectly complement the rich oxtail meat. The two wines have deep hints of vanilla that pull out the thyme and porcini and intensify the flavors of the roasted beef and the broth. **–K.P.**

Chile-Braised Beef Brisket

Serves 4 to 6

Brisket is commonly used to make corned beef, but I find that it lends itself well to other preparations. And once it's in the oven, you can forget about it for hours—it's that easy to prepare. This brisket with a south-of-the-border kick is one of my very favorites. The meat actually tastes better to me when it sits overnight so all the flavors have more time to marry. It will hold well for a few days. While good reheated the next day, the meat served cold in a sandwich is a delicious alternative for leftovers.

I serve the brisket alone or alongside a grilled steak, as it emphasizes steak's meaty flavor. In either case, Crispy Potatoes with Romesco (page 148) is a wonderful accompaniment.

1 star anise	3 tablespoons extra-virgin olive oil
1 teaspoon fennel seed	1 medium onion, cut into fine dice
12 pasilla chiles, seeded	
4 pounds beef brisket, trimmed of excess fat and silver skin	3 ripe tomatoes, grated on the largest holes of a box grater (see page 42), or 1 (14-ounce) can canned crushed tomatoes with juice
Kosher salt and freshly ground black pepper	
3 cups boiling water	2 cups Chicken Stock (page 213)
1/4 cup sherry vinegar	

Preheat the oven to 350°F.

In a small skillet over a medium heat, toast the star anise and fennel seed. Move the pan across the heat, letting the spices gently roll inside. Do that for about 3 to 4 minutes or until you begin to smell the toasting spices. Transfer into a spice mill or a coffee grinder. Add 5 of the chiles and grind until finely ground. Season the brisket with salt and pepper, rub

with the spice blend, cover, and refrigerate while continuing with the recipe.

Put the remaining 7 chiles in a bowl and cover with the boiling water. Set aside and let soak until the chiles have softened, about 30 minutes. When soft, reserve the chiles and 1 cup of the reconstituting water. Discard the rest of the water. In a blender, liquefy the chiles, the 1 cup reserved soaking water, and the sherry vinegar. Set aside.

In a large Dutch oven, heat the olive oil over high heat and sear the brisket in the hot oil on all sides until well browned, about 5 minutes per side. Remove the brisket from the pan and set aside. Add the onions to the pan and sauté until they become translucent, about 3 minutes. Stir in the tomatoes, stock, and chile mixture and bring to a boil. Remove the pan from the heat, add the brisket, cover, and braise in the oven until fork tender, 3 1/2 to 4 hours, skimming occasionally to remove excess fat.

When done, slice and serve hot with the braising liquid alongside.

To Drink

The hot climate of southern Oregon produces one of my very favorite Spanish varietals, Tempranillo, which loves meat braised with tomatoes, ground chiles, and spices. The black-fruit flavors of this grape and the tannins stand up well to the braised beef. Two Oregon wineries, Abacela and Dominio IV, produce fine examples of this grape varietal. A companion choice would be a French Rhône wine from Chapoutier: Châteauneuf-du-Pape, Saint-Joseph, or Crozes-Hermitage. These wines have spice, smoke, and lingering tannins that speak to all the flavors of the brisket. **–K.P.**

Lamb and Hay, Hay and Lamb

West of Corvallis, Oregon's Willamette Valley is flat, but the horizon is shaped by the Coast Range. We are running a little late for our meeting with John Neumeister of Cattail Creek Lamb, but we want to drive slowly and take in the pastoral beauty—the occasional farm surrounded by grassy fields, the gentle hillsides dense with trees. At a break in the fenced-in fields, we turn onto a road that leads us up to a house on a hilltop amid lovingly planted gardens.

John is waiting there to greet us. He reminds us of Clint Eastwood, with the weathered good looks of a man who works outdoors. He is a second-generation lamb producer, and one of the first things you realize about him is that he's happy doing what he does.

Once we're settled around the table in his light-filled kitchen, John described how he grew up on a farm in southern Ohio. He left to go to college and found his way to work with progressive organizations in San Francisco before being drawn back to the land, first to a communal farm in Oregon and then his own. He remembers phoning his mother years later and admitting to her that he'd spent fifteen years re-creating the farm he grew up on.

Almost by default, he gravitated to farming sheep, as his father had. "I understand sheep," he explains simply. He tells a story about being with his father hauling market lambs to the Cincinnati stockyards. He would help his father run the animals to the scale and then

into the plant. Afterwards they'd go sit by "the guy at the big desk" and his father would ask the man, "What are you paying for lambs today?" John points out to me that the broker could say whatever he wanted, "What was my father going to do, go back into the plant and sort his lambs from the pack?" So he accepted whatever he was offered, and lost money every year.

Over time, John realized he was doing the same thing in Oregon. The local broker would offer pretty much what he wanted, usually one or two cents a pound above the auction price. "You drive sixty miles to deliver your lambs—you're not going to turn around and take them home. In another month they'll be too fat to sell." There had to be a better way to do this.

So he wrote a business plan and started making connections that would help him market his lamb in a new way—direct to consumers, especially high-end chefs like Alice Waters at Chez Panisse in Berkeley, California, who has been buying John's lamb since 1984. Once he started selling directly, his marketing advantage became crystal clear: only three places on earth allow a year-round supply of grass fed lamb—New Zealand, the south of England, and the Willamette Valley.

Everyone loved John's lamb, but his new markets brought new challenges. One problem was how to inspire his restaurant customers to use every cut of lamb. Loins and racks were a no-brainer, but shoulders, legs, and necks were a tougher sell. John listened to restaurant chefs and worked intensively with his processor to deliver cuts that were familiar to them (and, more importantly, to their customers) and some that stretched the dining experience—for example, neck and shank cuts prepared like osso buco. His new, smaller, pan-ready cuts were a big hit, and his lamb began to sell out. The new markets also taught John the necessity of striving to produce a consistent product of incomparable quality. Though he has many standing orders, he knows he has to keep his eye on the ball. "I appreciate the loyalty of the people I supply, but I also understand what I deliver has to be good," he says. "I have to earn your business every week."

John breeds portions of the flock three or four times a year so he can always have fresh, young, grass-fed lamb. His sheep always graze on grass, with two excep-tions: when the valley floor floods he feeds them alfalfa from eastern Oregon, and when he brings them into the barn at night he tosses them hay to keep them enter-tained. There is one spot in John's field where hay and lavender grow side by side, reminding me of my riff on the old French preparation *jambon au foin* (see page 108).

Our connection to Cattail Creek is straightforward. John raises the best possible lamb; our mission is to help him grow his business. We feel we are collaborating with John as we shepherd these animals through a harmoni-ous circle that starts with him and his flock and his land. It is profoundly satisfying. We respect his animals and every time we cook his lamb, we think of all he does to bring them to us. We cook them whole when we can, and introduce our customers to the cuts most people know least, like the necks. We know every bit of John's lambs will be undeniably delicious.

Shoulder of Lamb Roasted with Hay and Lavender

Serves 4 to 6

Jambon au foin (ham in hay) is a very old French cooking technique rarely practiced these days. It is almost impossible to find any written recipes for it. This adaptation for lamb uses hay with lavender (at its peak locally when the first hay of the season is baled). When I first prepared it, our kitchen was filled with butterscotch aromas. The result was so spectacular, so unusual, that I kept it on the menu for as long as lavender was in season.

I prefer to use organic hay from clover or alfalfa, though any type is fine as long as it is organic. Your local farmer's market is a good source for potential suppliers—ask around. Serve the dish with Stuffed Tomatoes Provençal (page 138).

5 pounds lamb shoulder, bone-in	2 cups white wine
4 quarts brine (see page 27)	1 cup Chicken Stock (page 213)
1 big bundle of hay (enough to make a generous bed and cover in a roasting pan)	6 stems fresh organic flowering lavender
Kosher salt and freshly ground black pepper	6 bulbs garlic
1/4 cup extra-virgin olive oil	2 tablespoons chopped Persillade (page 198), for accompaniment

Using a sturdy knife or cleaver, cut the lamb shoulder through the spine into 2 equal pieces. If the bones are stubborn, a small hacksaw can easily do the job, or ask your butcher to do it when you order the lamb. Place the pieces in a large container or soup pot, pour in the brine, and refrigerate, covered, for at least 24 hours.

Rinse the hay in a bowl of cold water. Shake off any excess water and use enough of the hay to make a generous bed of it in a roasting pan. Reserve the remainder.

Preheat the oven to 375°F.

Rinse the lamb under cold running water, dry well with paper towels, and season with salt and pepper. In a 12-inch skillet, heat the olive oil over medium heat. Sauté the lamb on all sides until dark brown, about 5 minutes per side.

Transfer the lamb to the roasting pan. Discard the grease from the skillet, add the wine and stock, and bring to a boil over high heat. Remove from the heat and pour the hot liquid into the roasting pan. Distribute the lavender all around the lamb and nestle the garlic bulbs close by. Cover the contents of the pan with a thick enough layer of hay so you cannot see the meat through it. Seal the pan tightly with aluminum foil.

Roast the lamb until the meat is tender enough to fall off the bone, about 3 hours. Remove from the oven and carefully remove and discard the top layer of hay.

To serve, gently transfer the lamb pieces to a serving platter and surround with the cooked garlic bulbs. Remove and discard the remaining hay. Strain the roasting juices and drizzle over the meat. Finish the lamb with a sprinkle of persillade and pass the rest, along with the remaining pan juices, at the table.

Leftover lamb makes a delicious sandwich the next day.

To Drink

This old French preparation for lamb reminds me of Brick House, the vineyard and home of Oregon winemaker Doug Tunnell. The aromas of hay, earth, and lavender are distinct on his property and apparent in his wine. The long finish and firm tannins of his Cuvee du Tonnelier Pinot Noir are in perfect sync with the gaminess of the lamb. Another choice would be Domaine Tempier Bandol Rouge La Tourtine from France. With spice, lavender, pepper, and clove fragrances, it allows the French heritage of the lamb to show through. **–K.P.**

Lamb Necks Braised in Pinot Noir

Serves 4 to 6

A good-quality butcher shop will have access to lamb necks, although you may need to pre-order them. Ask the butcher to cut the necks as called for in this recipe, which produces a round, evenly cut piece of meat that will be easier to brown. This stew goes well with Soft Polenta with Rosemary (page 130) or ricotta gnocchi (Herbed Ricotta Gnocchi with Dungeness Crab and Preserved Lemon Peel, made without the crab, page 81). The lamb must marinate for 24 hours before cooking.

2 large lamb necks (about 2 1/2 pounds each), cut across the spine into 2-inch-thick rounds

2 carrots, peeled

2 onions

1 (750 ml) bottle Pinot Noir

Kosher salt and freshly ground black pepper

Extra-virgin olive oil

3 tablespoons tomato paste

3 cups Veal Stock (page 207)

2 bulbs garlic, halved across their midsection

3 bay leaves

Place the lamb in a container. Coarsely chop 1 carrot and 1 onion and add them to the container. Pour in the wine, cover, and let marinate in the refrigerator for 24 hours.

Preheat the oven to 350°F.

Drain the lamb and the vegetables and set aside. Strain the marinade into a small saucepan and cook over high heat until reduced by half, 10 to 15 minutes, skimming off the scum that forms on the surface.

Season the lamb with salt and pepper. In an ovenproof roasting pan, sear the lamb in olive oil over medium heat until well browned on all sides, about 5 minutes per side. Remove from the pan and set aside. In the same pan, brown the drained vegetables from the marinade, about 5 minutes. Stir in the tomato paste. Deglaze the pan with the reduced marinade. Add the stock. Bring to a boil over medium-high heat. Return the lamb to the pan and add the garlic and bay leaves. Cover, place in the oven and braise until fork tender, about 3 hours.

Meanwhile, cut the remaining carrot and onion into small dice. In a skillet, sauté the vegetables in olive oil over low heat, stirring occasionally, until soft, about 15 minutes. Reserve.

When the lamb is done, gently remove the meat from the pan and let sit until cool enough to handle. Carefully remove the meat from the bone. Strain the braising liquid and discard the solids. Skim and discard whatever fat has formed on the surface.

In a large skillet, combine the meat with the sautéed carrot and onion, add the braising liquid, and bring to a simmer over medium-low heat. Adjust the seasoning, if needed, and serve in wide bowls.

To Drink

Hearty comfort food like this seems best with a wedge of crusty bread and a full-bodied Pinot Noir. All the Pinots from Cristom Vineyard in Oregon will suit this lamb dish, but their Reserve Pinot Noir, with dark fruit and earthy flavors, is a perfect match. Lighter in style and compatible in a different way are the well-balanced Pinots from Jean-Marc Boillot in Burgundy. In particular, I like his Volnay Premier Cru Pitures, perfumed with violet and raspberry-red fruit that marries the stock, bay leaves, and meat. **–K.P.**

Crispy Sweetbreads and Crayfish Boil

Serves 4 to 6

The French, who are famous omnivores, call sweetbreads *ris de veau.* "Sweetbread" sounds like a dessert and strikes me as a more misleading name than "veal rice"—though I suppose both euphemisms are more appealing than "thymus glands" or "pancreas." At any rate I learned to love sweetbreads in France and was determined to serve them in our restaurant. They lend themselves so easily to a variety of preparations, moods, and seasons. We have used them to fill ravioli, grilled and served them with barbecue sauce and baked beans, and pan-fried them to pair with creamed morels and asparagus. But this recipe, prepared Creole-style, is the most memorable.

As with most sweetbread recipes, this requires both commitment and advance planning. But as most steps can be done ahead, the effort is easily rewarded. While both veal and lamb sweetbreads are delicious, the veal ones have a creamy, delicate, and tender texture that I really like.

Crayfish

2 gallons water

1 tablespoon cayenne pepper

5 tablespoons kosher salt

4 bay leaves

5 pounds live crayfish

Crayfish Stock

1/4 cup extra-virgin olive oil

Reserved crayfish heads and tail shells

1 large onion, coarsely chopped

1 large carrot, peeled and coarsely chopped

1 large bulb fennel, coarsely chopped

1/4 cup tomato paste

2 bay leaves

Kosher salt and freshly ground black pepper

1 (750-ml) bottle white wine

Sweetbreads

1 1/2 pounds veal or lamb sweetbreads

1 small carrot, peeled and coarsely chopped

1 small onion, coarsely chopped

1 bay leaf

2 cups dry white wine

Kosher salt and freshly ground black pepper

2 cups cold water

12 baby fingerling potatoes

2 ears corn, husked, ears cut into thirds

4 ounces chanterelle mushrooms

6 ounces green beans, trimmed

12 baby carrots, peeled and trimmed

2 tablespoons crème fraîche

2 tablespoons finely chopped fresh tarragon

Canola or grapeseed oil, for pan-frying

1/2 cup all-purpose flour

2 tablespoons Persillade (page 198)

To prepare the crayfish, fill a large soup pot with the water. Add the cayenne, salt, and bay leaves, and bring to a boil over high heat. Add the crayfish all at once. Cook until the crayfish turn bright red and their tails start separating from their bodies, about 15 minutes. Using a slotted spoon, remove to a baking sheet to cool, reserving the cooking liquid. Transfer the cooking liquid to a container and set aside to cool (you will use the liquid for cooking vegetables later on).

Reserve and refrigerate a few whole cooked crayfish for final preparation of the dish. Twist the heads of the remaining crayfish to separate from the tails. Shell the tails and save the tail shells and crayfish heads for the stock. Devein the tail meat and refrigerate until ready to use.

To prepare the crayfish stock, in a large soup pot, heat the olive oil over high heat. Add the crayfish heads and tail shells. Smash the heads using a potato masher and stir until the contents of the pot are glistening with oil. Add the onion, carrot, fennel, tomato paste, and bay leaves. Season with salt and pepper, then pour in the wine and enough water to just cover the solid ingredients. Bring to a simmer, decrease the heat to medium-low, and simmer until the crayfish flavors are very pronounced, about 1 1/4 hours. Strain through a fine mesh strainer, discarding the solids. Cool in an ice-water bath until ready to use. If made a day ahead, keep refrigerated.

To prepare the sweetbreads, soak them in cold water to cover for at least 4 hours, or overnight, in the refrigerator. If the sweetbreads are frozen, defrost them first before soaking.

In a saucepan, add the sweetbreads, carrot, onion, bay leaf, wine, 1 tablespoon of salt, and 2 cups cold water. Bring to a boil over high heat. Remove from the heat and let the sweetbreads blanch slowly in the residual hot water and then cool, about 30 minutes. When cooled they will be springy to the touch. Drain them in a colander set over a bowl and leave in the colander. Discard the liquid and the vegetables.

Make a weight by setting a heavy object (an unopened can or bottle of juice) on a plate and set the plate on the sweetbreads. Weight the sweetbreads for at least 2 hours to press out excess moisture. Peel away the outer membrane from the sweetbreads and remove any fat (the sweetbreads will naturally separate into smaller pieces). Place the pieces in a bowl and reserve.

To prepare the final dish, in a large pot, bring the reserved crayfish cooking liquid to a boil over high heat. Add the potatoes and cook for 10 minutes. Add the corn, mushrooms, green beans, and baby carrots and cook until all are tender, another 5 minutes. Add the reserved whole cooked crayfish, turn the heat off, and cover to keep everything hot in the cooking liquid.

While the vegetables are cooking, prepare the crayfish sauce. In a 2-quart saucepan, add the crayfish stock and bring to a boil over high heat. Cook until the stock is reduced by half, about 10 minutes. Add the reserved meat from the crayfish tails and the crème fraîche. Turn the heat off and season with salt and pepper to taste. Add the tarragon, stir, and keep warm.

Have a plate lined with paper towels ready. To finish the dish, in a large skillet, heat 1 inch of oil over medium heat until it shimmers. Season the sweetbreads uniformly with salt and pepper, dredge in flour, and shake off the excess. Fry the sweetbreads in the oil until golden brown, about 5 minutes per side. Transfer them to the prepared plate to drain.

To serve, place the crispy sweetbreads into the middle of a large serving platter. Drain the vegetables and the cooked crayfish and place them around the sweetbreads. Discard the cooking liquid. Sprinkle everything with persillade and serve immediately, passing the crayfish sauce at the table.

To Drink

White wines from Arbois, in the heart of the Jura region along France's eastern border, are like no other. They showcase the unique, expressive qualities of the Savagnin grape. Their dry sherry notes and pronounced acidity beautifully show off the crayfish and the creamy, gamey quality of the sweetbreads. One of my favorites is Vin Jaune from Jacques Puffeney. From the south of France, Domaine Tempier Bandol Blanc evokes sea and sun, reflecting exactly the flavors of the crayfish boil. The wine itself smells like sweetbreads cooked in butter, with a warm honey acidity that balances the delicate meatiness.

Closer to home, I recommend the almond-like Alder Ridge Vineyard, Horse Heaven Hills Roussane from Syncline in Washington State. It has plenty of acidity to pair nicely with this dish and rounds out its complex Creole flavors.   **–K.P.**

Weekend with Fergus

Fergus Henderson is at the center of the "nose-to-tail" school of cooking (in fact, he coined the phrase). His London restaurant, St. John, is a showcase for the amazing things Fergus does with every bit of an animal. He is the kind of chef who inspires other chefs and helps us put into words just what we're doing, and why. In Fergus's case, I found out one memorable weekend that those words are almost like culinary haiku—at once stripped down and overflowing with meaning.

I first met Fergus in 2005 in New York during the James Beard Awards, where I got a signed copy of his book. Later that year, I persuaded him to be a guest speaker at the annual Wild About Game festival organized by a Portland game purveyor. I also proposed that he teach a class at a local cooking school and spend a day with us at Paley's Place. It seemed a lot to ask, but he didn't hesitate: "Cooking game is right up my alley and if I am there, you might as well use me."

Six months later I was picking up Fergus and his chef, Chris Gillard, at their Portland hotel. This weekend would be the first time I heard Fergus really talk about food. While his speech is direct, he can easily sail into a metaphor that at first makes you wonder if you've missed something and then falls perfectly into place. When asked what drives him, for example, he answered, "Little animals running in the fields without their backs, while their loins and tenderloins are being served to some unsuspecting persons somewhere." This was classic Fergus—celebrating guts (and heads, and tails) in a sound bite.

Back at the restaurant, boxes of game, offal and all, covered about two thirds of the kitchen floor: buffalo tails and tongues; buffalo hearts so fresh they seemed to still be beating; glistening deep-red elk shoulders still on the bone; boxes of neatly packed pig's feet; rabbits, partridges, and ducks with their heads and feet still on. I was a little intimidated by the scene, but Fergus's eyes lit up with excitement and approval.

Fergus, Chris, and I went from box to box working out what to do with each item and where each preparation would fit among the several meals planned for the weekend. I kept notes, resorting to shorthand to keep up with the terse, vivid inspirations pouring out of my two colleagues.

Fergus surveyed a box of Oregon buffalo tongue from Bob Stangel, the buffalo rancher. "I love the sound of buffalo tongue. We could salt it. Cook it in duck fat and press it. Or brine it. Poach it and grill it." Next up, buffalo heart. "Nothing expresses the beast better than its heart," Fergus exclaimed. Chris suggested slicing the heart thinly, marinating it with balsamic vinegar, olive oil, shallots, and thyme, and searing it quickly on both sides. "And," he finished, "serve it with string beans." I was not going to argue with the man; it sounded amazing.

I unearthed the buffalo fillets that I had salted three days earlier based on Fergus's phone instructions. They were almost black on the outside. This was not my dish and I didn't know what to expect. I began to worry. I washed off the salt and dried them with paper towels. I rubbed them with coarsely ground black pepper according to his prior instructions, then sliced off a small piece from the skinnier end. The center was deep, dark red surrounded by a band of black. We all tasted. The flavor was complex, salty, sweet, and rich, running from gamy to salt water toffee. Revelatory.

We moved on to duck salad, which we would need not only for the class, but for dinner the following day. Fergus laid it out: "Confit in duck fat gizzard. Heart. Neck. Wings. And leg. Make a salad with watercress. Confit bits. Roasted shallots and mustardy dressing. Plus slivers of breast, roasted pink. Make a duck liver and foie gras mousse. And spread it on bread toasted with duck fat."

"Should we pick the meat off the bone before mixing the salad?" I wondered.

Fergus made a gesture like a cartoon character with large exposed teeth gnawing on the bone: "We have to engage the diners. They need to pay attention and think about food. We will leave all the bones in."

I agreed with my whole heart, and in that moment it coalesced for me, what this weekend with Fergus was about. For one evening, in our restaurant, the American dissociation with our food would cease to exist—the plastic-wrapped, mega-mart nightmare would be utterly vanquished and we would make food say what we wanted, no holds barred.

I had no time for philosophy though—it was on to the next box. When Fergus saw the partridges, he outlined a plan for roasting and serving them with bread sauce for the class: "Stuff butter and sage into cavity of a partridge. Season the bird. Roast till flesh has just lost translucency. Heat milk with clovey onion,"

("Clovey," did he say? Clovey. Right.)

"when hot, add bread crumbs. Mash together and let sit until it is about calm."

(Did he say cook until "calm?" Okay, just keep going.)

"Just before serving return to heat. Add butter, salt and pepper, and ahhh."

(Me too. Ahhh.)

As we moved toward rabbits (a specialty at St. John), Fergus seemed to be speaking about every eighth word he was thinking: "Class. Dinner. Both. Rabbit wrapped in fennel twigs and bacon. Splash the rabbits with oil. Season enthusiastically with salt and pepper. Surround with the dried fennel. End to end. Tummy to back. Wrap in strips of streaky bacon. Lay in a deep-ish roasting pan. Nestle garlic next to the rabbit. Pour in the wine and stock, and cook until giving."

(Giving, I thought. I get that.)

"Chop the rabbit into chunks and serve with bacon, garlic, and the jug of the juices from the pan."

He had me. I only wanted to cook and eat.

One rabbit followed another. As Fergus talked of fried rabbit with lemon, I thought it sounded a little simpler. But experience reminds me that with two or three ingredients on a plate there is nowhere to hide— if the preparation and the technique are not precise, the simple becomes just plain.

"Baby rabbit. Deep-fried. Jointed. And poached gently in pig's-trotter enriching stock. Bread-crumbed with the finest of crumbs. Dijon mustard in the egg wash. Serve with lemon."

Pig's trotters (pig's feet) are central to Fergus's cooking; he jokingly calls trotter stock his "trotter gear." The stock imparts wonderful layers of flavor to whatever he poaches in it. The next preparation would be based on the logic of trotter gear.

When we came to the stack of boxes containing large chunks of elk shoulder, it registered that neither Fergus nor I had ever cooked elk shoulder before. The lean, dark-red meat was cut in cross sections that resembled giant pieces of osso buco.

Fergus paused for a moment, then launched into an inventory of actions: "Make the rabbit stock from bones. Cook the trotters in the rabbit stock."

(Uh-oh. Don't lose me.)

"Poach the rabbit in the trotter stock. Pick the trotters' meat. Cook it again in the same, already a very rich flavorful stock, while braising the elk shoulder."

I could see that new flavors would develop in the stock each time we cooked it, this layering being the genius tying the whole dish together.

What vegetable would we serve with the elk shoulder? Fergus deliberated, then let his imagination run: "So the elk was strolling the forest nibbling on mushrooms. Hopping through fields of cabbage."

So be it. We would serve braised shoulder of elk and pig's trotters, garnished with mushrooms and cabbage. It happened that beautiful chanterelles and savoy cabbage had been delivered to the kitchen that morning. I told myself I was either lucky or clairvoyant.

These morning plans set a tone of nonstop excitement for the whole weekend, which ended with a kitchen full of spent, euphoric cooks washing down the leftovers with bottle after bottle of champagne. The few who got to eat this food were as lucky as my cooks and I were to prepare it. That weekend we would fully express the values Fergus's ideas echoed in our own cooking: sustainability, respect for the whole animal, common sense, and sheer joy. Our souls drew nurture from this encounter, and on that evening, we knew we had been able to pass it on.

Braised Elk Shoulder with Mushrooms and Cabbage

Serves 4 to 6

Elk usually appears on our menus in early fall, paired with seasonally abundant wild mushrooms. I like to braise the lean elk meat with pig's feet (trotters) for their smooth richness, and savoy cabbage, as it holds up well over long, slow cooking and imparts depth of flavor.

If you don't hunt, farm-raised elk is available by mail order (see Resources, page 222), or substitute lamb shoulder. Pig's feet are available in ethnic markets or quality grocery stores, but may require a special order.

While this wonderfully rustic dish is meant to be a one-pot meal, Soft Polenta with Rosemary (page 130) makes a fine side dish. When making this dish, plan ahead, as the meat will need to marinate for some time before braising.

1 (750-ml) bottle red wine, preferably Pinot Noir	3 tablespoons extra-virgin olive oil
1 carrot, peeled and sliced into 1/2-inch rounds	3 cups Chicken Stock (page 213)
1 onion, quartered	4 large shallots, halved
1 bay leaf	1 small (about 1 1/2 pound) fresh pig's foot
5 sprigs of thyme	8 ounces chanterelle or other wild or cultivated mushrooms
1 tablespoon whole black peppercorns	1/4 head (about 8 ounces) savoy cabbage, cored and sliced into 1-inch ribbons
2 1/2 pounds elk shoulder, bone-in	
Kosher salt and freshly ground black pepper	

To prepare the marinade, in a large container or pot, combine the wine, carrot, onion, bay leaf, thyme, and peppercorns. Submerge the elk shoulder in the mixture, cover, and refrigerate for at least 6 hours or overnight.

Remove the shoulder from the marinade, pat it dry with paper towels, and set aside. Strain the marinade into a 2-quart saucepan and discard the solids. Cook the marinade over medium-high heat until reduced by half, skimming often to remove scum, about 10 minutes.

Preheat the oven to 350°F.

Season the meat generously with salt and pepper. In a large Dutch oven, heat the oil over high heat and sear the meat until brown on both sides, about 4 minutes per side. Remove the meat and set aside. Discard the cooking oil.

Add the reduced marinade and stock to the Dutch oven, and bring to a boil over high heat. Add the shoulder, shallots, and pig's foot, cover tightly, and place into the oven.

Braise for 1 hour, then turn over the elk shoulder and pig's foot and add the mushrooms and cabbage. Cover again and continue to braise until the elk is fork tender and the meat from the pig's foot is falling off the bone, about 1 1/2 hours longer.

Remove from the oven. Transfer the pig's foot to a bowl and set aside until cool enough to handle. Everything but the bones is edible. Carefully pick the meat from the bones (of which there are many) and tear into bite-sized pieces.

Return the meat from the pig's foot to the Dutch oven and mix with the elk meat. On the stove, gently bring the braised mixture to a simmer over medium-low heat. Season with salt and pepper if needed and serve family-style in a large, deep platter.

To Drink

Tony Rynders, formerly of Domaine Serene in Oregon, makes concentrated and deeply satisfying wines. One such example is the limited-production Domaine Serene Evenstad Pinot Noir. This full-bodied wine, layered with tobacco and dark-fruit aromas is perfect for a one-pot meal of braised elk, pig's feet, and cabbage. Or try Louis Jadot Beaune Clos des Couchereaux from France. It shows black cherry, soft tannins, and a bit of fat that holds up well against the earthy mushrooms and other savory ingredients in the dish. **–K.P.**

Chicken Roulade

Serves 4 to 6

This is an incomparably delicious dish—chicken breast stuffed with a savory forcemeat and swaddled in lacy, net-like caulfat. Caulfat, which is the lining of a pig's abdominal cavity, contains the chicken and keeps it beautifully moist, then melts away during cooking. This dish can be served hot or prepared ahead, sliced, and served cold with mustard. I usually accompany it with Savory Bread Pudding (page 131). You might also try it with Ken's Potato Galette (page 146), Creamed Brussels Sprouts and Bacon (page 151), or for those occasions when time is short, just a simple salad. Caulfat can be found at many ethnic groceries and most quality butcher shops.

1 large sheet caulfat

1/4 cup extra-virgin olive oil

8 ounces fresh wild mushrooms, such as chanterelles, morels, or porcini, cleaned and coarsely chopped

Kosher salt and freshly ground black pepper

1 (4-pound) chicken, boned (see page 208)

1 small onion, coarsely chopped

4 cloves garlic

2 bunches fresh thyme, 1 stripped of its leaves and chopped, the other left in whole branches

1/4 cup Persillade (page 198)

Place the caulfat sheet in a large bowl and cover it with cold water. Let it soak for about 1 hour to rid it of excess blood. Change the water if it discolors.

In a large skillet, heat 2 tablespoons of the olive oil over medium heat. Add the mushrooms, season with salt and pepper, and sauté until the mushrooms have cooked through and turned golden, about 5 minutes. Set them aside to cool completely.

With a meat grinder feeding into a large bowl, grind the chicken leg meat together with its skin, the onion, garlic, and cooked mushrooms. Fold in the chopped thyme leaves and persillade, season with 1 teaspoon of salt and 1/2 teaspoon of pepper, and mix well to incorporate.

Squeeze the sheet of caulfat dry and spread it out on a cutting board. Halve it vertically. Place a generous portion of the ground chicken mixture near the bottom of 1 half-sheet of caulfat. Season 1 chicken breast on both sides with salt and pepper and set it on the ground chicken mixture, skin side up. Pat it down to flatten. Pull the breast skin back and spread another portion of the ground

chicken mixture directly on the breast meat. Fold the skin back over it. Moving the wing tip out of the way, carefully wrap the stuffed breast several times with caulfat to create a neat package. Do not wrap too tightly or the caulfat will crack during cooking. Repeat with the other breast. If there is any ground chicken mixture left over, cook it for breakfast and serve with eggs, or incorporate it into a pasta sauce for dinner.

Preheat the oven to 400°F.

In a large skillet, heat the remaining 2 tablespoons of olive oil over medium heat. Sauté both roulades on all sides until uniformly golden brown, about 10 minutes total. Line a small roasting pan with the remaining thyme branches. Lay the chicken roulades on the thyme and roast, uncovered, until their internal temperature reaches 160°F, 35 to 45 minutes. Remove from the oven, cover loosely with aluminum foil, and let the chicken rest for 5 minutes before slicing and serving.

Chef's Tip

If you don't have a meat grinder, have your butcher bone your chicken and grind the leg meat for this recipe, then chop the onion, garlic, and mushrooms finely before mixing with the ground meat. Don't use a food processor, as it will produce too fine a paste.

To Drink

Which wine to pair with chicken? There are two schools of thought: a young, fruity red Burgundy or a classic Chardonnay. For the red, I like Beaujolais, which is from Burgundy. Try a fragrant and lively Fleurie, St-Amour, Morgon, or Côte de Brouilly—all will let the earthy mushrooms in the forcemeat assert themselves. Or go with a white wine—my choice is Domaine Drouhin Arthur Chardonnay from Oregon. It carries a long finish with crisp green apple overtones and a hint of vanilla that cuts through the richness of the bird and complements its juiciness. Try either: red or white, you can't go wrong. **–K.P.**

Roast Duck with Cherries

Serves 4

I absolutely love a one-pot meal, and this one is particularly soul-satisfying for me to make and to eat. The tender duck and vegetables are bound together with nothing more than aromatic spices. Slowly stewed cherries cut through the gamy flavor of the duck and the rich vegetables, making everything seem lighter while echoing the spices of the dish.

Pinch of ground cloves

6 star anise, ground, plus 2 whole

1 teaspoon ground cinnamon

2 large Yukon gold potatoes, peeled and cut into large chunks

2 carrots, peeled and sliced into 1/2-inch rounds

1 large onion, quartered

1 large turnip, peeled and quartered

1 large sweet potato, peeled and cut into large chunks

Kosher salt and freshly ground black pepper

6 tablespoons extra-virgin olive oil

1 (4- to 5-pound) whole Muscovy duck

Duck neck and organs (not the liver) (optional)

6 sprigs of thyme

2 bay leaves

3 cinnamon sticks

3 cups Bing cherries, stemmed and pitted

3 cups red wine

1/4 cup sugar

2 bulbs garlic, separated into cloves

Preheat the oven to 350°F.

In a small bowl, stir together the cloves, ground star anise, and ground cinnamon. In a roasting pan large enough to hold the duck, place the potatoes, carrots, onion, turnip, and sweet potato. Sprinkle with half of the spice mixture, some salt and pepper, and 3 tablespoons of the olive oil. Mix the vegetables until they are uniformly seasoned, covered with spices, and glistening with oil.

Rinse the duck in cold water and pat dry. Rub the duck all over with the remaining spice mixture and 3 tablespoons of olive oil. Season it generously inside and out with salt and pepper. Place it, breast side up, on top of the vegetables in the roasting pan. Add the neck and organs, along with the thyme, bay leaves, and 2 of the cinnamon sticks.

Cover the pan tightly with aluminum foil and roast for 2 hours.

In a saucepan, combine the cherries, red wine, sugar, the remaining cinnamon stick, and the whole star anise and cook over low heat until the cherries are soft and the wine has reduced to a syrupy consistency, about 30 minutes. Reserve about 3 tablespoons of the syrup for glazing the duck. Transfer the rest to a small serving bowl. Set aside and keep warm.

After the duck has cooked for 2 hours, remove the foil carefully (so you don't get burned by the steam) and baste the bird with the pan juices. Add the garlic cloves, cover the bird again with the foil, and cook until the meat starts pulling away from the bone, about 2 more hours.

Uncover once more, and brush the duck with the cherry-wine syrup. Remove the foil, and roast until the skin gets crispy and a dark, rich brown, another 15 minutes.

Carefully transfer the duck onto a large serving platter. Let it rest, uncovered, while assembling other parts of the dish. Use a slotted spoon to transfer the vegetables to a large bowl.

Pick off the meat of the neck and add it to the vegetables. Thinly slice the giblets and add them to the vegetables. Mash the vegetables and picked meat, season with salt and pepper, and transfer to a serving bowl.

For an impressive presentation, carve the duck at the table. Pass the mashed vegetables separately, along with the cherry–red wine compote.

To Drink

Evesham Wood Pinot Noir Cuvee J is a sublime marriage with this dish. Russ Rainey's Oregon Pinot in the Burgundy style plays nicely to the spice and gaminess of duck. A French counterpart is Domaine Robert Arnoux Nuits-Saint-Georges—redolent of cassis and dark cooked cherries. **–K.P.**

Roasted Rabbit with Mustard Sauce

Serves 4

Our time in France taught us that rabbit has always been a staple in French cooking. The meat of a rabbit is very lean, pale, and mild in flavor, so it lends itself easily to a variety of sauces. Some of the most famous preparations include rabbit stew enriched with blood, rabbit with prunes, or Kimberly's favorite (which she prepared for my 39th birthday)—rabbit with Dijon mustard.

A good butcher shop may stock rabbit or you can purchase it by mail (see Resources, page 222).

4 rabbit hindquarters

Kosher salt and freshly ground black pepper

1 tablespoon unsalted butter

2 tablespoons extra-virgin olive oil

1 large onion, halved and thinly sliced

1 large carrot, peeled and sliced into 1/4-inch rounds

4 sprigs of thyme

1 bay leaf

3/4 cup white wine

3/4 cup Chicken Stock (page 213)

3 tablespoons Dijon mustard

3 tablespoons crème fraîche

Preheat the oven to 375°F.

Season the rabbit with salt and pepper. In a large cast-iron skillet, melt the butter along with the oil over medium heat. Place the seasoned rabbit in the skillet and turn it a few times to coat the pieces in fat.

Scatter the sliced onions and carrots over and around the rabbit. Place the thyme and bay leaf into the pan as well. Cover tightly and roast for 1 hour. Uncover and roast for another 30 minutes to give the rabbit a bit of color.

Transfer the rabbit and vegetables onto a serving platter. Cover with aluminum foil to keep warm while finishing the sauce.

Pour the wine and stock into the skillet and simmer over medium heat until reduced by half, about 10 minutes. Whisk in the mustard and crème fraîche. Increase the heat and bring the sauce to a boil; remove from the heat. Pour the sauce over the rabbit and serve.

To Drink

Chablis and rabbit is a classic wine-food pairing. A Chablis produced by Frédéric Magnien in France has balanced acidity and just a hint of wood so as not to overwhelm the flavors of the lean meat. When you taste it, it reminds you of wet stones, which offsets the mustard and cream. Verget Bourgogne Blanc, another white Burgundy, offers green apple acidity for the mustard and the smoky, caramel essence of hearth-cooked meat. The wines of Verget never come off our list. From Oregon, the classic Burgundian-style Chardonnay produced by Cameron Winery pairs admirably with a dish with similar Burgundian roots, yet retains a signature that is pure Oregon. **–K.P.**

Roasted Guinea Fowl with Chapelure de Legumes and Apple Cider Sauce

Serves 4 to 6

While working in France, I prepared a crusty coating for a bird made from dried vegetable flakes called *chapelure de legumes* (vegetable "bread crumbs"). They added a wonderful, unexpected fragrance. I found the idea so brilliant and clever that I vowed to repeat it when I had my own restaurant.

2 small bulbs fennel

2 small onions

1 large celery root, peeled

2 tart apples, such as Granny Smith, peeled and cored

2 small carrots, peeled

12 small red or fingerling potatoes, halved

1 large bulb garlic, separated into unpeeled cloves

Kosher salt and freshly ground black pepper

1/4 cup plus 1 tablespoon extra-virgin olive oil

2 guinea fowl (2 pounds each)

1 bunch thyme or winter savory

1 cup fresh apple cider

2 tablespoons unsalted butter

2 tablespoons Persillade (page 198)

Preheat the oven to 150°F.

To make the vegetable flakes, set a mandoline over a large bowl. Slice 1 fennel bulb paper-thin, then slice 1 onion, 1/2 of the celery root, and 1 of the apples to the same thickness. Switch to a vegetable peeler, and working over the same bowl, peel 1 carrot into thin ribbons. Mix the vegetables and spread them evenly on a baking sheet. Place the sheet in the oven to dry the vegetables until completely brittle, about 2 1/2 hours. (If you have an oven with a convection function, this will shorten the drying time to 1 hour.)

Transfer the vegetables to the work bowl of a food processor fitted with the metal blade and pulse until reduced to flakes. Store, covered, at room temperature. This can be done 1 day ahead.

Preheat the oven to 400°F.

To prepare the birds, halve the remaining fennel, onion, carrot, and celery root, then cut them again into several small wedges. Place them in a large baking dish along with the potatoes and garlic. Generously season with salt and pepper. Drizzle with 3 tablespoons of the olive oil and mix to coat.

Season the guinea fowl with salt and pepper inside and out. Stuff the cavities with whole sprigs of thyme. Rub them all over with the remaining 2 tablespoons of olive oil. Place the birds on the bed of vegetables. Roast, uncovered, for 45 minutes, basting occasionally with pan juices.

Cut the remaining apple into several wedges and add it to the roasting pan. Continue roasting and basting until the skin on the birds turns golden brown, another 20 minutes. Remove the birds from the oven, sprinkle them generously with dried vegetable flakes, then continue to roast until the juices run clear, another 10 minutes. Transfer the birds and roasted vegetables to a serving platter. Cover loosely with foil and let rest while preparing the sauce.

To make the pan sauce, pour the pan juices into a small saucepan. Skim and discard as much fat off the top as possible. Over medium-low heat, deglaze the roasting pan with the cider and simmer for 5 minutes, scraping the bottom of the roasting pan to loosen the browned bits. Add the hot cider from the roasting pan to the pan juices, and over high heat, reduce the liquid by half. Stir in the butter, season with salt and pepper, and pour it into a sauce boat. Sprinkle the birds and the vegetables with persillade. Carve the guinea fowl at the table and serve with the cider sauce.

To Drink

Bergström Winery Pinot Noirs from Oregon have the necessary aromatics to stand up to this fragrant dish. Any single-vineyard Savigny les Beaune from Domaine Maurice Ecard in France would also pair well with the earthiness of the bird. **–K.P.**

Duck Wellington with Mole Sauce

Serves 4

This dish was born when I was participating in an important wine dinner that also featured game birds and mushrooms. I needed to create something to match a local Syrah. Kimberly and I got to work, swirling, sniffing, tasting. The wine's scent was redolent of cinnamon and clove, its taste assertive with black pepper and cayenne. We detected creamy butter, chocolate, and tobacco that gave way to a pleasant earthy taste of fungus. Leather and prune finished it, with flavors that seemed to go on forever. "Seared duck breast," I mused, "with prune and mushroom duxelles. I'll wrap it in puff pastry." I was on the right track, but it felt incomplete. How could I introduce a note of chocolate, which we had tasted in the wine? Kimberly had it: "How about garnishing the dish with a spicy mole sauce?" Spice, rich chocolate, gaminess, earthiness, dried fruit—we could make this dish sing in unison with the wine. But what to call it? "It's a madman's Wellington with mole sauce," I said, and laughed out loud.

Mole Sauce

1/2 teaspoon ground cinnamon

Pinch of ground cloves

2 star anise, ground

1/2 teaspoon cayenne pepper

6 pasilla chiles, stemmed and seeded

2 tablespoons sherry vinegar

1 cup Chicken Stock (page 213)

Kosher salt and freshly ground black pepper

2 tablespoons honey

2 ounces dark chocolate, broken into small chunks

1/2 cup hazelnuts, toasted and finely ground

Duck

2 boneless Pekin duck breasts, skinned (skin reserved)

1 cup cold water

Kosher salt and freshly ground black pepper

1 pasilla chile, stemmed, seeded, and ground

1/2 teaspoon unsweetened cocoa powder

2 large shallots, finely diced

2 large fresh porcini or king oyster mushrooms, cleaned and finely diced

6 large pitted prunes, coarsely chopped

Generous dash of brandy

1/2 cup cream sherry

Olive oil to finish (see Chef's Tip) (optional)

2 very long russet potatoes, peeled (optional)

10 by 12-inch sheet of puff pastry, thawed if frozen

2 large eggs, beaten, for egg wash

To prepare the mole sauce, in a small bowl, combine the cinnamon, cloves, star anise, and cayenne pepper to make the spice mix. Reserve.

Place the chiles in a bowl, cover with boiling water, and let sit about 30 minutes. Drain the chiles, reserving 1 1/2 cups of the soaking liquid.

In a blender, liquefy the chiles, the reserved soaking liquid, and the vinegar. Transfer to a saucepan, add the stock, and stir in 1 tablespoon of the spice mix. (Reserve the rest of the spice mixture for the duck.) Season generously with salt and pepper.

Bring to a simmer over medium heat, and cook about 5 minutes. Decrease the heat to low and stir in the honey, chocolate, and hazelnuts. Cook, stirring frequently, until the flavors intensify and the sauce thickens, about 45 minutes. Adjust the seasoning with salt and pepper. Set aside while preparing the duck.

To make the duck, set a fine mesh strainer over a small bowl and have ready. Finely chop the duck skin. Place it in a small saucepan, add 1 cup of cold water, and cook over low-to-medium heat, stirring frequently to keep the bits of skin from sticking, until the water evaporates and all that is left in the pan is rendered fat and pieces of skin. Continue to cook and stir just until the bits of skin turn crispy and golden brown. The whole process will take about 25 minutes. Strain the fat in the prepared bowl and reserve. Transfer the cracklings into a separate bowl, season them with salt, and set aside to cool.

In a small bowl, combine the reserved spice mixture with the ground chile and cocoa powder. Halve the duck breasts lengthwise to form 2 long strips each. Season the breast pieces with salt and pepper and sprinkle liberally all over with the spice mixture. In a large skillet, heat 1 tablespoon of reserved duck fat over high heat and briefly sauté the duck breast strips on all sides until browned, but not cooked through, about 10 seconds per side. Set aside to cool.

In another large skillet, melt another 2 tablespoons of duck fat over low heat and gently sauté the shallots until translucent, about 5 minutes. Add the mushrooms, increase the heat to medium, and sauté until soft, another 5 minutes. Stir in the prunes. Remove from the heat, pour in the brandy, and ignite the alcohol with a fire starter or long kitchen match. When the flame has subsided, return the pan to the burner and add the sherry to deglaze the pan. Decrease the heat to low and cook until the liquid has dried up, about 10 minutes. Fold in the cracklings. Adjust the seasoning with salt and pepper. Set aside to cool.

Preheat the oven to 350°F.

Using a mandoline or the slicing blade of a food processor, slice the potatoes lengthwise $1/8$ inch thick. Brush a baking sheet with a little duck fat and season it with salt and pepper. Vertically line up 4 equal-sized potato slices so they overlap each other by $1/2$ inch. Repeat the process 3 more times. Brush the top of the potatoes with the remaining duck fat, season with salt and pepper, and bake until just pliable and soft, but still raw, about 5 minutes. Leave the 4 potato "sheets" intact. Set aside to cool.

Increase the oven temperature to 450°F.

Spread 1 heaping tablespoon of the prune mixture horizontally across each potato sheet. Place 1 seared duck breast piece on top of each potato sheet. Roll the potatoes over the duck to wrap tightly.

Grease a baking sheet and have ready. Cut the puff pastry into 4 equal rectangles. Brush them with egg wash. Place a potato-wrapped duck breast in the center of each piece of pastry. Roll to wrap tightly.

Pinch the seams closed and fold the ends under. Place the rolls, seam sides down, at least 3 inches apart on the prepared baking sheet. Brush the outside of each roll with the egg wash. Poke the top of each roll with a small paring knife to create a stem vent. Bake until golden brown, about 20 minutes.

To serve, make a little pool of the sauce on the bottom of each dinner plate. Carefully slice the duck Wellingtons and arrange the slices on top of the sauce. Serve immediately.

Chef's Tips

Keep the puff pastry cold until the last possible moment before using it. It will be easier to work with. If the puff pastry sheet seems too small to wrap the roll, just stretch it gently and it will fit.

Rendering fat by cooking it in water is a technique we use at the restaurant. It helps to gently render all the fat while minimizing the potential to burn. If you run out of duck fat to finish the dish, use olive oil instead.

To Drink

The tasting notes from winemaker Tony Rynders for Domaine Serene's Rockblock Syrah includes references to chocolate, cinnamon, licorice, and smoke—the hallmark flavors of a good mole. It almost leads the wine to this dish. All I can say is that the wine and this duck rock together. A French wine with a similar flavor profile—from Domaine du Vieux Télégraphe, Château de Beaucastel, or producer Domaine Jean-Louis Chave—expresses the soul of the southern Rhône. The spicy duck encourages an appreciation for the inherent spicy quality of the grapes from this region. If the occasion for having a wine from these producers merits a splurge, go for it. **–K.P.**

Chapter 6
Vegetables and Side Dishes

Soft Polenta with Rosemary

Serves 4 to 6

Polenta is simple to make, and while you can flavor it many ways depending on the season or your whim, this is how I prepare it when I crave something straightforward and undemanding. Adding rosemary gives it a woodsy tone that works well with braised meats or mushrooms.

I prefer the Corn Grits–Polenta from Bob's Red Mill. It cooks beautifully, developing a pleasant texture and rich corn flavor. It is widely available in well-stocked markets or by mail order (see Resources, page 222).

2 1/2 cups whole milk

2 1/2 cups Chicken Stock (page 213)

Kosher salt and freshly ground black pepper

1 cup stone-ground yellow polenta

2 tablespoons unsalted butter

1/3 cup grated Parmesan cheese

1 1/2 teaspoons finely chopped fresh rosemary

In a saucepan, combine the milk and the stock, season generously with salt and pepper, and bring to a boil over high heat. Gradually whisk in the polenta.

Decrease the heat to medium and continue to whisk until the mixture thickens, about 5 minutes. Decrease the heat to low, and continue cooking, whisking occasionally to prevent scorching, until the polenta has lost its crunch and is very creamy, about 1 hour. If it becomes too thick during the cooking and difficult to stir, add a little hot water to thin it out.

When the polenta is cooked to your liking, remove from the heat and stir in the butter, Parmesan, and rosemary. Adjust the seasoning with salt and pepper and serve right away.

Chef's Tip

I am a big fan of cooking polenta even longer than an hour. If I have time, I will let it go for 1 1/2 hours or more to let the flavors really develop. The texture becomes luxuriously silky.

If there is any polenta left over, spread it in a greased pie tin or small casserole, wrap well, and refrigerate. The next day cut it up and fry in olive oil. It will get delightfully brown and crispy on the outside and creamy inside.

Savory Bread Pudding

Serves 6 to 8

Born of necessity (a restaurant can only use so many bread crumbs made from leftover bread), this became the restaurant's most requested recipe. In summer, we substitute sweet onion for the leeks and serve the dish topped with chopped tomatoes. It only tastes better with age—perfect for entertaining. If you make it a day ahead, gently reheat it in a 350°F oven.

The mushrooms and leeks will leach out some water as they cook. It is important to let the vegetables reabsorb this liquid so that it does not dilute the custard. The additional cooking makes them even more tender and concentrates their flavors.

3/4-pound loaf day-old sour-dough bread, crusts removed, cut into 1-inch cubes

5 tablespoons unsalted butter, melted

10 sprigs of winter savory or thyme, leaves only, finely chopped

1/4 cup plus 1 tablespoon extra-virgin olive oil, plus more for brushing

1 pound Fresh Pork Sausage (recipe follows)

2 leeks, white parts only, halved lengthwise, washed, and sliced into 1/4-inch half-moons

1 pound small fresh chanterelle mushrooms, cleaned and dried

Kosher salt and freshly ground black pepper

1 large green apple, peeled, cored, and thinly sliced

2 cups heavy cream

5 large eggs

1/4 cup balsamic vinegar

1 1/2 cups grated Parmesan cheese

3 tablespoons Persillade (page 198)

Preheat the oven to 350°F.

In a bowl, toss the bread cubes with the melted butter and chopped savory. Transfer to a baking sheet and toast until crispy and golden, about 30 minutes. Increase the oven temperature to 375°F.

In a 12-inch skillet, heat 2 tablespoons of the olive oil over medium heat. Break up the sausage into silver–dollar–sized pieces, add to the pan, and cook thoroughly, about 10 minutes. Remove and set aside to cool. Add the remaining 3 tablespoons of olive oil to the same skillet. Add the leeks and mushrooms, season with salt and pepper, and cook,

stirring, until all the liquid has been absorbed, about 10 minutes. Stir in the apple and set aside to cool.

Brush a 9-inch-square ovenproof casserole with olive oil. In a large bowl, mix the toasted bread cubes, sausage, and leek-mushroom mixture. Transfer to the casserole.

In a bowl, whisk together the cream, eggs, balsamic vinegar, 3/4 cup of the Parmesan, 1 tablespoon salt, 1 teaspoon pepper, and the persillade. Pour the mixture over the bread mixture, cover tightly with aluminum foil, and bake for about 1 hour. Test for doneness by inserting a small paring knife into the middle of the pudding. If it comes out clean it is done. If it does not, cook longer, checking for doneness every 15 minutes. Uncover the pudding and sprinkle evenly with the rest of the Parmesan. Preheat the broiler and broil the pudding until it turns golden, about 3 minutes. Cut into squares and serve.

Fresh Pork Sausage

Makes about 1 1/4 pounds

1 pound ground pork shoulder

5 large cloves garlic, finely chopped

1 small onion, finely diced

1 tablespoon ground fennel seed

1/2 teaspoon ground cinnamon

1/2 teaspoon ground ginger

1/2 teaspoon ground allspice

1/2 teaspoon red pepper flakes

1 tablespoon salt

1/2 teaspoon freshly ground black pepper

In a bowl, combine all the ingredients, mixing thoroughly. Gather the sausage in a ball, cover, and refrigerate. The sausage is best when made 1 day ahead to let the flavors marry. The uncooked sausage will freeze well for up to a month.

Buckwheat Crêpes Stuffed with Turnips and Truffles

Serves 6

We like to offer guests a new view of humble vegetables—in this case, turnips. We cook the turnips in butter with shallots and honey, then elevate them with truffles. Once the crêpes are filled, we dip them in egg and pan-fry them until crispy. The resulting packet is a surprise of flavors, textures, and aromas.

Buckwheat flour in the batter produces a slightly sturdier crêpe that will better hold the stuffing and stand up to frying. Because making crêpes can be tricky, this recipe produces more than you'll need here.

$1/2$ cup buckwheat flour

1 cup all-purpose flour

6 large eggs

2 cups milk, plus more if needed

1 tablespoon unsalted butter, melted, plus $3/4$ cup, melted, to fry the crêpes

3 tablespoons truffle butter (see Resources, page 222)

2 shallots, thinly sliced

1 large Oregon black or white truffle (about 2 ounces), coarsely chopped

1 pound turnips, peeled and coarsely grated

$1/3$ cup honey

$1/2$ cup cider vinegar

Kosher salt and freshly ground black pepper

2 cups Chicken Stock (page 213)

To make the crêpe batter, sift the flours with a pinch of salt into a bowl. Make a well in the center of the flour and add 3 of the eggs. Using a whisk, slowly incorporate the flour into the eggs so the batter develops without lumps. Add 1 cup of the milk, whisking until smooth, the remaining 1 cup milk, and 1 tablespoon of the melted butter. Cover and set the mixture aside for 30 minutes at room temperature.

To make the stuffing, in a large skillet, melt the truffle butter over medium heat without browning. Add the shallots and truffle, and cook until the shallots are translucent but not colored, 4 to 5 minutes. Add the turnips, honey, and cider vinegar. Season with salt and pepper. Add the stock and bring to a boil over high heat, stirring to mix the ingredients.

Decrease the heat to low, cover, and simmer very gently, stirring occasionally to prevent sticking and browning, until the turnips are very soft, about 1 hour. Adjust the seasoning if necessary. Transfer the stuffing to a bowl and set aside to cool. The stuffing can be done a day in advance and refrigerated until ready.

To cook the crêpes, heat a 10-inch nonstick crêpe pan or skillet over high heat until hot, about 5 minutes. Brush the pan with melted butter. Remove from the heat and pour $1/4$ cup of the batter into the center of the pan, rotating the pan so the batter runs evenly to the edges in a thin layer. Return the pan to the heat. Cook the crêpe until the edges brown, about 2 minutes. Slip a flexible spatula under the crêpe, carefully flip it over, and cook on the other side for 30 seconds. Transfer the cooked crêpe to a plate. Repeat until all the batter is used, stacking the crêpes as they are done.

To stuff the crêpes, place 1 on a work surface, set a generous spoonful of turnip-truffle mixture in the center, and spread it to within 1 inch of the edge of the crêpe. Fold the filled crêpe in half and then in half again. Repeat with the remaining crêpe and stuffing.

Preheat the oven to 200°F.

Place the remaining 3 eggs in a shallow pie plate, beat them with a fork, and have ready. To fry the crêpes, heat 2 tablespoons of the melted butter in a large nonstick pan over medium-high heat. Carefully dip one stuffed, folded crêpe into the beaten eggs, turning it to coat on all sides. Lift the crêpe with your fingers, allowing excess egg to drip back into the bowl, and place the crêpe in the hot skillet. Fry until crisp and browned on both sides, 45 seconds to 1 minute per side. Transfer to a baking sheet and keep warm in the oven while cooking the rest. Repeat the procedure, using more melted butter as needed to fry the remaining crêpes. Serve hot.

Asparagus with Smoked Salmon–Dill Butter

Serves 4 to 6

When asparagus is in season, this recipe is a sure winner. If the grill is going, give the asparagus the taste of summer by finishing them over a hot fire and serving family-style on a big platter. Smoked salmon in the butter echoes the charred flavors of the grill. Hot-smoked salmon is more intense than its cold-smoked counterpart so is a good match for grassy asparagus. I like to save the delicate cold-smoked salmon for when I am in the mood to have it with a warm bagel and cream cheese.

1 pound thick asparagus

1/4 cup unsalted butter, softened

1 ounce hot-smoked salmon, preferably from the belly or collar of the fish, coarsely shredded

Finely grated zest of 1 lemon

Juice of 1/2 lemon

1 1/2 tablespoons chopped fresh dill, plus large dill sprigs, for garnish

Kosher salt and freshly ground black pepper

Extra-virgin olive oil (optional)

Sea salt, for finishing

Align the asparagus stalks at their tips. Cut off and discard the woody fibrous ends so the trimmed stalks are all the same length.

To make the salmon-dill butter, in a small bowl combine the butter, salmon, lemon zest, lemon juice, and chopped dill. Using a fork, blend it all together into a coarse paste. Season with salt and pepper and set aside at room temperature.

Have a plate lined with paper towels ready. To prepare the asparagus in a skillet, fill a large skillet 2 inches deep with water, season with enough salt so you can taste it, and bring to a boil over medium-high heat. Add the asparagus and cook until tender, about 5 minutes. Transfer to the prepared plate to drain and dry.

If grilling, preheat an outdoor grill. Brush the blanched spears with a bit of olive oil and place them on the grill. Roll them across the grate to give them grill marks and heat them through, about 3 minutes.

To serve, before they cool, transfer the asparagus to a serving platter and season with sea salt. Spoon out the butter in small pieces and scatter atop the asparagus. Garnish with dill sprigs and serve.

Peas and Carrots with Bacon

Early summer is prime time for a bountiful harvest of peas. Young, tender carrots appear at the same time. When I frame the combination with bacon and herbs, the dish almost vibrates with color and flavor.

The method for glazing carrots is a tried-and-true French technique to gently coax them into giving up all their flavor. Serve this dish with Bacon-Crusted Razor Clams with Basil Aioli (page 96) and prepare yourself for something very special.

Kosher salt and freshly ground black pepper	1 tablespoon extra-virgin olive oil
10 ounces sugar snap peas, stems and strings removed	6 ounces unsmoked bacon, cut into 1/4-inch dice
6 ounces fresh English peas, shelled	6 fresh basil leaves, hand-torn, for garnish
8 ounces small new carrots, peeled and trimmed	6 fresh mint leaves, hand-torn, for garnish
1 tablespoon unsalted butter	
1 tablespoon sugar	

Have a bowl of ice water ready. Bring a 4-quart pot of well salted water to a boil over high heat. Add the sugar snap peas and cook until tender yet still crunchy, about 4 minutes. Remove the peas from the water with a slotted spoon and immediately refresh in the ice-water bath to stop the cooking and help the peas retain their bright color. Repeat the process with the English peas. Drain and dry on paper towels and set aside.

Have ready a 10-inch round of waxed paper or parchment paper. In a 10-inch skillet, place the carrots, butter, sugar, a large pinch of salt, and enough cold water to come halfway up the carrots. Loosely cover the carrots with the paper. Cook on medium heat until the water has evaporated, 4 to 5 minutes. Discard the paper. Shake the pan to roll and glaze the carrots, moving it back and forth across the heat for about 1 minute. Set aside to cool.

In another large skillet, heat the olive oil over medium heat. Add the bacon and cook until browned and crispy, about 10 minutes. Drain the bacon on paper towels and discard all but 1 tablespoon of bacon fat. Wipe the pan clean.

Add the bacon fat back into the pan, followed by the sugar snap and English peas, carrots, and the cooked bacon. Season with salt and pepper. Warm for about 3 minutes over medium-high heat, stirring occasionally. Transfer to a serving platter, garnish with basil and mint, and serve.

Sauté of Market Vegetables with Miso Butter

Serves 4 to 6

Carrots, cauliflower, summer squash, eggplant, baby turnips, beets, potatoes, kohlrabi, Walla Walla onions, torpedo onions, shallots, garlic. A gazillion varieties of tomatoes, corn, and green beans. It is hard to restrain yourself when shopping for vegetables at the Portland Farmer's Market in the height of summer. So I don't. I buy everything in sight, as I know that my cooks and I will find creative uses for it all.

This dish is inspired by Japanese cooking, where miso seems to make food taste salty without any salt. Butter rounds out flavors but lets the miso speak. Use these vegetables as a guide. Support your local farmer's market and buy what is fresh and in season.

1/4 cup unsalted butter, softened

1/4 cup blond miso

Kosher salt and freshly ground black pepper

1/2 pound green beans, stems trimmed

1 small head broccoli, separated into small florets

1 small head cauliflower, separated into small florets

1 bunch green onions, white parts only

1/2 cup plus 2 tablespoons extra-virgin olive oil

1 large green zucchini, ends trimmed

1 large yellow zucchini, ends trimmed

24 baby carrots, peeled, trimmed, and glazed (see page 136)

1/4 cup Persillade (page 198)

To make the miso butter, place the butter and miso into a small bowl and mix with a fork until well blended. Cover, and set aside at room temperature.

Have a large bowl of ice water ready. To cook the vegetables, bring a large pot of water to a boil. Season it with salt until you taste it. Add the green beans all at once and cook until tender yet still brightly colored, about 5 minutes. Remove the beans from the water with a slotted spoon and immediately refresh in the ice-water bath to stop the cooking and help the beans retain their bright color. Drain and dry with paper towels, then set aside.

Repeat the process with the broccoli, cauliflower, and green onions. Taste for doneness and be mindful of the cooking time, as it will vary from vegetable to vegetable.

Quarter the green and yellow zucchini lengthwise, then slice into 1/2-inch pieces. In a large skillet over high heat, add the 1/2 cup of olive oil and heat until it shimmers. Add the green and yellow zucchini pieces, season with salt and pepper, and cook, stirring, until they turn golden brown, about 3 to 4 minutes. Remove with a slotted spoon to drain on paper towels. Discard the oil and wipe the pan clean.

In the same skillet over medium heat, warm the remaining 2 tablespoons of olive oil. Add all the vegetables, including the carrots, to the skillet to warm them through, about 5 minutes.

Stir in the miso butter until it melts, and then the persillade. Transfer the vegetables to a large serving platter and serve immediately.

Stuffed Tomatoes Provençal

Serves 4

In my mind, this dish captures the true flavors of southern France. I enjoy it on its own or as an accompaniment to grilled meats. At Paley's, we might serve it with spit-roasted suckling lamb or Shoulder of Lamb Roasted with Hay and Lavender (page 108). The one thing to remember when stuffing tomatoes is to fill them loosely or they will split during baking.

4 firm, large, ripe tomatoes

1/4 cup plus 2 tablespoons extra-virgin olive oil

1 onion, finely diced

2 cloves garlic, finely chopped

Pinch of red pepper flakes

4 anchovy fillets, drained and finely minced

Kosher salt and freshly ground black pepper

1/2 cup bread crumbs (see Chef's Tip, below)

1/2 cup loosely packed fresh basil leaves, coarsely chopped

2 tablespoons Persillade (page 198)

1 hard-boiled egg, peeled and coarsely grated on the largest holes of a box grater

1 tablespoon grated Parmesan cheese

Preheat the oven to 400°F.

To prepare the tomatoes, slice off their caps with stems intact, reserving the stems and caps for garnish. To ensure that the tomatoes lay flat while they bake, shave off a slice from the bottoms. Chop the trimmings and save them as well.

Hollow the inside of each tomato, being careful not to pierce the bottom, by scooping out the flesh and seeds. Reserve the flesh and seeds on a cutting board along with the chopped tomato bottoms. Set the tomato shells aside.

To make the filling, in a small skillet, heat 1/4 cup of the olive oil over medium heat. Add the onion and garlic, sprinkle with red pepper flakes, and cook, stirring, until softened, about 5 minutes. Add the anchovies and chopped tomato, and continue cooking until the liquid evaporates, another 15 minutes. Season with salt and pepper. Cool slightly, then transfer to a small bowl. Add the bread crumbs, basil, persillade, and grated egg.

Mound the stuffing in each tomato, patting the tops by hand. Place the stuffed tomatoes in an ovenproof gratin dish. Sprinkle each tomato with Parmesan cheese. Place the reserved tomato tops, stem side up, in the gratin dish as well. Drizzle all with the remaining 2 tablespoons of olive oil and bake until the tomatoes are soft to the touch and the cheese browns a bit, about 20 minutes. Replace the tops and serve.

Chef's Tip

To make breadcrumbs, preheat the oven to 300°F. Cut a day-old loaf of bread into 1-inch cubes. Place them on a baking sheet and bake for 1 hour to toast. Let cool, then pulverize in batches in a food processor until you have fine crumbs. Store in an airtight container at room temperature for 2 days or freeze for up to 1 month.

Summer Ratatouille

Serves 4 to 6

When eggplant season begins, ratatouille promptly appears on our menu. It's a versatile dish that we serve cold as an appetizer or hot as a side dish. The eggplant needs to be cooked through, and my technique is to bake it slowly, drizzled with olive oil and accompanied by lots of garlic. As the eggplant bakes, it soaks up the sunny flavors of the peppers and tomatoes that surround it. When it is done, I slowly uncover the roasting pan, place my face right above it, and inhale deeply—my Provençal "facial." Each time I catch those first intoxicating aromas, I'm certain there is no better dish to capture the spirit of summer.

1 large eggplant, cut into 1-inch cubes

Kosher salt and freshly ground black pepper

1/2 cup extra-virgin olive oil, plus more if needed

1 large red bell pepper, stemmed, cored, and coarsely diced

1 medium green zucchini, ends trimmed, cut into 1-inch cubes

1 large onion, cut into 1-inch cubes

6 large cloves garlic, minced

1 bunch thyme, finely chopped

2 large ripe tomatoes, grated on the largest holes of a box grater

1/2 cup loosely packed fresh basil leaves

Preheat the oven to 400°F.

Place the eggplant in a large bowl, sprinkle with 2 tablespoons of salt, and toss to coat. Transfer to a colander set over a bowl or the sink, letting it drain its water, about 15 minutes.

In a large skillet, heat 1/4 cup of the olive oil over high heat. Add the bell pepper, season it with salt and pepper, and cook, stirring, until it has softened and starts to brown, about 3 minutes. Use a slotted spoon to transfer it to a large roasting pan.

Add more oil as needed and repeat the process, sautéing the zucchini, onion, and the drained eggplant separately, and transferring the sautéed vegetables to the roasting pan. Cook in batches if necessary to ensure the vegetables develop even coloring.

Add the garlic, chopped thyme, and tomatoes to the roasting pan, drizzle with 1/4 cup of the olive oil, and mix everything together.

Roast until the vegetables give up their liquid, cook dry, and are very tender, about 1 1/2 hours. Stir the vegetables gently as they cook so they maintain their distinct shapes.

To serve, transfer the ratatouille to a serving bowl. Coarsely chop the basil and gently stir into the vegetable mixture. Serve hot or at room temperature.

Total Potatoes

Once a week for more than ten years, Gene Thiel and his son Patrick have traversed much of Oregon's breadth, driving 300 miles west from his farm near Joseph to Portland, then back again the next day. Starting early Friday morning, they travel along two-lane county roads and eventually join the interstate at La Grande. They wind up over the summits of the Blue Mountains, where the road descends to bare flatlands in the state's high, dry center. The landscape here is marked by scrub-dotted buttes.

The road finally joins and follows the course of the Columbia River all the way to Portland. The road along this magnificent river—which defines much of the border between Oregon and Washington before turning north to its Canadian headwaters—passes dams and natural waterfalls, ancient forests, and fertile valleys. It's one of the most beautiful routes in the nation.

This five-hour-long commute to Portland and back every week has proved to be a salvation for Gene and his wife, Eileen, after years of struggling to farm potatoes sustainably in a marketplace that overwhelmingly treats potatoes as cheap, mass-produced commodities. Facing the need to create his own market moved Gene to knock on Portland's restaurant doors one by one. He convinced chefs to try his potatoes by speaking about the tubers with a thoughtful authority they had never encountered, and between restaurant customers and farmer's market

sales, he quickly established a guaranteed market for whatever he could produce. At the Portland Farmer's Market, Gene stacks his potatoes on a modest table, many of them unusual varieties like Heartha, la Ratte (a French heirloom variety), and Alby's Gold. His potatoes are amazing, and he brings them to market with an unassuming wit and a dignified desire to educate his customers about the characteristics of each variety and the ideal ways to prepare them.

Gene Thiel is gentle man. Physically, he embodies the qualities of a sturdy tree, lean and taut and bursting with *élan vital*. He doesn't fidget, but you feel the hum of his concentration. When he sits, he crosses his hands in an automatic and disciplined gesture. As he speaks, his hands unfold to move in a parallel language.

This is a man who ministers to dirt. The damp scent and familiar feel of loose loam seem to be his tonic and the pillar upon which his spirit rests. He is a third-generation potato farmer, the descendent of German immigrants who migrated west by train, settling in Idaho and Oregon because they recognized good soil when they saw it. The soil he grew up on was rich and well maintained from one generation to the next. What Gene has learned from a lifetime of observing soil, season, and geography has given him the strength and insight he has needed over the years to come to terms with both change and constancy. Farming anchors him to the present, connects him to the past, and carries him through a thousand uncertainties.

The Thiels farm sixty acres in the Wallowa Valley; they moved to Oregon from Idaho in 1975. Their son Patrick, also a farmer, describes the county as not heavily farmed. "This means there's a lot of healthy soil here that hasn't been ruined for organic agriculture and that doesn't need expensive fertilizers." The surrounding mountains provide a good supply of water. Each year the Thiels work thirty-five acres of exceptionally rich soil while the remaining acres lie fallow. Eileen says, "This amount of acreage has been sufficient to support us and small enough for Gene to watch his crops on a very personal basis." She swears he knows every plant and what it's doing every day.

In his intelligent reliance on the wisdom of tradition and his steady care for his soil, Gene is in a minority among his generation of American farmers. In the 1950s, when Gene was a young man ready to take his place in the world, agriculture was making an historic shift: it was becoming agribusiness. Chemical inputs like fertilizers and pesticides promised to increase crop yields astronomically (and they did so, though at a cost to soil health and ecosystems), new varieties developed in corporate laboratories would yield uniform potatoes bred to be stored and shipped (flavor and nutrition were at best secondary considerations), and centralized distribution would expand markets (and, as it happened, consolidate economic power in the hands of brokers, bankers, seed companies, and the like, leaving farmers with little control over either what they spent or what they earned).

Sixty years later, we're increasingly aware of the immense and irretrievable social, economic, and ecological costs of this shift. But young men of Gene's generation were destined to work for their fathers until one or the other of them died. Their social order was closed. They had been to war, and away to college, and it was difficult to come back to a system where their thinking would be branded as wrong, where no one was open to new, modern ideas, and where they had to wait their turn. When business wooed these young men with a sales pitch of, "You can do anything," the message fell on ready ears. Science and technology, along with market innovations, offered them new ways of solving old problems and a chance at success on their own terms.

In retrospect, it's clear that the marriage of farming and agribusiness that shaped the development of commodities thinking also gave rise to the idea of organic farming and voice to the idea of sustainability. When Gene was growing up, food marketed as "organic" did not exist. Organically produced food was, nevertheless, what a long tradition of farming yielded. Farmers have always known that good, fertile soil is active, alive, and capable of producing a superior crop, or as Gene says, "Good soil is good economy." He believes that chemical-drenched, industrial-scale farming impoverishes the soil, so that only more and more chemicals will make it yield. It's a vicious cycle of dependency and destruction that Gene Thiel wants no part of.

After they moved to Oregon in the seventies, the Thiels, in conjunction with a few other growers, formed an organization called the Northwest Organic Growers Association (NOGA), committing to paper what they knew of traditional farming methods. NOGA gave shape to the present day Oregon Tilth system, which certifies organic practices.

Gene approaches farming as he always has—by relying on the ecosystem and working with it. He is adamant that the use of chemicals is a trap that inevitably leads to blight, a naturally occurring condition that kills potato plants or stunts their growth when the natural balance is disturbed. Healthy soil, which requires a healthy ecosystem including weed plants in symbiosis with crop plants, keeps blight in check. If it's managed through good soil husbandry (rather than fought with chemicals), blight may affect yields but it won't devastate crops. Patrick says many potato farmers locked into the system can't risk a dip in yield: "In the potato industry there are many farmers and only a few major buyers, so you tend to work for a company and not for yourself, and that drives you into nonsustainable practices. Organics is a totally separate world." But Eileen says she gets more and more calls from farmers asking about organic farming and how to go about changing over.

Gene gets emphatic and even emotional when he talks about potatoes. He tells me that commercial potatoes are designed to be uniform in appearance, and that they contain few if any antioxidants, whereas a good potato is loaded with them. Potatoes derive taste from a number of factors, he says. Plant genetics are primary,

but bacteria, fungi, and the chemistry of healthy soil all interact to produce texture and flavor. A potato takes what it needs from the soil in 80 to 120 days, depending on the variety. It is enough time for the acids that produce flavor to appear. Gene speaks of the pleasing esters present in potatoes, explaining that they affect both taste and smell. In addition, certain potatoes can continue to develop flavor even after harvest. He harvests by hand, slipping tubers out of the ground fairly clean, and avoiding flooding them with water, which can alter their flavor while they are tender. He cures them under the eastern Oregon sun for a few hours to further develop their flavor and nutrient content and to toughen their skins. He brushes them when they are dry and gathers them in string bags to sell at his market table. He still feels a thrill every time he harvests a potato, knowing what natural riches are concentrated in each tuber.

I tell him stories from my childhood, of how I used to accompany my grandfather to a farm each fall. We gathered enough potatoes to last through the winter. In our basement my grandfather constructed a clever maze of compartments that would keep the tubers in the cold and dark. Among the many potato dishes that my grandmother prepared, one in particular stands out in my memory. It was simply tiny pancakes made from grated raw potatoes mixed with eggs and fried in duck fat. I stood by the stove whenever she prepared them, like a hungry puppy panting for food, and always got the first few pancakes as they came out of the fat. Cooled only slightly by sour cream, they burned my fingers as I ate them. Once I had my fill, the more patient members of our clan had their turn.

Gene doesn't hesitate to share his own favorite method of preparing potatoes. The night before he wants them for breakfast, he parboils Alby's Gold until they are nearly cooked. In the morning he shreds them and shapes a potato pancake the size of his skillet, cooking it crisp on each side in a mixture of olive oil and butter. Separately, he scrambles an egg, embellishing it as the mood strikes with sun-dried tomatoes, shallots, herbs, and salt and pepper. When the pancake is done, he covers it with the egg mixture, then moistens a slice of bread with good organic vinegar and rests it atop everything in the pan. He inverts a plate over the skillet, and while the bread steams, the plate warms. He savors each bite and insists that the combination of potato and vinegar contributes to his good health and gives him the energy he needs to work the land.

Gene is now in his seventies, and he began picking potatoes when he was six years old. He remains energized by the consciousness that there is always more for him to learn. He believes the intention of a new generation of young organic growers, focused on sustainable objectives, is correct. His own commitment, a window into the soul of a farmer who must still rely on the practical response of the market, is total. Consumers help farmers like him gain ground whenever we demand the very best food, uncontaminated by chemicals and brimming with nature's distilled vibrancy.

Potato-Mushroom Cake

Makes one 10-inch cake or 12 individual cakes

This dish closely resembles the potato latkes that my grandmother made. We prepared something similar when I worked in France, but as one large cake that also included mushrooms. I like this version a number of ways: on its own, as a side dish, and with cold smoked salmon and sliced onion. My favorite, though, is as little pancakes straight out of the pan and slathered with sour cream, as my grandmother made them. If duck fat isn't available, I substitute olive oil.

6 tablespoons duck fat, plus more if making individual cakes

1 large fresh porcini or king oyster mushroom, coarsely diced

Kosher salt and freshly ground black pepper

1 pound Alby's Gold or Yukon Gold potatoes, peeled and cut into $1/4$-inch dice

1 large shallot, coarsely chopped

2 cloves garlic, finely minced

1 large egg, lightly beaten

3 tablespoons chopped fresh Italian parsley

In a large skillet, heat 2 tablespoons of the duck fat over medium heat. Add the mushrooms, season with salt and pepper, and sauté until soft and lightly colored. Drain on paper towels and set aside to cool.

Preheat the oven to 400°F.

In the work bowl of a food processor fitted with the metal blade, add the cooked mushrooms, potatoes, shallot, garlic, egg, and 2 tablespoons of the parsley. Season liberally with salt and pepper. Pulse 8 to 10 times until the mixture is pureed.

To make one large potato cake, in a 10-inch nonstick skillet, melt the remaining duck fat over low-to-medium heat. Pour in the pureed potato mixture and spread it evenly to the edges with a rubber spatula. Cook the cake, undisturbed, until the edges turn light brown, about 5 minutes. Place a large shallow platter or flat pot lid over the pan and flip the pan so the cake falls onto the platter. Gently slide the cake back into the skillet, place it in the oven, and bake until the potatoes are completely done and the cake gets springy to the touch, about 30 minutes.

Slide the cake onto the serving platter and slice it into wedges. Sprinkle with remaining parsley and serve.

To make individual potato cakes, melt duck fat in a skillet over medium heat. Drop in small dollops of potato batter and brown 2 to 3 minutes per side. Repeat until all the batter has been used up, adding more duck fat as needed. Serve hot or at room temperature.

Ken's Potato Galette

Serves 6

My friend Ken Forkish has a tiny artisan bakery located several blocks from the restaurant. A couple of years ago we collaborated on a dinner entitled "All Things Bread." He prepared this galette, which he learned to make in Paris using puff pastry (good French bakers always have more than bread in their repertoires), but made it even more luscious by adding farmer Gene Thiel's Dutch yellow potatoes. They are rich and buttery, with a vibrant yellow flesh. I thought I knew potatoes, but it was like I was tasting them for the first time.

We continue to serve this galette in our restaurant as an accompaniment to Roasted Rabbit with Mustard Sauce (page 123).

5 medium yellow-fleshed potatoes such as Dutch yellow (about 2 pounds), peeled

1 tablespoon salt

1 small onion, finely diced

8 sprigs of thyme, picked and finely chopped

2 tablespoons unsalted butter, melted

2 sheets puff pastry, 10 by 8 inches and 11 by 9 inches

1 large egg, beaten, for egg wash

1/4 cup plus 2 tablespoons crème fraîche

Preheat the oven to 375°F.

Slice the potatoes 1/8 inch thick, using a mandoline if you have one, or the slicer attachment of a food processor. In a bowl, toss the slices with the salt, then place them in a colander set over a bowl or the sink to drain for about 30 minutes. (It is important to rid the potatoes of any excess moisture that will make the pastry soggy during baking.) In a bowl, mix the potato slices with the onion, thyme, and butter, and set aside.

Line a baking pan with parchment paper. Lay the 10 by 8-inch sheet of pastry on a work surface.

Spread the potato mixture evenly over the pastry, leaving a 1-inch border all around. (You might think that you have too much potato, but pile it on, as the mixture loses volume during cooking.) Brush the border with egg wash and top with the 11 by 9-inch sheet of pastry, stretching it over the potatoes.

Crimp the edges with a fork to prevent the pastry sheets from separating. Trim off any excess pastry and generously brush the top with egg wash. Poke a small vent hole in the center of the pastry to ensure an even rise. Crisscross the top with the back of the knife for decoration.

Bake until golden brown, about 60 minutes. Test the potatoes for doneness by inserting a small paring knife into the galette. If they are done, so is the pastry. If there is any sign of resistance, decrease the oven temperature to 300°F and bake, testing frequently, another 15 minutes.

To serve, carefully transfer the galette to a large serving platter. Slice horizontally all around to separate the top and bottom crusts. Lift the top crust to expose the potatoes. Spoon crème fraîche evenly over them, reposition the top crust, and serve immediately. Slice the galette at the table.

Chef's Tip

You can buy frozen puff pastry made with vegetable shortening at your grocery store. However, I would encourage you to make friends with your local baker. If he is as nice as Ken, I am sure he will sell you some freshly made with real butter. You'll taste the difference.

Crispy Potatoes with Romesco

Serves 4

When Kimberly and I traveled through Spain, we tried a dish of roasted potatoes with a pepper and fried almond condiment called romesco. When I created my version of this taste memory, I sought simple and satisfying tastes that exploded with flavor.

Dark red and mild, nyora peppers are authentic to this recipe. When I can't find nyoras I look for other dried peppers with mild taste. Or, I will use only fresh bell peppers.

8 dried nyora peppers (or any mild, dried red chile), seeded	1 tomato, peeled and seeded
2 cups boiling water	1/8 cup sherry vinegar
2 red bell peppers	Kosher salt and freshly ground black pepper
1 1/4 cup extra-virgin olive oil	1 cup mixed olives, such as Arbechina and Lucques, pitted
1/2 cup almonds	
2 tablespoons bread crumbs	2 pounds Yukon gold potatoes
2 cloves garlic, peeled and coarsely chopped	2 tablespoons Persillade (see page 198)

Snap the stems from the nyora peppers. Shake and discard the seeds. Place the chiles in a bowl and cover with boiling water. Cover with a small plate to keep the chiles submerged until softened, about 20 minutes. Discard the soaking liquid. Set the chiles aside.

To peel the bell peppers on a gas burner, place them on a burner set on high heat. Using tongs, rotate them on all sides until they become uniformly blackened. To roast and peel the peppers in the oven, roast them in a 350°F oven until the skins brown and loosen, about 30 minutes.

For either method, place the cooked peppers in a bowl, cover with plastic wrap, and let sit until cool enough to handle, approximately 10 minutes. Peel off the skins, remove the seeds and stems, and set the peppers aside.

In a small skillet, heat 1/4 cup of the olive oil, add the almonds, and cook over medium heat, shaking the pan a few times, until the nuts are lightly

browned, about 4 minutes. Drain the almonds and let cool slightly. Discard the oil.

In the work bowl of a food processor fitted with the metal blade, place the chiles, roasted bell peppers, almonds, bread crumbs, garlic, tomato, vinegar, and the remaining 3/4 cup olive oil. Season generously with salt and pepper. Pulse to obtain a smooth puree. Transfer the pureed romesco mixture to a container, cover, and refrigerate until needed.

Preheat the oven to 425°F.

To prepare the potatoes, place them in a saucepan with enough cold water to cover them by 1 inch. Add a generous sprinkle of salt. Cook over medium heat until the potatoes are barely done and still a bit firm when pierced with a long wooden skewer or small paring knife, about 25 minutes. Drain, cool slightly, then peel them and cut into wedges.

Transfer the potato wedges to a baking sheet and season generously with salt and pepper. Drizzle with the remaining 1/4 cup olive oil to coat the potatoes evenly. Bake on the upper rack of the oven until browned and crispy, about 40 minutes.

To serve, place the potatoes in a serving bowl, scatter with olives, and top with half of the romesco. Sprinkle with persillade and pass the potatoes around the table, accompanied by the rest of the romesco.

Chef's Tips

Many cooks peel roasted bell peppers under running water, which I think is a big mistake. The water washes off essential oils, and the flavor you've just lovingly imparted by roasting. I peel them by hand, being as thorough as I can, then wash my hands, not the peppers.

I always buy olives with pits. I find that pitted olives are flabby in texture and lackluster in flavor. To pit olives I place them on cutting board and smash them gently, one at a time, using the bottom of a coffee cup.

Roasted Beets with Horseradish Cream

Serves 4 to 6

Dishes like this, with ingredients (like horseradish) that my grandfather used to prepare, bring back my fondest childhood memories. Even on special holidays, beets would appear in many forms at the family dinner. I grew up eating them as salad with vinaigrette, as borscht, or as a topping for pickled herring.

I prefer to roast beets, not boil them, because roasting concentrates their sugars and intensifies flavor. I think it's hard to overcook beets, so I don't worry if I forget them a little in the oven. The longer they roast the sweeter they get. Roast as many varieties of beets as you can find for a colorful presentation.

1 1/2 pounds medium mixed beets

3 tablespoons extra-virgin olive oil

1/2 cup sour cream

1/4 cup Prepared Horseradish, slightly drained (page 202)

Juice of 1/2 lemon

Kosher salt and freshly ground black pepper

2 tablespoons Persillade (page 198)

Preheat the oven to 400°F.

Set the beets in a roasting pan and drizzle with olive oil. Cover with aluminum foil and bake until tender, about 2 hours.

Remove from the oven and let them cool while you whisk together the sour cream, horseradish, and lemon juice in a small bowl. Season with salt and pepper.

Remove the skin from the beets while they are still warm, rubbing them with a kitchen towel or paper towels. Cut each beet into bite-sized wedges and transfer them to a serving bowl.

To serve, drizzle the beets with half of the horseradish cream and sprinkle them with persillade. Serve the remaining horseradish cream on the side. I favor the taste of just-roasted beets and serve them slightly warm; however, the dish can also be prepared a day in advance.

Braised Red Cabbage

Serves 4 to 6

To me, cabbage is an undervalued vegetable. We use it raw in coleslaw, that American lunch staple, but rarely venture any further. When cabbage is cooked gently for a long time, something magical happens. It develops earthy and meaty aromas, a sweetness that is both familiar and exotic, and a melt-in-your-mouth texture. With the addition of smoked bacon and apples, it can stand proudly next to any holiday dish. I think of this recipe as part of a holy trinity of sides—along with Savory Bread Pudding (page 131) and Creamed Brussels Sprouts and Bacon (page 151)—for a special Thanksgiving meal. You can braise the cabbage up to a day ahead and reheat it in a 350°F oven.

1 head red or green cabbage, tough outer leaves removed	1 green apple, peeled, cored, and thinly sliced
1 tablespoon extra-virgin olive oil	1 cup cider vinegar
1 pound Smoked Bacon (page 204), cut into 1-inch cubes	1/4 cup honey
	Kosher salt and freshly ground black pepper
1 onion, halved and thinly sliced	

Preheat the oven to 350°F.

Quarter, core, and thinly slice the cabbage. Set aside. In a large Dutch oven, heat the olive oil over medium heat. Add the bacon and cook until crispy, about 10 minutes. Transfer the bacon to paper towels to drain, leaving the bacon fat behind. Add the onion and the apple to the pan and sauté, stirring, until softened, about 5 minutes. Add the cabbage and toss

well until it is glistening with bacon fat. Return the bacon to the pan and stir in the vinegar and honey. Season with salt and pepper, cover, and bake until the cabbage is meltingly tender, about 2 hours. If the cabbage is still quite watery, uncover, and on high heat on the stove, cook until the pan is almost dry. Season with salt and pepper. The cabbage should develop an intense sweet-and-sour flavor.

Transfer to a large platter and serve immediately.

Creamed Brussels Sprouts and Bacon

Serves 4 to 6

In an attempt to be militant about seasonal cooking, virtually the only green vegetable we use in our kitchen in winter is Brussels sprouts. As cooks, we've learned that something special comes out of working under such stringent restrictions. But how to make so humble an ingredient sing with excitement and not be repetitive? We get creative. We cook them in orange juice with smoked ham hock, with sour cream and horseradish, with whole-grain mustard and butter. We roast them briefly in the oven at a high temperature until they taste smoky and meaty. But this is our favorite preparation—so good, so satisfying, so simple.

1 pound Brussels sprouts	Juice of 1/2 lemon
1 tablespoon extra-virgin olive oil	Kosher salt and freshly ground black pepper
8 ounces Smoked Bacon (page 204), cut into 1/2-inch dice	1 tablespoon Persillade (page 198), for garnish
1 cup crème fraîche	

Trim off the browned root end of each sprout and peel away and discard any discolored outer leaves.

Have a bowl of ice water ready. Bring a pot of well salted water to a boil. Cook the Brussels sprouts until they soften and loose their bitterness, about 5 minutes. With a slotted spoon, transfer the sprouts to the ice water to stop the cooking.

In a 12-inch skillet, heat the olive oil over medium heat and cook the bacon until crispy, about 10 minutes. Pour off and discard half the bacon fat. Add the Brussels sprouts, crème fraîche, and lemon juice. Cook until the cream thickens, about 5 minutes. Season with salt and pepper.

To serve, transfer to a large platter, garnish with persillade, and serve immediately.

Chapter 7

Desserts

Cheese Is Milk Continued

Central Point, Oregon, is a cowboy town in the southern part of the state, nothing fancy. Since the 1930s, though, some of the best American artisanal cheese has started life there. This cheese is alive—98 percent of it is raw-milk cheese, never pasteurized or brought to a temperature above that of the milk when it came out of the cow.

"We have a contract partnership with one farm that has a closed herd. Getting milk is a simple system—we know exactly where it comes from, and healthy milk makes healthy cheese," explains David Gremmels, co-owner of Rogue Creamery, located in Central Point. In 2002, David and his partner, Cary Bryant, bought the creamery from the founding Vella family and have, if anything, intensified the company's dedication to hand-crafting premium cheeses.

David is leading Kimberly and me on a tour of his operation, a collection of converted farm storage buildings permeated by the smells of flowers and cream. "Pasteurizing takes one critical thing away, the sense of place," he says as he leads us into the blue cheese aging cave. "Ig is very proud of this building," he says, referring to Ignazio Vella, the eighty-year-old son of founder Tom Vella, who created the classic Vella Monterey Dry Jack in the 1930s. Ig has been referred to as the godfather of American artisanal cheese making, and he still works for Rogue Creamery. Tom Vella learned the craft

of making blue cheese in Roquefort, France, and at the end of his stay was gifted with a manila envelope of the Roquefort strain of mold. He built this aging facility to the highest specifications of the period, releasing his first blue cheeses in 1957. "Maytag has us beat by only three years," David notes, referring to Iowa's Maytag Dairy Farms, which also produces a noteworthy blue cheese.

Wheels of cheese line rows of metal racks in the dim, cavernous space. The smell is haunting and familiar, sweet yet salty. This cave has been in continuous operation since 1956. "Notice the mold," says David. "That is *Penicillium roqueforti* fungus, and *B. linens.* That is a lot happening. We wipe the walls down once a week but never sanitize. When we replace a coil, we replace one at a time. When we paint a floor, we paint a quarter of it, and we always keep a piece of cheese in the room. We don't know where the magic comes from, but we know that it starts here. We preserve the relationship between the cheese and this environment."

David describes the aging process, which is active and exacting. "We salt the wheels on all sides and flip them for a week, creating the right pH and environment for the mold inside. The wheels are spaced an inch apart. The airflow helps the mold breathe better. Then we turn each wheel a quarter-turn every day by hand for about six weeks depending on how the mold is developing. We perforate each wheel at about four to six weeks to bring more oxygen to the starving mold. And it just grabs." These white round things sitting on these shelves were not merely cheeses. They are like children, growing, maturing, requiring intense nurturing and full attention.

When the mold has developed optimally, David says, "We hand dip our wheels four times in wax to create a complete seal. This moves the cheese into an anaerobic state and starves the mold. It is one of the key secrets in releasing flavor in the blue. Then they get boxed up and into long-term storage to mature." The cheese makers taste every lot before it is released, holding it back if it's not ready yet.

He points to a stack of five-gallon buckets. "To conclude the life cycle of the cheese, we put each wheel into a bucket of hot water to loosen the wax. We use knives to peel it. Using surgical tweezers, we also pull the wax out of every perf-hole. Then each wheel goes onto a sheet of foil to be hand-wrapped and then labeled. We wrap it in parchment, hand stamp the lot number, and then send it out."

"Wow!" I say. "With all the work that goes into every wheel I am surprised the cheese is reasonably priced."

David smiles. "If we knew then what we know now. Cary and I had no idea. When we bought the creamery, the distributor price was only $3.20 per pound. At that price we could not even pay for electricity, and we had to double the price. The beauty is that Ig helped me out at the counter one day. About six months after we bought the creamery, a customer came in to buy some cheese. When he saw the new price he exclaimed, "What do you think this is, gold? I've been buying this cheese for years. I am not even going to pay, forget it." And he started to walk away. Ig happened to be at the counter and said, 'Sir, if I could just explain. My father never raised the price in the last twenty years. You can do that when you have thirteen million in the bank. These fellows, they don't have the money to do that. They are trying to make a real go of it and make a viable business for the community. If you want this creamery to be here next week, you pay the price.' He bought it and is now a regular." In the few years that Cary and David have owned Rogue Creamery, they have placed the American artisanal cheese movement the Vellas started firmly on the map. Fortunately for us, they are right here in Oregon.

We proudly serve a number of Rogue Creamery cheeses in the restaurant, both from the kitchen and as components of a cheese course. Here are some of our favorites, with tasting notes.

Rosemary Cheddar

The recipe for this cheese was passed from Zolita Vella, Ig's mother, to Ig and then to David and Cary. She flavored the cheese with Italian long-leaf rosemary that the Vellas brought from Sicily. Now the herb grows on their property.

The cheese is very delicate and clean on the palate. It is mild, floral, and sweet, with the highest butterfat in the history of the creamery. It melts luxuriously when you cook with it. Use it to stuff a butterflied leg of lamb lined with prosciutto, tied, and then baked.

Oregonzola

Both the recipe and the molds for this cheese came from Italy, making it akin to a real Gorgonzola. They do not add cream to finish, as in a dolce, but they do hold the

milk still for two days, allowing the cream to rise, then use that cream to make the cheese. This gorgeous cheese looks a bit waxy because of its high butterfat content. It gets sweeter and creamier as it ages. When I tasted it at 180 days, I got a hint of oats up front. Then I got a nutty flavor, followed by fruit, particularly berries. The blue flavor comes next, spreading across the palate, and Rogue's signature sweet cream finishes the taste, making you want more.

Oregon Blue

Produced since 1957, this is Rogue's number-one seller, which has become the foundation of this creamery and a Pacific Northwest classic. It is a versatile cheese that can be eaten as part of a cheese plate, added to a salad, or used in a blue cheese dressing. It is approachable, remaining subtle and sweet with a sharp and vividly tangy blue flavor. It has less butterfat than the Oregonzola and is much brighter in color. Over fifty years later, it still gives you a real sense of place.

Crater Lake Blue

This is David and Cary's new signature blue, following in the footsteps of their predecessors (Ig Vella created Oregonzola and Tom Vella started it all with Oregon Blue). Crater Lake Blue contains a spectrum of mold, creating a brilliant depth of flavor. I tasted it when it had been aged about four months and found it bursting with refreshing sweet, salty, and acidic flavors. It is deep, complex, and well integrated with herbaceous tastes of summer and winter savory.

Rogue River Blue

This is the blue cheese of my dreams, made once a year in the fall when the cows are grazing on blackberry, maple leaves, weeds, and flowers and the last bits of forage and vegetation. The cheese makers wrap each wheel in syrah leaves from Carpenter Hill Vineyard soaked in Clear Creek pear brandy.

This blue is bold and regal in hues of deep gold and purple—almost black. It reveals the soul of that cave, with soft yet vibrant, full, and defined blue notes that play across the palate for a good long time. If you can locate this hard-to-find cheese, it will be a revelation.

Smokey Blue

Because this is the first smoked blue cheese in the world, it has drawn the attention of every blue cheese producer. The cheese makers slowly smoke it for sixteen hours over hazelnut shells, then age it for thirty days to mellow out the smoke. It is surprisingly mild and balanced, with notes of grass, meat, and bacon—not rendered or crispy bacon, but mellow, like raw bacon. Unlike many other blue cheeses, the flavor of smoke spikes and lingers, tempering the sharpness of the blue. The smokiest flavor is found closest to the rind.

Pecan Carrot Cake with Plumped Cherries

Makes one 9-inch layer cake; serves 8 to 10

Not too long ago, carrot cake seemed to appear on every menu. I think it lost many fans from overexposure, but this grown-up version just might win them back. Our version is pretty and exceptionally tasty because we use young, sweet heirloom carrots in shades of yellow and orange. Toasted pecans stand in for the usual walnuts, and tart dried cherries for the raisins. More dried cherries are plumped in red wine and verjus (see Chef's Tip) and serve as an accompaniment to the cake.

2 cups all-purpose flour, plus more for the pans

2 teaspoons baking soda

1/2 teaspoon salt

1 tablespoon ground cinnamon

4 large eggs

2 1/3 cups granulated sugar

1 cup mild extra-virgin olive oil

3 cups packed grated carrots (preferably a mix of heirloom varieties)

1/2 cup unsweetened applesauce

1/2 cup pecans, lightly toasted and coarsely chopped

2 cups dried tart cherries

18 ounces cream cheese, softened

3/4 cup (1 1/2 sticks) unsalted butter, softened

1 1/2 teaspoons vanilla extract

1 1/2 cups confectioners' sugar

3 cups verjus

2 cups red wine

Preheat the oven to 375°F. Butter and flour two 9-inch round cake pans or coat them with nonstick vegetable spray.

In a small bowl, sift the 2 cups flour with the baking soda, salt, and cinnamon. Set aside.

In a large bowl, mix together the eggs, 2 cups of the granulated sugar, and olive oil. Whisk until smooth. Add the sifted flour mixture, stirring just to combine. Fold in the carrots and applesauce followed by the toasted pecans and 1/2 cup of the dried cherries. Mix well to evenly distribute the ingredients. Divide the batter between the 2 prepared pans.

Bake until a skewer inserted in the center comes out clean, 45 to 50 minutes. Remove from the oven to a wire rack and cool in the pans for 10 minutes. Remove from the pans and cool completely on the rack.

While the cakes are cooling, make the cream cheese frosting. Combine the cream cheese and butter in the bowl of a stand mixer fitted with the paddle attachment. Mix on low speed, gradually increasing to medium, and beat until well combined and free of large lumps. Add the vanilla. Sift the confectioners' sugar directly into the mixer bowl and thoroughly combine on low speed. Scrape down the sides of the bowl and continue mixing until very smooth and uniform.

To plump the cherries, in a saucepan, combine the remaining 1 1/2 cups cherries, verjus, red wine, and the remaining 1/3 cup granulated sugar. Bring the mixture to a boil over medium-high heat, then decrease the heat to low. Simmer until the liquid has reduced by about two thirds and has a syrupy consistency, about 90 minutes. Serve at room temperature. The cherries can be made ahead and stored in the refrigerator for up to 1 week.

Frost the cake layers and refrigerate, uncovered, for 30 minutes or until the frosting is set. Serve cold with the plumped cherries and some of their syrup.

Chef's Tip

Verjus (French for "green juice") is made from the juice of unripe grapes. The French often use it in dishes calling for wine or vinegar. We've added it to the fruit in this carrot cake. A touch of acid enlivens the natural flavor of the cherries and seems to lighten the richness of the creamy frosting. Verjus can be purchased in specialty groceries that carry wines or by mail order (see Resources, page 222).

Cherry–Olive Oil Polenta Cake

Makes one 10-inch cake; serves 8

A cake with olive oil and cornmeal is a typical Italian sweet. Whether to use extra-virgin or regular olive oil is personal preference. Extra-virgin imparts a fruitier, more pronounced flavor, while regular yields a milder taste.

During the summer, use the abundance of fresh fruit available—berries, sliced plums, peaches, and nectarines are all good choices. The fruit is what keeps this cake from being overly dry and crumbly, so be generous.

3 large eggs

1 1/2 cups sugar

1 tablespoon vanilla extract

3/4 cup extra-virgin olive oil

Finely grated zest and juice of 1 lemon

3 cups all-purpose flour

3/4 teaspoon baking soda

3/4 teaspoon salt

1/3 cup polenta or cornmeal

2 1/2 cups fresh cherries (about 1 pound), pitted and halved

Cinnamon-Cherry Ice Cream (page 182) or crème fraîche, for accompaniment

Preheat the oven to 350°F. Spray a 10-inch round cake pan with nonstick vegetable spray or lightly coat with butter or oil.

In the bowl of a stand mixer fitted with the paddle attachment, combine the eggs and sugar. Beat on medium-high speed until light in color, about 4 minutes. Add the vanilla, olive oil, lemon zest, and lemon juice.

In a separate bowl, sift together the flour, baking soda, and salt. Add to the egg mixture along with the cornmeal and mix until combined.

Pour two thirds of the batter into the prepared pan. Evenly distribute the cherries over the batter, covering it completely. Spoon the remaining batter over the cherries allowing the fruit to peek through in spots. Bake until the top and edges are lightly golden and a skewer inserted in the center comes out clean, 50 to 60 minutes. Remove from the oven to a wire rack and cool in the pan for 10 minutes. Remove from the pan and cool completely on the rack.

Serve with Cinnamon-Cherry Ice Cream or a dollop of crème fraîche.

Goat Cheese Cheesecake with Strawberries and Basil

Makes 8 individual cakes or one 10-inch cake

The tang of fresh goat cheese gives this cheesecake a more complex flavor than traditional recipes made with cream cheese, with a texture every bit as smooth and creamy. Use a good-quality, light, mild, and tangy cheese, but don't feel compelled to search out a fancy, artisanal one.

Saba is made by slowly cooking grape must (the juice of unfermented grapes). It is usually available at fine markets where balsamic vinegar is sold (see Resources, page 222).

Crust
1 1/4 cups all-purpose flour

1/2 cup sugar

1 1/2 teaspoons baking powder

1/4 teaspoon salt

1/2 cup (1 stick) unsalted butter

Finely grated zest of 1 lemon

1 large egg

Filling
12 ounces goat cheese

3/4 cup sugar

1 1/2 cups sour cream

3 large egg yolks

Garnish
1 pint fresh strawberries, stemmed and sliced

3 tablespoons sugar

1/4 cup loosely packed fresh basil leaves, hand-torn

1/4 cup saba (optional)

To make the crust, sift the flour, the 1/2 cup sugar, baking powder, and salt into the bowl of a stand mixer fitted with the paddle attachment. Cut the butter into small pieces and add to the mixer bowl with the lemon zest. Mix on low speed until the mixture resembles cornmeal.

Add the egg and mix until the dough comes together to form a ball. Wrap the dough in plastic wrap and chill until firm, about 30 minutes. Halfway through the chilling time, preheat the oven to 350°F.

To make the filling, combine the goat cheese and the 3/4 cup sugar in the mixer bowl and mix on low speed to incorporate. Add the sour cream and increase the speed to medium, mixing until smooth. Add the egg yolks, 1 at a time, mixing in each and scraping down the sides of the bowl before adding the next.

To make individual cheesecakes, coat 8 cups of a muffin tin with butter or nonstick vegetable spray. Divide the dough evenly into 8 pieces the size of golf balls and press 1 piece into the bottom of each prepared muffin cup. Work the dough without tearing about 1 inch up the sides.

Fill each cup almost to the top with the filling and smooth with a small knife or spatula. Bake in the lower third of the oven until the edges are puffy, lightly browned, and the centers are slightly jiggly, 35 to 40 minutes. Transfer to a wire rack and let cool in the muffin tin to room temperature. As they cool, the tops sink. Cover with plastic wrap and chill at least 4 hours or overnight.

To make 1 large cheesecake, coat a 10-inch springform pan with butter or nonstick vegetable spray. Pat the crust evenly over the bottom of the pan and work the dough without tearing about 1 inch up the sides. Pour the filling into the crust and smooth the top with a small knife or spatula. Bake the cake in the lower third of the oven until the edges are puffy, lightly browned, and the center is slightly jiggly, 45 minutes to 1 hour.

Remove from the oven and set on a wire rack to cool in the pan to room temperature. As the cake cools, the top will sink.

For the garnish for both size cakes, toss the strawberry slices with the 3 tablespoons sugar. Add the basil and saba and toss again.

To serve the individual cheesecakes, run a small paring knife around the edges of the muffin cups to loosen the cakes. Gently lift the cakes from the tin, and set each on a dessert plate.

For the 10-inch cake, release and remove the sides of the pan. Slice the cake into wedges and arrange on a serving plate.

To garnish either size cake, spoon the strawberries and juices over the individual cakes or large cake. Drizzle with extra juices and serve.

Huckleberry Kuchen with Cassis-Huckleberry Sauce and Crème Fraîche

Makes 12 to 14 individual cakes

Suzanne Bozarth, a bartender at the restaurant for years, used to describe our *Kuchen* (cakes) as "blueberry muffins gone to heaven." Wild huckleberries are plentiful in Oregon during late summer. For the Native Americans who gather them in the Pacific Northwest, they are an essential food, and the people bless them before bringing them to market. We don't revere berries gathered elsewhere in that way.

We find the acidity of the wild berry nicely complemented by the buttery, sweet taste of the cake. Blueberries or other local seasonal berries work well when we don't have huckleberries.

2 cups all-purpose flour

2 teaspoons baking powder

1/2 teaspoon salt

3/4 cup (1 1/2 sticks) unsalted butter, softened

2 cups sugar

4 large eggs, at room temperature

1 teaspoon vanilla extract

2 pints huckleberries (about 4 cups), plus additional berries for garnish

Cassis-Huckleberry Sauce (recipe follows)

Crème fraîche, for topping

Preheat the oven to 350°F. Butter and flour individual baking dishes or ramekins, or a standard 12-cup muffin tin, or spray with nonstick vegetable spray.

In a bowl, sift together the flour, baking powder, and salt and set aside.

In the bowl of a stand mixer fitted with the paddle attachment, combine the butter and sugar and beat on medium-high speed until the mixture is light and fluffy, about 4 minutes. Add the eggs, one at a time, scraping the sides of the bowl as necessary and combining well after each addition. Add the vanilla,

then the flour mixture, and combine on low speed. Divide the batter evenly between the baking dishes or the cups of a muffin tin, filling each one about two-thirds full. Cover the batter with 1/4 to 1/3 cup of berries per cake.

Bake the cakes until a skewer inserted in the middle comes out clean, 30 to 40 minutes. To serve, invert the warm cakes onto individual plates, top with 2 to 3 tablespoons of sauce, and a dollop of crème fraîche.

Cassis-Huckleberry Sauce

Makes about 1 1/4 cups

2 tablespoons water

1/2 cup sugar

Grated zest and juice of 1 lemon

Pinch of salt

1 pint huckleberries (about 2 cups)

1/4 cup crème de cassis or loganberry liqueur (preferably Clear Creek)

In a small, nonreactive saucepan, combine the water, sugar, lemon zest, and salt. Add the huckleberries, bring the mixture to a boil over medium heat, and simmer until the fruit begins to collapse, about 10 minutes.

Pour the cooked berry mixture into a blender. Add the cassis and the lemon juice and liquefy. Strain through a fine mesh strainer into a small container, cover tightly, and refrigerate until ready to use. This sauce can be made up to 2 days in advance.

Tres Leches Cake with Blackberries and Maple-Glazed Almonds

Makes one 9 by 13-inch cake; serves 12

From Latin America, this moist cake melts in your mouth because it is soaked in three kinds of milk—*tres leches*. Our version uses heavy cream, sour cream, and whole milk. We could have added rum, which is traditional, but instead use a healthy dose of local Clear Creek Kirschwasser (cherry brandy), because we like how it perfumes the milk. This cake keeps well in the refrigerator for up to four days and only gets better with time.

Cake
9 large eggs, separated

2 cups sugar

1 teaspoon vanilla extract

2 teaspoons almond extract

1 tablespoon baking powder

1/2 cup whole milk

2 cups all-purpose flour, sifted

1/2 teaspoon salt

Filling
3 3/4 cups heavy whipping cream

3/4 cup sugar

5 large egg yolks

1 cup sour cream

1 tablespoon vanilla extract

2 teaspoons almond extract

6 to 8 tablespoons Kirschwasser (such as Clear Creek)

1/2 teaspoon salt

Blackberry Coulis (recipe follows), for topping

Almond Cream (recipe follows), for topping

Maple-Glazed Almonds (recipe follows), for garnish

Fresh blackberries, for garnish

Preheat the oven to 350°F. Spray a 9 by 13-inch baking pan with nonstick vegetable spray or lightly coat with butter. Set aside.

To make the cake, in the bowl of a stand mixer fitted with the paddle attachment, beat the 9 egg yolks and 2 cups sugar on high speed until the mixture becomes thick and pale in color, about 5 minutes. Add the 1 teaspoon of the vanilla extract and 2 teaspoons of almond extract and mix on low speed until incorporated. Transfer the mixture to a bowl and set aside.

In a small bowl, combine the baking powder with the milk and stir. In 3 batches, using a large spatula, fold the flour and milk mixture alternately into the yolk mixture, beginning and ending with flour.

Using the clean, dry bowl of a stand mixer fitted with the whisk attachment, whip the 9 egg whites on medium speed until frothy. Stop the mixer, add the 1/2 teaspoon salt, and whisk at high speed until the whites form soft peaks. Using a large spatula, in 3 batches, gently fold the whites into the flour mixture.

Pour the batter into the prepared pan and bake the cake until golden brown, 45 minutes to 1 hour. The edges of the cake will have pulled away from the sides slightly.

Transfer to a wire rack to cool completely in the pan. Run a small knife around the edge of the pan, but do not remove the cake.

To make the cream filling, in a saucepan, combine the heavy cream and 3/4 cup sugar and bring to a simmer over medium heat. Simmer until the sugar dissolves, about 3 minutes. Remove from the heat.

Put the 5 egg yolks in a bowl and whisk to combine. Slowly whisk in the hot cream mixture to temper the yolks.

In another bowl, combine the sour cream, 1 tablespoon vanilla extract, 2 teaspoons of almond extract, the Kirschwasser, and 1/2 teaspoon salt. Whisk smooth and slowly add the yolk-cream mixture, whisking to combine.

To finish the cake, poke holes with a wooden skewer over the entire surface. Slowly ladle a cup of the cream filling over the surface. Repeat until all the cream filling has been evenly absorbed. Refrigerate, covered, until ready to serve.

Spread the cooled cake with almond cream or use it to garnish each individual serving. To serve, cut the chilled cake into wedges, and garnish with Blackberry Coulis and fresh blackberries. Sprinkle with Maple-Glazed Almonds.

Blackberry Coulis

Makes 2 cups

2 pints blackberries, plus more for garnish

1/4 to 1/3 cup sugar

2 teaspoons freshly squeezed lemon juice

Pinch of salt

Place all the ingredients in a blender and liquefy. Strain through a sieve to remove any seeds. Taste and adjust for sweetness. Refrigerate until ready to use.

Almond Cream

Makes about 2 cups

1/2 cup sour cream

1/4 cup sugar

1/4 teaspoon salt

1 teaspoon almond extract

1 1/4 cups heavy whipping cream

In the bowl of a stand mixer fitted with the whisk attachment, combine the sour cream, sugar, salt, and almond extract on low speed until blended. Increase the speed to medium and slowly add the cream. Increase the speed to high and whisk until the cream forms soft peaks. Spread the almond cream over the entire surface of the cake, or use it to garnish each individual serving.

Maple-Glazed Almonds

Makes 2 cups

2 cups sliced almonds

2 tablespoons maple syrup

Pinch of salt

Preheat the oven to 375°F.

Lightly oil a baking sheet or line with parchment paper. In a bowl, add the almonds, drizzle with maple syrup, and sprinkle with salt. Toss to combine and coat the nuts.

Spread the nuts on the prepared pan. Bake until golden, 10 to 15 minutes. Cool and store in an airtight container.

Chef's Tip

I often use Clear Creak Distillery's Kirschwasser and apple brandy for cooking. Their pear brandy is also superb. It feels fat in the mouth and is also rich with the essence of pear. I encourage you to check with your local liquor store as to the availability of these handcrafted brandies. Or contact Clear Creek directly (see Resources, page 222) to find out where it's sold in your area.

Grilled Lemon Pound Cake with Lemon Verbena Ice Cream and Fresh Berries

Makes one 9 by 5 by 3-inch loaf; serves 8

What we call pound cake, the French call *quatre quarts* (four parts), named for the proportion of its ingredients—one part each of butter, sugar, eggs, and flour. A true pound cake is at once dense and soft, with a crumb perfumed with the serious flavor of excellent butter.

We were inspired by that image when we devised this lemon cake to cook on an outdoor grill. We adjusted the traditional proportions to make it more grill-friendly—that is, with a sturdy crumb that rendered toasty notes when grilled, yet still delicate in the spirit of true pound cake. We love the results.

Pairing the cake with summer herbs and berries—raspberries in particular, but any berry in season is every bit as wonderful—seems to intensify everything, cake, fruit, and cream.

Cake
3 cups all-purpose flour

2 teaspoons baking powder

3/4 teaspoon salt

2 cups sugar

2 lemons, for zesting

1 cup (2 sticks) unsalted butter, softened

4 large eggs

1 cup whole milk

Lemon Verbena Syrup
1/4 cup freshly squeezed lemon juice

1/4 cup water

1/2 cup sugar

2 large sprigs of lemon verbena

Topping
1 pint fresh raspberries

2 tablespoons sugar

Juice of 1/2 lemon

Melted butter or extra-virgin olive oil, for grilling

Lemon Verbena Ice Cream (page 180), for accompaniment

Preheat the oven to 350°F. Butter and flour a 9 by 5 by 3-inch loaf pan or spray it with nonstick vegetable spray.

To make the cake, in a bowl, sift the flour with the baking powder and salt and set aside.

In the bowl of a stand mixer fitted with the paddle attachment, add the sugar. Grate the zest of the lemons with a microplane zester into the sugar in the bowl. Use your fingers to rub the zest into the sugar and moisten it with the essential oils in the zest. Add the butter and beat on medium-high speed until the mixture is light and fluffy, about 4 minutes.

Add the eggs, one at a time, scraping the sides of the bowl as necessary. It's fine if the mixture appears curdled after adding each egg. In 3 batches, add the flour mixture alternately with the milk and blend briefly on low speed after each addition, beginning and ending with the flour mixture.

Pour the batter into the prepared pan. Bake until the loaf is a deep brown with a cracked top and a skewer inserted in the center comes out clean, about 1 hour and 10 minutes.

While the cake is in the oven, prepare the lemon verbena syrup. In a small saucepan, combine the lemon juice, 1/4 cup water, 1/2 cup sugar, and lemon verbena. Simmer over medium-low heat stirring occasionally until the sugar dissolves, about 3 minutes. Remove from the heat.

Transfer the finished cake to a wire cooling rack. Remove the lemon verbena sprigs from the syrup. Using a skewer, poke holes all over the top of the loaf and immediately brush it with half of the syrup. Let stand 10 minutes, invert the loaf onto the rack, and generously moisten the bottom and sides. Turn the loaf right-side-up and brush the top with any remaining syrup. The amount of syrup might seem excessive, but the hot cake readily accepts it. Cool completely.

To serve, for the topping, toss the berries with the sugar and lemon juice.

Preheat an outdoor grill to high. Slice the loaf into 8 pieces, each about 1 inch thick. Lightly brush each slice of pound cake on both sides with butter or olive oil. Toast the pieces on the hot grill, turning once, until lightly toasted and golden, about 2 minutes per side. If desired, rotate the slices a quarter turn after 1 minute to create a crosshatch of grill marks.

To serve, place a slice of cake on individual plates and top with a scoop of Lemon Verbena Ice Cream. Spoon the fresh berries and their juices over the ice cream and drizzle any remaining juices around the plate.

Pairing Wine with Cheese and Dessert

The following are some of our favorite dessert wines. If you cannot find them in your local wine shops, we encourage you to make your own discoveries.

From Oregon: Andrew Rich Gewürztraminer Dessert Wine; Solèna Late Harvest Reisling; Sokol Blosser Muscat; Madrone Mountain LBV Red Dessert Wine; Francis Tannahill Passito Gewürztraminer

From France: Any Sauternes you can afford; Château de Beaulon Pineau de Charentes; Banyuls, La Tour Vieille; Domaine de Coyeux, Muscat De Beaumes de Venise

When liquid dessert is all you want, we suggest you drink it on its own. Try any of the following from Steve McCarthy of Clear Creek Distillery, whose facility is just a few blocks away from the restaurant: Williams Pear Brandy; Grappa Moscato; Eau de Vie de Pomme (barrel-aged for eight years); or Eau de Vie of Mirabelle Plum.

Hazelnuts Make Everything Taste Better

A hazelnut orchard, with row upon row of long, shaded alleys, is a beautiful sight. The symmetrically planted trees create natural arches with dappled light. In the heat of summer, the dense canopy creates a refreshing coolness evoking old cathedrals—silent, sculpted, and inviting.

Barb and Fritz Foulke own a sixty-acre hazelnut farm west of Corvallis in a small valley called Little Luckiamute. As we entered the valley, we could see, three or four miles in the distance, the dark square of the Foulkes' farm. Hazelnuts are as much a part of Oregon's culinary identity as salmon or berries. The state produces about 10 percent of the world's crop (France, Italy, and Turkey supply the rest), and Oregon hazelnuts are considered premium. The orchard is a sort of maze, and once you're inside it, you could easily lose your sense of direction. The six thousand trees on Barb and Fritz's sixty acres are about thirty years old, and you get the impression that the farmers know every single one of them. The trees are planted in a grid pattern, twenty by twenty feet apart. Every tenth tree is a pollinator because hazelnuts are not self-pollinating. The entire landscape is impeccable. You get the feeling that if Barb had a sixty-acre house, it would be as tidy as this orchard. "The day we stop chain sawing is the day we start shredding. The day we stop chipping is the day we start mowing. We just finished picking up all the prun-

ing," Barb explained. They chop the branches and mow repeatedly so that grass and wood chips disintegrate back into the soil.

Barb grew up ten miles from this spot and can tell stories about her grandfather who had a farm "right down at the end of this valley" and used dogs to herd sheep to Albany, about twenty miles away. All of her family still lives here, and most are farmers. Fritz, on the other hand, is a city boy who grew up in Corvallis.

For the first few years on the farm they did all their work by hand. "There are no breaks, no weekends," Fritz said. "Barb's great-grandmother came West over the Oregon trail," he continued, "and at some point I realized Barb would make it too. I've never seen anyone work the way she does." After the first year in business they sold five hundred pounds of nuts. The second year they sold five thousand. In the third year, they landed a huge crop, but were offered a terrible price by the commodity buyers. Barb credits that blow as the start of her success. She talked to other farmers in her family about farmer's markets and then did some math. Processing their own nuts to sell directly to the consumer, she found, would allow them to actually make money, rather than just breaking even as commodity farmers selling their nuts for forty-five cents a pound. So Barb has developed into a grower-processor, taking on the new challenges and rewards of product development, marketing, and distribution.

Nowadays, their harvest takes two days and yields 80,000 to 250,000 pounds of hazelnuts. The trees are never picked. The farmers wait for the nuts to fall to the meticulously kept orchard floor, then sweep the ground with a machine that blows nuts, twigs, and leaves from the tree line to the middle of the row.

"We bring in the tractor pulling a harvester that just sucks the nuts up," Fritz said. The harvester blows all the debris away, dropping the nuts onto conveyor belts that empty into big boxes.

"This is my baby," Barb said proudly as she fired up her hazelnut shelling line, a loud, Willy Wonka–type machine that makes it possible for her to shell, sort, and grade a ton of nuts in an hour and a half. Once the nuts are processed, Barb keeps them refrigerated. She tells us, "I take no shortcuts, so the quality of the final product is evident." Barb and Fritz also traveled to Italy and invested in a state-of-the-art machine that allows them to custom roast. While there, they saw the products the Italians make from nuts and began producing a hazelnut pesto, and are working to produce hazelnut oil. "Part of my work is to inform the public about the integrity of what we do," Barb summarized. She believes the consumer is smart enough to know when something is different and better. "We count on that."

Hazelnut-Yogurt Cake with Honey-Poached Quinces and Raspberries

Makes one 10-inch cake; serves 8 to 10

This cake has much to recommend it: It can be made in one bowl in ten minutes or less. It lends itself well to many variations. And its texture and flavor both improve as it sits.

The hazelnut harvest coincides with the first appearance of quinces and the late-season raspberries, lending the combination a natural harmony. The crème fraîche topping mirrors the tang of the yogurt in the cake.

2/3 cup hazelnuts, lightly toasted

1/2 cup granulated sugar

1 1/3 cups all purpose flour

1 tablespoon baking powder

1/2 teaspoon salt

1/2 cup packed brown sugar

1 cup plain yogurt

3 large eggs

1 teaspoon vanilla extract

1/2 cup (1 stick) unsalted butter, melted

Honey-Poached Quinces (recipe follows), for accompaniment

1 pint raspberries (about 2 cups), for accompaniment

Lightly whipped crème fraîche, for topping

Preheat the oven to 350°F. Generously butter a 10-inch round cake pan and set it aside.

Combine the hazelnuts and granulated sugar in a food processor fitted with the metal blade and process briefly to finely grind the nuts (don't overprocess or you'll make hazelnut butter). Reserve. In a bowl, whisk together the flour, baking powder, and salt.

In a second bowl, vigorously whisk together the brown sugar, yogurt, eggs, and vanilla until the mixture is very well blended. With a rubber spatula, fold in the flour mixture, then the melted butter. When the butter is completely incorporated, the batter will be thick and smooth with a slight sheen. Scrape the batter into the prepared pan and smooth the top.

Bake until golden brown and a skewer inserted in the center comes out clean, 50 to 60 minutes. Transfer the pan to a wire rack and let sit for 5 minutes. Run a knife around the edges and invert onto the rack to cool completely.

Serve the cake with several Honey-Poached Quince slices. Drizzle some of the poaching liquid around the plate and scatter with fresh raspberries.

Honey-Poached Quinces

Makes 4 cups

4 medium quinces, peeled, cut into 1/4-inch wedges, and cored

3 cups water

1 cup dry white wine

1/2 cup sugar

1/2 cup honey

In a large saucepan, combine the quince wedges, the 3 cups water, white wine, sugar, and honey. Cover the fruit with a round of parchment paper the diameter of the pot.

Bring the mixture to a boil over high heat, decrease the heat to medium-low, and cook until the quinces are tender, about 1 hour. Allow the fruit to cool in the poaching liquid.

Chef's Tip

Quinces are a pale yellow-green fruit about the size of an apple or pear. Unlike apples and pears, quinces have to be cooked to be eaten. Gently poaching them in sugar water brings out their rich floral fragrance. The fruit is very hard when raw, so it takes some skill to peel and core them. I find that a sharp knife and a sturdy peeler make the job easier. The pale flesh discolors when exposed to the air, but I find this contributes to the beautiful deep amber color it takes on when cooked.

Warm Chocolate Soufflé Cakes

Makes twelve 6-ounce cakes

This is the original warm chocolate cake with the gooey center. Along with Crème Brulée (page 185), it has been a constant on our dessert menu since we opened the restaurant. Chocoholics agree that its rich, oozing goodness feeds their addiction.

This recipe is versatile and forgiving. The batter can be made ahead and refrigerated, covered with plastic wrap, for up to three days. It will need a slightly longer baking time than if used right away because it goes into the oven cold.

15 ounces bittersweet chocolate (64 percent cocoa solids)

3/4 cup (1 1/2 sticks) unsalted butter

6 large eggs, separated

1/2 cup plus 1/3 cup sugar

Pinch of salt

Honey-Vanilla Ice Cream (page 180), for accompaniment

In a double boiler, melt the chocolate and butter over low heat. Set aside to cool to room temperature.

Place the egg whites in a small bowl. Place the egg yolks in the bowl of a stand mixer fitted with the whisk attachment. With the mixer on medium speed, add 1/2 cup of the sugar and a pinch of salt and mix until the yolks are slightly thicker and lighter in color, 2 to 3 minutes. Set aside.

Wash and dry the mixer bowl. Add the egg whites and whisk on low speed, gradually adding half of the remaining 1/3 cup of sugar. Increase the speed to medium, and whisk until the whites form soft peaks, 3 to 4 minutes. Slowly add the remaining sugar, increase the speed to high, and whisk until stiff peaks form.

Check that the chocolate and beaten egg yolks are the same temperature. Using a spatula, fold the beaten yolks into the chocolate. In 3 additions, fold in the whites until just combined.

Preheat the oven to 400°F. Lightly butter twelve 6- to 8-ounce individual baking dishes or spray with nonstick vegetable spray.

Fill the dishes three-fourths full. Bake until just set and a bit jiggly in the center, 12 to 14 minutes. Serve immediately with Honey Vanilla Ice Cream.

Chocolate-Caramel-Almond Tart

Makes one 10-inch tart; serves 8 to 10

A slice of this chewy tart is a study in shades of brown: the deep dark chocolate of the cookie crumb shell, the bittersweet ganache topping, the golden hue of caramel, and the rich brown of toasted almonds.

9 ounces bittersweet chocolate

2 tablespoons unsalted butter, melted

2 cups finely ground chocolate cookie crumbs

1 large egg

1 large egg yolk

1 tablespoon vanilla extract

1/4 teaspoon salt

1 1/2 cups sugar

1/4 cup water

Pinch of cream of tartar

2 cups heavy whipping cream

2 cups whole almonds, toasted

Honey-Vanilla Ice Cream (page 180), for accompaniment

Preheat the oven to 375°F. Spray a 10-inch tart pan with removable bottom with nonstick vegetable spray.

To make the crust, in a double boiler or bowl fitted over a pan of lightly simmering water, melt 3 ounces of the chocolate and the 2 tablespoons butter over low heat. Add the cookie crumbs and stir to combine. Pat the crumbs into the bottom and up the sides of the prepared pan. Bake until lightly toasted and with a chocolatey aroma, 10 to 15 minutes. Set aside on a wire rack to cool completely. Decrease the oven temperature to 325°F.

Put a bowl in the freezer. In another bowl, whisk together the egg, egg yolk, vanilla, and a pinch of salt until well combined. Set aside.

To prepare the caramel, in a deep, heavy-bottomed saucepan, mix the sugar and water, add cream of tartar, and stir again. Cook the sugar mixture over medium heat, brushing the insides of the pan with a pastry brush dipped in water to eliminate any sugar sticking to the sides. When the sugar has dissolved and the liquid is clear, about 5 minutes, increase the heat to high and cook, without stirring, until the sugar turns a light golden brown. Remove the pan from the heat.

Very slowly, drizzle in 1 1/4 cups of the cream a little at a time. Be careful, it will sputter if you add it too quickly. Stir with a heat-resistant spatula or wooden spoon to keep the bubbles down and thoroughly combine. Remove the bowl from the freezer and pour in the caramel to cool.

When the caramel has cooled slightly, slowly whisk it into the egg mixture. Add the almonds and pour into the prepared crust. Bake until the filling bubbles slightly around the sides, 30 to 40 minutes. The center should still be jiggly; watch closely, as the center goes from being loose to set very quickly. Remove from the oven and cool completely on a wire rack before finishing with ganache.

To make the ganache, put the remaining 6 ounces of chocolate in a bowl. In a saucepan, gently heat the remaining 3/4 cup of cream with the remaining pinch of salt over low heat; do not let it boil. When the cream is hot, pour it over the chocolate, let it sit briefly, and stir until smooth.

To finish the tart, with a spatula, spread the ganache in a smooth layer on the cooled tart. Chill it in the refrigerator, uncovered, until the top has set, at least 1 hour. Serve cold with Honey-Vanilla Ice Cream.

Peanut Butter Pie

Makes one 10- or 11-inch tart; serves 10 to 12

This signature Paley's dessert pays tribute to peanut butter and chocolate, a combination of flavors loved by young and old. The tart has a crumbly cookie crust that offsets the dense filling of peanut butter and cream cheese and the rich chocolate ganache topping.

7 ounces bittersweet chocolate, finely chopped

2 tablespoons unsalted butter

2 cups finely ground chocolate cookie crumbs

1 1/2 cups cold heavy cream

8 ounces cream cheese, softened

1 cup crunchy-style natural peanut butter, at room temperature

1/2 cup sugar

2 teaspoons vanilla extract

Banana Ice Cream (page 181), for accompaniment

Preheat the oven to 375°F. Spray a 10- or 11-inch tart pan with a removable bottom with nonstick vegetable spray or lightly coat with butter or vegetable oil.

To make the crust, in a double boiler, melt 3 ounces of the chocolate and the 2 tablespoons butter over low heat. Add the cookie crumbs and stir to combine. Pat the crumbs into the bottom and up the sides of the prepared pan. Bake until crisp, 10 to 15 minutes. Set aside on a wire rack to cool.

To make the filling, in the bowl of a stand mixer fitted with the whisk attachment, whip 1 cup of the cream to stiff peaks. Put the whipped cream into another container and refrigerate. In the mixer bowl used to whip the cream (no need to clean the bowl), add the cream cheese, peanut butter, sugar, and vanilla. Fit the mixer with the paddle attachment and beat until smooth and uniform in color, about 4 minutes.

Using a spatula, in 3 additions, gently fold the whipped cream into the peanut butter mixture. Spread the filling evenly in the cooled tart shell. Cover the tart with plastic wrap gently pressed against the filling and chill until set, about 3 hours, or overnight.

To finish, put the remaining 4 ounces of chocolate in a small bowl. In a small saucepan, bring the remaining 1/2 cup cream to a boil over medium-high heat and pour it over the chocolate to melt. Whisk until smooth. When the chocolate has cooled to lukewarm, pour the mixture over the tart, distributing it evenly with a small spatula.

Refrigerate the tart until the chocolate sets, about 45 minutes. Slice into wedges and enjoy chilled with Banana Ice Cream.

Apple Pandowdy with Maple Syrup and Crème Fraîche

Makes one 12-inch oval dish; serves 6

Pandowdy, a deep-dish dessert of fruit sweetened with molasses or maple syrup, is traditional, no-frills Yankee fare. The fruit is topped with a flaky pastry crust that has been scored into squares (dowdied) and lightly pressed into it. Its name could also come from the plain, old-fashioned appearance of the dessert.

We choose a firm apple that holds its shape when cooked, like Cox's Orange Pippin, Belle de Boskoop, Gravenstein, or Pink Lady. If these aren't available, use Granny Smith.

For this simple dessert, we prefer dark amber Grade B maple syrup because it has a heartier flavor.

3 ounces cold cream cheese, cut into small chunks	1/2 teaspoon salt
6 tablespoons cold unsalted butter, cut into small chunks	1 teaspoon ground cinnamon
	1/2 teaspoon allspice
3/4 cup all-purpose flour, plus more for sprinkling	1/4 teaspoon freshly grated nutmeg
Pinch of salt	2 1/2 pounds apples, peeled, cored, and sliced 1/2 inch thick (about 6 medium apples)
1 1/2 tablespoons heavy whipping cream	
3/4 cup Grade B pure maple syrup	2 tablespoons unsalted butter, softened
1 1/2 teaspoons cornstarch	Crème fraîche, for topping

To make the dough, in the work bowl of a food processor fitted with the metal blade, add the cream cheese, butter, flour, and salt. Pulse the mixture several times until it resembles cornmeal. Add the cream and pulse a few more times, until the dough forms a ball. Flatten the dough into a 1-inch-thick disk, wrap with plastic wrap, and chill for at least 1 hour.

Preheat the oven to 400°F.

In a bowl, whisk together the maple syrup, cornstarch, salt, cinnamon, allspice, and nutmeg. Add the sliced apples and stir to coat well. Place the apple–maple syrup mixture in a 12-inch oval gratin dish with 2-inch sides and dot the top with the 2 tablespoons of butter.

On a lightly floured surface, roll the dough into a 1/8-inch-thick square slightly larger than the baking dish. Lay the dough over the apples and turn the extra dough under itself along the edges. Using a sharp paring knife, lightly score the dough in a diamond pattern without cutting through it.

Place the pan on a baking sheet and bake for 30 minutes. Take the pandowdy out of the oven and generously baste the crust with the juice from the apples underneath. The crust may break, which is okay. Return the pan to the oven and bake until the crust is golden brown and the apples and juices underneath are bubbling, another 15 to 20 minutes. Serve warm with a dollop of crème fraîche.

Apricot, Sage, and Cornmeal Cookies

Makes 3¹/₂ dozen cookies

There's a different taste discovery with each bite of this cookie. That's what makes it unique. It has a pleasant chewy texture and a surprise of dry fruit and pungent, savory herb— a nibble with a complexity that seems bigger than its size.

¹/₂ cup (1 stick) unsalted butter, softened

²/₃ cup sugar

1 large egg

³/₄ cup all-purpose flour

¹/₂ teaspoon baking soda

¹/₂ teaspoon salt

¹/₂ cup fine cornmeal

¹/₂ cup dried apricots, finely diced

2 tablespoons finely chopped fresh sage leaves

In the bowl of a stand mixer fitted with the paddle attachment, beat the butter with the sugar until pale and fluffy, about 2 minutes. Scrape down the sides of the bowl. With the mixer running, add the egg, mix to incorporate, and scrape once more.

In a bowl, sift the flour with the baking soda and salt and add to the mixer bowl along with the cornmeal. Mix on low speed until just combined. Add the apricots and sage and mix to combine. (Don't worry if the dough is slightly sticky.) Shape it into a disk, wrap with plastic wrap, and chill several hours.

Remove the dough from the refrigerator. Preheat the oven to 350°F. Line a baking sheet with parchment paper greased with nonstick vegetable spray.

Pinch off pieces of dough the size of large marbles and roll them into balls. Place the dough balls about 2 inches apart on the prepared baking sheet to allow the cookies to spread. Bake until light golden brown around the edges, about 10 minutes. Transfer to a wire rack to cool.

Bourbon-Pecan Tea Cookies

Makes 5 dozen small cookies

Our version of Mexican wedding cakes or Russian tea cakes makes heavenly, crumbly cookies. They melt in your mouth before you can chew them, and leave a fruity note of nuts. Although they are best the day they are made, they can be kept in an airtight container for a day or two, but will require another dusting of confectioners' sugar before serving. The dough (or the cookies themselves) can be frozen for up to two months. Thaw the frozen dough in the refrigerator one day before you want to bake the cookies.

2 cups all-purpose flour

1/4 teaspoon salt

1 cup (2 sticks) unsalted butter, slightly softened

1/2 cup confectioners' sugar, sifted

1 tablespoon bourbon

3/4 cup finely chopped toasted pecans

In a small bowl, sift the flour with the salt and set aside.

In a stand mixer fitted with the paddle attachment, cream the butter and confectioners' sugar on medium speed until smooth and creamy, about 2 minutes. Add the flour mixture and mix briefly. Stir in the bourbon and pecans, working the dough as little as possible. (The less you work the dough, the more crumbly and light the cookies will be.)

Scrape the dough onto a piece of plastic wrap and form it into a ball. Wrap and chill until firm, at least 2 hours.

Preheat the oven to 375°F. Line two baking sheets with parchment paper.

Pinch off pieces of dough the size of large marbles and roll them into balls. Lightly coat each ball with confectioners' sugar. Arrange the cookies close together on the prepared baking sheets.

Bake until the bottoms are just golden and the rest of the cookie is almost firm but without color, 10 to 12 minutes. Transfer them to a wire rack. When cooled to room temperature, roll each one again in confectioners' sugar, shaking to remove excess sugar.

Ginger Pillows

Makes about 4¹/₂ dozen small cookies

Molasses plus ginger two different ways produce a cookie with a soft chew and subtle sophistication. The ginger fills your palate with a pleasant warmth.

This dough freezes beautifully. Don't hesitate to make and freeze more dough than you're planning to bake, and you can be nibbling warm cookies just twenty minutes after the craving for them hits.

2 cups all-purpose flour

1 tablespoon ground ginger

1¹/₂ teaspoons ground cinnamon

¹/₂ teaspoon ground cloves

2 teaspoons baking soda

¹/₄ teaspoon salt

²/₃ cup unsalted butter, softened

1¹/₄ cups sugar

1 large egg

¹/₄ cup molasses

¹/₄ cup finely chopped crystallized ginger

In a bowl, sift the flour with the ground ginger, cinnamon, cloves, baking soda, and salt. Set aside.

In the bowl of a stand mixer fitted with the paddle attachment, beat the butter at medium speed until smooth, about 2 minutes. Add 1 cup of the sugar and beat until the mixture is pale and fluffy, another 2 minutes. Scrape the sides of the bowl. With the mixer running, add the egg, and when incorporated, scrape the bowl again. Add the molasses and mix briefly.

Mix in the flour mixture until just combined, then the chopped crystallized ginger. The dough will be soft and malleable. Shape it into a disk, wrap in plastic wrap, and refrigerate until firm, about 3 hours.

Preheat the oven to 350°F. Line 2 baking sheets with parchment paper.

Scoop or pinch off pieces of dough the size of large marbles. Roll them into balls, coat with the remaining sugar and place them 1 inch apart on the prepared baking sheets. Bake the cookies, rotating the pans after 5 minutes, until they spread and the tops crack, about 10 minutes. They are ready when the edges have darkened slightly, and the centers remain soft and chewy. Let the cookies rest for 2 to 3 minutes before lifting them onto a wire rack to cool completely.

Cacao Nib Biscotti

Makes about 7 dozen small cookies or 3$1/2$ dozen large ones

Biscotti fall under a category of cakes and cookies that are twice cooked. We like them small, so we roll the log 1$1/2$ inches wide. You can make them any size you like. If they're not snatched up and eaten immediately, they last up to a week (longer, if frozen).

Cacao nibs are roasted, crushed cocoa beans–tiny brown nuggets similar in size to buckwheat kernels. They are not sweet, but lend an intense nutty, chocolate flavor to the recipes in which they are used. Scharffen Berger is a popular and widely available domestic brand (see Resources, page 222).

2$1/4$ cups all-purpose flour	1 tablespoon grated orange zest
1$1/2$ teaspoons baking powder	1 tablespoon orange liqueur
$1/4$ teaspoon salt	1 teaspoon vanilla extract
$1/2$ cup (1 stick) unsalted butter, softened	$1/4$ cup cacao nibs
$3/4$ cup granulated sugar	Confectioners' sugar, for dusting (optional)
2 large eggs	

Preheat the oven to 375°F. Line a baking sheet with parchment paper.

In a bowl, sift together the flour, baking powder, and salt and set aside.

In the bowl of a stand mixer fitted with the paddle attachment, cream the butter and sugar together on medium speed until very smooth, about 2 minutes. Add the eggs and continue to beat until the mixture is light and creamy, about 2 minutes. Scrape the bowl, add the zest, orange liqueur, and vanilla extract and mix to combine. Decrease the speed to low and add the flour mixture, beating until just incorporated. Scrape again, add the cacao nibs, and mix just to blend.

Form the dough into a disk, cover with plastic wrap, and chill until firm, at least 1 hour. Divide it into 3 equal pieces and roll each into a log approximately 10$1/2$ inches long and 1$1/2$ inches wide. If the dough is sticky as you shape the logs, dust it with confectioners' sugar.

Arrange the logs about 4 inches apart on the baking sheet. Bake until firm and lightly golden, 18 to 20 minutes. Transfer the pan to a wire rack and let the logs cool for 10 minutes. Decrease the heat to 325°F.

With a long serrated knife, cut each log straight across into $1/2$-inch-thick slices. Arrange the slices on the baking pan and bake until barely golden, about 5 minutes on each side. Transfer the cookies to a wire rack to cool completely.

Thumbprint Cookies

Makes about 4 dozen cookies

These buttery cookies have a soft crumbly texture like short-bread that is further enhanced with a nickel-sized blob of jam. Raspberry and apricot are particularly good, but try several flavors until you find a favorite.

1^3/$_4$ cups all-purpose flour

^{1}/$_2$ teaspoon salt

^{3}/$_4$ cup (1^1/$_2$ sticks) unsalted butter, softened

^{3}/$_4$ cup confectioners' sugar

Yolk of 1 large egg

Zest of ^{1}/$_2$ lemon

1 tablespoon bourbon

2 teaspoons vanilla extract

About ^{1}/$_2$ cup jam or marmalade of your choice

In a bowl, sift the flour with the salt and set aside.

In the bowl of a stand mixer fitted with the paddle attachment, cream the butter with the confectioners' sugar on medium speed until smooth and well combined, about 2 minutes. Scrape down the bowl, add the egg yolk, and mix to incorporate. Add the lemon zest, bourbon, and vanilla, and mix again. On low speed, add the flour mixture, mixing only until combined.

Form the dough into a disk, wrap in plastic wrap, and chill until firm, about 2 hours.

Remove the dough from the refrigerator. Preheat the oven to 350°F. Line 2 baking sheets with parchment paper.

Pinch off pieces of dough the size of large marbles and roll them into balls. Place them 2 inches apart on the prepared baking sheets. Steadying each cookie with the thumb and a finger of one hand, use the pinkie of your other hand (or the end of a wooden spoon) to make an indentation in the center of each cookie, without poking all the way through.

Fill each indentation with about ^{1}/$_2$ teaspoon jam. Bake until lightly golden on the bottom and only slightly colored on the surface, 12 to 15 minutes. If they appear underdone, it is fine; this is a cookie that should not be overbaked. Transfer to a wire rack to cool completely.

Basic Vanilla Bean Ice Cream

Makes about 1 quart

Ice cream that you make at home is better than anything you'll find in the store. We make our ice cream using a fresh supple vanilla bean and often flavor the custard any number of ways (see Variations). We have been known to infuse the cream with tea leaves or lavender, or to fold in goodies like sherry-plumped cherries a minute or so before the ice cream is fully churned.

3 cups heavy whipping cream

1 cup half-and-half (or $^1/_2$ cup cream and $^1/_2$ cup whole milk)

1 plump vanilla bean, split and scraped, or 1 tablespoon vanilla extract

Pinch of salt

8 large egg yolks

1 cup sugar

In a heavy-bottomed saucepan, bring the cream, half-and-half, vanilla bean (seeds and pod), and salt to a simmer over medium heat. Cover the pan, remove from the heat, and set aside for 30 minutes to allow the vanilla bean to infuse the cream mixture. (If using vanilla extract, warm only the cream and salt. The extract is added later.)

Meanwhile, in a medium bowl, whisk together the egg yolks and sugar until the mixture is well blended and slightly thickened. Whisk in 1 cup of the warm cream mixture to the yolks. Whisking continuously, slowly pour the egg yolk mixture back into the saucepan with the remaining warm cream mixture.

Have a bowl of ice water ready. Return the saucepan to the stove and cook the custard over low heat, stirring constantly with a wooden spoon or heatproof spatula. Stir without stopping until the custard thickens slightly and coats the spoon, leaving a trail if you run your finger down the back, about 5 minutes. Immediately remove the pan from the heat and strain the custard into a 2-quart bowl. Place the bowl in the ice-water bath to cool completely. If you didn't use a vanilla bean, add the vanilla extract.

Cover the custard with plastic wrap and refrigerate until thoroughly chilled, at least 4 hours.

Transfer the cold custard into the bowl of an ice cream maker and churn according to the manufacturer's instructions. Pack the ice cream into a container, cover, and freeze until it is firm enough to scoop, about 2 hours.

Variations

To make **Honey-Vanilla Ice Cream,** replace $^1/_2$ cup of the sugar with $^1/_2$ cup honey. The sweetness of this ice cream is softened by the perfume of whichever local honeys we find at our farmer's market; we serve it with our Warm Chocolate Soufflé Cakes (page 169).

To make **Lemon Verbena Ice Cream,** prepare the Basic Vanilla Bean Ice Cream recipe, replacing the vanilla bean with 1 cup loosely packed fresh lemon verbena leaves. Bring the cream mixture to a simmer, add the lemon verbena leaves, and remove from the heat. Cover and infuse for at least 30 minutes. Proceed as directed in the recipe.

To make **Lavender Ice Cream,** prepare the Basic Vanilla Bean Ice Cream recipe, replacing the vanilla bean with the lavender flowers. Bring the cream mixture to a simmer, add $^1/_4$ cup fresh lavender flowers, or 2 tablespoons dried, and remove from the heat. Cover and infuse for 10 minutes. Taste and strain. If you'd like a more pronounced lavender flavor, cover and let infuse another 10 minutes. Proceed as directed in the recipe.

We make **Black Tea Ice Cream** with Earl Grey tea; it is a natural companion to desserts that feature chocolate. Loose tea leaves offer a more complex flavor than tea bags. To prepare it, replace the vanilla bean in the Basic Vanilla Bean Ice Cream recipe with $^1/_4$ cup plus 2 tablespoons loose Earl Grey tea leaves, or about 3 tea bags. Bring the cream mixture to a simmer, add the tea leaves, and remove from the heat. Cover and set aside for at least 30 minutes to infuse the cream mixture. (Consider the steeping time here only as a guideline; let the cream infuse until the flavor is as intense as you like.) Taste and strain. Proceed as directed in the recipe.

Banana Ice Cream

Makes about 1 quart

Is there a kid who doesn't like bananas? If any such exist, I was not one of them. Bananas are so much fun to eat—peeling the skin partway, then nibbling away at the odd-looking but lusciously sweet fruit. When we flavor ice cream with it we get a two-for-one pleasure for kids of all ages. Pairing banana with lime juice in this ice cream seems to heighten its exotic tropical origins.

3 cups heavy whipping cream

1 cup half-and-half (or 1/2 cup cream and 1/2 cup whole milk)

1 tablespoon vanilla extract

Pinch of salt

8 large egg yolks

1 cup sugar

3 medium ripe bananas

Juice of 1 lime

In a heavy-bottomed saucepan, bring the cream, half-and-half, and salt to a simmer over medium heat. Cover the pan, remove from the heat, and set aside.

In a medium bowl, whisk together the egg yolks and sugar until the mixture is well blended and slightly thickened. Whisk in 1 cup of the warm cream mixture to the yolks. Whisking continuously, slowly pour the egg yolk mixture back into the saucepan with the remaining warm cream mixture.

Have a bowl of ice water ready. Return the saucepan to the stove and cook the custard over low heat, stirring constantly with a wooden spoon or heatproof spatula. Stir without stopping until the custard thickens slightly and coats the spoon, leaving a trail if you run your finger down the back, about 5 minutes. Immediately remove the pan from the heat and strain the custard into a 2-quart bowl. Place the bowl in the ice-water bath to cool completely. Stir in the vanilla extract. Cover the custard with plastic wrap and refrigerate until thoroughly chilled, at least 4 hours.

Puree the bananas with the lime juice. Transfer the cold custard into the bowl of an ice cream maker, add the banana–lime juice puree, and churn according to the manufacturer's instructions. Pack the ice cream into a container, cover, and freeze until it is firm enough to scoop, about 2 hours.

Cinnamon-Cherry Ice Cream

Makes about 1 quart

Made with fresh cherries soaked in sherry, this is an ice cream for grown-ups. To keep them soft, we soak them in sherry before folding them into the ice cream. There is something very appealing about the way the cherries take on the flavor of the sherry. The leftover cherry soaking liquid gets reduced to a syrupy consistency and drizzled on top.

1 cup sweet cream sherry	3 cinnamon sticks
2¹/4 cups fresh cherries, pitted and halved	Pinch of salt
3 cups heavy whipping cream	8 large egg yolks
1 cup half-and-half (or ¹/2 cup cream and ¹/2 cup whole milk)	1 cup sugar

In a bowl, pour the sherry over the cherries, cover with plastic wrap, and let them soak overnight.

In a heavy-bottomed saucepan, bring the cream, half-and-half, and salt to a simmer over medium heat. Add the cinnamon sticks, remove from the heat, cover, and set aside for at least 30 minutes to develop a pronounced cinnamon flavor. If you'd like more cinnamon flavor, let infuse longer, until it is to your liking. Taste and strain.

Meanwhile, in a bowl, whisk together the egg yolks and sugar until the mixture is well blended and slightly thickened. Whisk in 1 cup of the warm cream mixture to the yolks. Whisking continuously, slowly pour the egg yolk mixture back into the saucepan with the remaining warm cream mixture.

Have a bowl of ice water ready. Return the saucepan to the stove and cook the custard over low heat, stirring constantly with a wooden spoon or heatproof spatula. Stir without stopping until the custard thickens slightly and coats the spoon, leaving a trail if you run your finger down the back, about 5 minutes. Immediately remove the pan from the heat and strain the custard into a 2-quart bowl. Place the bowl in the ice-water bath to cool completely.

Cover the custard with plastic wrap and refrigerate until thoroughly chilled, at least 4 hours.

Transfer the cold custard into the bowl of an ice cream maker and churn according to the manufacturer's instructions. Strain the cherries, reserving the liquid, and fold them into the fully churned cinnamon ice cream before putting it in the freezer to firm up.

Meanwhile, in a saucepan, cook the cherry soaking liquid over medium heat until reduced to a syrupy consistency. Allow to cool completely before serving the ice cream with a drizzle of cherry sauce.

Margarita Sorbet

Makes about 3 cups

We use a tiny store-bought ice cream machine that makes just one quart of ice cream or sorbet at a time. We do not have a lot of freezer space, yet somehow we always manage to have a great range of ice creams and sorbets on hand. We allow what is in season to inspire us and we are always willing to experiment. This sorbet is perhaps the ultimate frozen cocktail. The bright, crisp flavor of tequila (we like Sauza Hornitas) enhances the citrus flavors of orange and lime. I'd avoid using a tequila with subtle flavor as the nuances would be lost with freezing. This sorbet can be prepared and frozen up to two days ahead without losing its smooth texture. We always have a batch of simple syrup in-house, so making sorbet is that much easier.

1 1/2 cups Simple Syrup (page 192)

1/2 cup freshly squeezed orange juice (from 1 to 2 oranges)

1 cup freshly squeezed lime juice (from 6 to 8 small limes)

2 tablespoons finely grated lime zest

6 to 8 tablespoons tequila

Large pinch of salt

In a bowl, combine the simple syrup, orange and lime juices, lime zest, tequila, and salt. Cover and refrigerate until cold, about 2 hours.

To prepare in an ice cream maker, pour the sorbet mixture into the ice cream maker and freeze according to the manufacturer's instructions. Pack the sorbet into a container, cover, and freeze until it is firm enough to scoop, about 2 hours.

If you don't have an ice cream maker, make a granita, an Italian frozen dessert like shaved ice. Add 1/2 cup water to the sorbet mixture. Freeze the mixture in a bowl until semi-firm, about 3 hours, whisking occasionally. Cover and freeze until solid, at least 6 hours or overnight. Using a fork, scrape the surface of the granita to form crystals. Scoop the crystals into frozen glasses and serve immediately.

Meyer Lemon–Gin Sorbet

Makes about 3 cups

Meyer lemons have a captivating perfume. Available during the winter months, they are smaller and rounder than the standard lemon variety found at the market, with a thinner skin. We always incorporate the zest to capture every nuance of unique Meyer lemon flavor.

We use Aviation or Desert Juniper gin for this sorbet because they are made locally. Otherwise, try gins with spicy citrus nuances, like Tanqueray No.10 or Beefeater, that complement the fragrance of the lemon.

1 1/2 cups Simple Syrup (page 192)

1 1/2 cups freshly squeezed Meyer lemon juice (from about 8 lemons)

2 tablespoons finely grated Meyer lemon zest

1/2 cup gin

Pinch of salt

In a bowl, combine the simple syrup, lemon juice and zest, gin, and salt. Cover and refrigerate until cold, about 2 hours.

To prepare in an ice cream maker, pour the sorbet mixture into the ice cream maker and freeze according to the manufacturer's instructions. Pack the sorbet into a container, cover, and freeze until it is firm enough to scoop, about 2 hours.

If you don't have an ice cream maker, make a granita, an Italian frozen dessert like shaved ice. Add 1/2 cup water to the sorbet mixture. Freeze the mixture in a bowl until semi-firm, about 3 hours, whisking occasionally. Cover and freeze until solid, at least 6 hours or overnight. Using a fork, scrape the surface of the granita to form crystals. Scoop the crystals into frozen glasses and serve immediately.

Strawberry-Bourbon Lemonade Sorbet

Makes about 1 quart

Strawberry lemonade, made with equal parts tart and sweet, is a warm weather favorite. In the summer, we like to make it into a smooth frozen treat spiked with bourbon. We use Jack Daniels or Jim Beam, but you can try it with whatever bourbon you have on hand.

2 cups ripe strawberries, fresh or frozen, stemmed

1 1/2 cups Simple Syrup (page 192)

2/3 cup freshly squeezed lemon juice (from about 4 lemons)

3 tablespoons finely grated lemon zest

1/2 cup bourbon (optional)

Pinch of salt

In a blender, put the strawberries and 1 cup of the simple syrup and blend to a coarse mixture. Add the lemon juice, bourbon, and salt and blend to a smooth puree. Strain the puree and add the remaining 1/2 cup simple syrup and lemon zest, stirring until smooth. Transfer to a bowl, cover, and refrigerate until cold, about 2 hours.

Pour the sorbet mixture into an ice cream maker and freeze according to the manufacturer's instructions. Pack the sorbet into a container, cover, and freeze until it is firm enough to scoop, about 2 hours.

Crème Brûlée

Serves 6

This classic dessert with its velvety custard and crackly sugar crust is the only dish you are "allowed" to burn. It has always had a place on our menu.

The cooking time will vary considerably according to the size and depth of the dishes the custard cooks in. Ramekins, which are deep and narrow, can take twice as long as the wide, shallow (1 inch high) baking dishes traditionally used for crème brûlée.

3 cups heavy cream	6 large egg yolks
1/2 vanilla bean, split and scraped	1 cup plus 2 tablespoons sugar
3/4 teaspoon salt	

In a heavy saucepan, combine the cream, vanilla bean seeds and pod, and the salt and bring to a boil over medium-high heat. Remove from the heat, cover, and set aside for 30 minutes to allow the cream to infuse with the flavor of the vanilla. Return the cream to a boil before continuing.

In a bowl, whisk the egg yolks with 3/4 cup of the sugar until light in color. Drizzle in about 1/2 cup of the hot cream to temper (warm) the yolks, while stirring gently with a wooden spoon. Slowly add the remaining cream, stirring all the while. Strain the custard into a container and cool slightly before using.

When ready to bake, preheat the oven to 325°F.

Divide the custard between six 6-ounce ramekins or shallow baking dishes, filling each about two-thirds full. Place them in a roasting pan lined with a few paper towels. Place the pan in the oven, and with oven door still open, add enough hot water to come halfway up the sides of the dishes. Cover the pan loosely with aluminum foil and bake until the centers are set, 35 to 40 minutes for shallow dishes, 45 to 50 minutes for ramekins. When the ramekin is tapped, the custard should hold firm and the center should be barely set.

Lift the dishes from the water onto a wire rack and let cool to room temperature. Cover each dish with plastic wrap and refrigerate for at least 3 hours. The custard will not caramelize unless it has been thoroughly chilled.

Evenly sprinkle the surface of each custard with about 1 tablespoon of sugar. Heat with a kitchen torch until the sugar bubbles and turns caramel in color. Serve at once.

Chef's Tip

Like most puddings and custards, crème brûlée is baked in a hot water bath to prevent overcooking and ensure a silky texture. If you line a pan with paper towels and place the ramekins on them before adding the hot water, the dishes won't slip around.

Ricotta Doughnut Holes with Chocolate Sauce

Makes 16 to 20 doughnut holes; serves 4 to 5

For most people, deep-frying at home is intimidating. After testing a few deep-frying recipes myself using a big soup pot and candy thermometer, I went out and bought a good-quality home deep-fat fryer. Now I have total control over the temperature of the oil and don't have to lug around a pot of hot oil and risk getting burned.

That said, this is an easy recipe for producing doughnut holes that melt like cotton candy. The hint of cinnamon in the batter connects at once with a rich chocolate sauce. They are cloudlike and irresistible, and in the end, worth the effort.

1 cup Fresh Ricotta Cheese (page 219)	Pinch of salt
2 large eggs	1 cup sugar
1/2 tablespoon Kirschwasser, preferably Clear Creek	1 teaspoon ground cinnamon
1/2 cup all-purpose flour	12 cups canola oil, for deep-frying
1/2 tablespoon baking powder	1 cup warm Chocolate Sauce (recipe follows)

In a bowl, whisk together the ricotta, eggs, and Kirschwasser. In another bowl, sift together the flour, baking powder, and salt. Gently fold the flour mixture into the ricotta mixture. In a separate bowl, mix the sugar and cinnamon and set aside.

In an 8-quart heavy-bottomed soup pot, heat the oil over medium heat until it reaches 350°F on a deep-fat thermometer. Divide the batter into 2 batches. Using 2 teaspoons, drop rounded spoonfuls of the batter into the hot oil and fry until golden on all sides, about 5 minutes. Remove the fried doughnuts with a slotted spoon and drain on paper towels. While hot, roll them in cinnamon-sugar until well coated. Repeat until all the batter is used.

Transfer to a serving platter and serve immediately with warm Chocolate Sauce on the side for dipping.

Chocolate Sauce

Makes 2 cups

1/3 cup water	1/3 cup unsweetened cacao powder (preferably Dagoba)
1 cup heavy cream	4 ounces dark chocolate (preferably Dagoba 68 percent cacao), coarsely chopped
2/3 cup sugar	

In a saucepan, combine the water and cream and simmer over medium heat about 5 minutes. Add the sugar, cacao powder, and chocolate. Remove from the heat, stir to dissolve, and melt until smooth. The sauce keeps, refrigerated, for up to 1 week.

Chef's Tip

As a result of my experience of first frying the doughnuts in a big pot, I drew some conclusions that will prove helpful if you deep-fry them the same way:

- Fill the pot no more then one-third full with oil.
- Be patient. Heat the oil slowly over moderate heat for better control.
- Above all, do not move the pot of hot oil around.
- Fry in small batches to help the oil maintain a steady temperature.
- Save the empty oil bottles and strain the oil back into them when it has cooled.

Ricotta-Orange Blintzes with Roasted Rhubarb

Makes 1¹/₂ dozen 7-inch blintzes; serves 9

When I was growing up, fresh milk was delivered weekly to our house still warm from the cow and topped with glistening cream. What we could not drink, my grandmother let sour to make fresh cheese for blintzes that she served with stalks of rhubarb that grew in our backyard. If I could go back in time and eat only one thing again, these blintzes would be it.

In the effort to turn back the clock and reproduce those precious tastes, I encountered some challenges. Today's pasteurized milk will not sour on its own. It needs help from lemon juice and heat. The results are quite pleasing and produce a respectable version of the cheese I remember.

Once it is folded into a blintz, fried, and served warm with rhubarb, it brings me right back to that tiny one-room house of my youth.

Blintzes
1 cup all-purpose flour

1 cup whole milk

3 large eggs

2 tablespoons brown butter, slightly cool (see Chef's Tip)

2 teaspoons sugar

¹/₂ teaspoon coarsely ground black pepper

¹/₄ teaspoon salt

3 to 4 tablespoons melted butter

Cheese Filling
10 ounces (1¹/₄ cups) Fresh Ricotta Cheese (page 219)

2 ounces (¹/₄ cup) cream cheese

1 large egg

2 tablespoons sugar

1 tablespoon Grand Marnier

¹/₄ teaspoon salt

Grated zest of 2 oranges

Rhubarb Topping
1 pound rhubarb, washed, leaves and ends trimmed, and cut into ¹/₂-inch dice

¹/₂ cup sugar

Juice of 1 of the zested oranges

Aged balsamic vinegar, for drizzling

Coarsely ground black pepper, for finishing

To make the blintz batter, in a blender, combine the flour, milk, eggs, brown butter, sugar, pepper, and salt. Blend until smooth, about 1 minute. Strain the batter into a small bowl, cover, and let rest for 30 minutes at room temperature, or cover and refrigerate overnight. The batter will keep for a few days.

To make the ricotta filling, in the work bowl of a food processor fitted with the metal blade, combine the ricotta cheese, cream cheese, egg, sugar, Grand Marnier, salt, and orange zest and process until the misxture is a smooth puree. Place in a container, cover, and chill until you are ready to assemble the blintzes.

To fry the blintzes, remove the batter from the refrigerator to warm slightly. Heat a crêpe pan or a small (6 to 7-inch) nonstick skillet. Add about 1 teaspoon of the melted butter to lightly coat the pan and wipe out the excess to keep the first blintz from sticking (you won't have to do it again). Lift the pan off the heat and add 3 tablespoons of batter. Immediately tilt and rotate the pan so the batter spreads and fully covers the bottom of the pan in a thin, even layer.

Brown the first side for about 1 minute. Flip the blintz over and quickly brown the other side. Stack them as you fry. Wrap them tightly in plastic wrap. They keep for several hours at room temperature, or overnight in the refrigerator.

To roast the rhubarb, preheat the oven to 400°F. In a bowl, toss the diced rhubarb with ¹/₂ cup sugar and the orange juice. Arrange the coated rhubarb pieces in a single layer on a baking sheet and roast until tender, about 20 minutes. Gently shake the pan every 5 minutes or so to rotate the rhubarb, and check for doneness after 15 minutes. The pieces of rhubarb should be soft enough to eat, yet hold their shape. Lightly sprinkle the warm rhubarb with additional sugar if it is too tart; it will dissolve in the residual heat. Set aside.

To fill the blintzes, set a blintz on a work surface and spoon about 1¹/₂ tablespoons of ricotta filling in the center. Fold the top edge down and the bottom up so they meet in the center of the blintz and cover the filling. Then fold in the sides to make a square.

To brown the blintzes, brush the bottom of a large nonstick skillet with melted butter. Over medium heat, sauté a few blintzes at a time, seam side down, until golden brown, about 1 minute. Turn the blintzes over and brown the other side, another 45 seconds. Repeat with the remaining blintzes.

To serve, place 2 blintzes on each plate and top with a spoonful of roasted rhubarb. Drizzle aged balsamic vinegar over and around the edge of the plate and garnish with a coarse grinding of black pepper.

Chef's Tips

When choosing rhubarb for this recipe, look for stalks of uniform thickness. Early in the season, you may be able to find tender, pencil-thin stalks that can be sliced in equal lengths, about 1/2 inch. If the rhubarb stalks look more like fat pieces of celery, cut them into 4-inch lengths and split each length down the middle. If the pieces are still overly large, split them down the middle again and dice into 1/2-inch pieces. The chunks don't need to be perfectly diced or perfectly alike, but they should be roughly the same size so that they cook evenly. You should have about 3 cups.

Browning butter is not difficult. There is a moment, though, when it gets too dark and burns. To get to the perfect browning point, heat the butter over medium heat, constantly moving the pan across the burner. First, the butter melts, then starts to foam, and then begins to turn brown. Pull it off the heat at that moment, and pour it into a small bowl to stop the cooking.

Chapter 8
Bar and Pantry

Simple Syrup

Makes about 2 cups

Typically made from a 1:1 ratio of sugar to water, simple syrup is handy to have in the refrigerator. Use it to sweeten tea or cocktails, toss it with fresh fruit, or in a last-minute sorbet.

2 cups water
2 cups sugar

Combine the water and sugar in a saucepan and bring to a boil over high heat, stirring occasionally, until the sugar is completely dissolved. Transfer the mixture to a clean heatproof container, let it cool to room temperature, then cover tightly and refrigerate. The syrup will keep, refrigerated, in a covered container for up to 1 month.

Fresh Cranberry Juice

Makes about 10 cups

When we start seeing fresh cranberries around Thanksgiving, we anticipate making fresh juice, one of my favorite preparations. I prepare it traditionally, as an infusion.

As a kid, I remember watching my grandmother gently simmer the berries in sugar water until they popped their skins, leached their festive color, and infused the liquid with a bittersweet flavor. This neon red liquid, called kissel in Russian, was the drink of choice for our winter holiday meals and special occasions. A pitcher of kissel always stood proudly next to bottles of vodka and other festive libations that graced our table. Kissel can be made using any red fruit or berries, although cranberries are the first choice among aficionados.

2 pounds fresh cranberries, picked over
4 quarts water
1 1/2 cups sugar

In a 6-quart soup pot, place the cranberries, water, and sugar. Bring to a boil over high heat, decrease the heat to medium-low, and simmer until the cranberry flavor is pronounced, about 45 minutes.

Line a colander with a double layer of cheesecloth and set over a bowl. Strain the cranberry juice several times, discarding the solids.

Serve the juice well chilled or mix it with your favorite beverage. It will keep, refrigerated, up to 2 weeks and frozen for up to 3 months.

Fresh Heirloom Tomato Juice

Makes about 2 cups

Once I started making this juice, I could never go back to the canned variety. It is simple to prepare and has incomparable flavor when tomatoes are at their peak. The addition of just a hint of olive oil prevents it from separating. Drink it chilled on its own, or use it to create a delicious House Bloody Mary (page 196).

4 large heirloom tomatoes, such as Aunt Ginny's Purple Brandywine, Paul Robeson, or Black Krim
4 teaspoons extra-virgin olive oil
Kosher salt and freshly ground black pepper

Halve the tomatoes across their midsection. Squeeze the halves to remove the seeds. Holding the rounded portion of a tomato half against your palm, grate it over a bowl using the largest holes of a box grater. Stir in the olive oil and season with salt and pepper. Transfer the mixture to a blender jar and liquefy. Strain through a fine mesh strainer or cheesecloth. Serve chilled. The juice will keep, refrigerated, for about 2 days.

Fresh Strawberry Puree

Makes approximately 1³/4 cups

1 pint fresh strawberries, stemmed and coarsely sliced
2 tablespoons sugar

Place strawberries and sugar in a blender and liquefy. Strain contents through a fine mesh strainer into a container. Cover tightly and refrigerate until ready to use. This puree can be made up to 2 days in advance.

Housemade Maraschino Cherries

Makes approximately 50 cherries

Toward the end of the cherry season we marinate several large containers full so we have housemade maraschino cherries well into the fall. We use them as garnishes for our cocktails, including Paley's Old Fashioneds (page 196), Manhattans, and Collins; and in desserts and as a topping for ice creams. They can also be eaten straight out of the jar as a snack. We use firm, ripe Bing cherries because they are always big, sweet, and plump, though any firm, dark cherry variety will work. There are two brands of maraschino liqueur widely available: Maraska, the sweeter of the two, and Luxardo. Either will make a fine choice for this recipe.

$3^1/2$ cups fresh Bing cherries, with pits and stems intact
$3/4$ cup maraschino liqueur
1 cup Simple Syrup (page 192)

Have ready a clean 1-quart glass jar with removable lid and a round of waxed paper sized to fully cover the top of the cherry mixture.

Fill the jar with cherries. In a small bowl, mix the maraschino liqueur and Simple Syrup and pour into the jar. Cover the cherry mixture with the waxed-paper round. Fasten the lid. Punch 1 hole in the lid to slow fermentation. Macerate in the refrigerator for at least 1 month. Once done, they will keep for up to 3 months in the refrigerator.

Cocktails

The bar at Paley's Place operates as a tiny stage for the bartender. A nonstop performance—no intermissions—unfolds nightly. Our bar recipes reflect our commitment to local, seasonal ingredients. Outstanding local spirits like Desert Juniper gin, Clear Creek pear brandy, M vodka, and Aviation gin give distinction to our cocktails, as do heirloom tomatoes in our House Bloody Mary (page 196) or Housemade Maraschino Cherries (page 194) in our Old Fashioned (page 196). The end result: delicious, classic, handcrafted cocktails with a twist. If you can't find the brands of spirits we call for, you may of course substitute your own favorites.

Tennessee Rose

Serves 1

2 ounces Jack Daniels whiskey
1 teaspoon Simple Syrup (page 192)
4 ounces freshly squeezed grapefruit juice
1 ounce freshly squeezed lemon juice
Splash of Clear Creek crème de cassis
Lemon wedge, for garnish

In a shaker filled with ice, combine all the ingredients except the lemon wedge and shake vigorously until well chilled. Strain into a 12-ounce glass filled with fresh ice. Garnish with the lemon wedge, and serve.

Cosmo-Not

Serves 1

2 ounces M vodka
1 ounce Cointreau
Splash of Simple Syrup (page 192)
1/2 ounce freshly squeezed lime juice
1 1/2 ounces freshly squeezed orange juice
Splash of Fresh Cranberry Juice (page 192)
Lime wedge, for garnish

In a shaker filled with ice, combine all the ingredients except the lime wedge and shake vigorously until well chilled. Strain into a chilled 7-ounce martini glass. Garnish with the lime wedge, and serve.

House Bloody Mary

Serves 1

3 dashes Worcestershire sauce
1/2 teaspoon Prepared Horseradish (page 202)
2 dashes Tabasco (optional)
1 lime wedge
1 lemon wedge
2 ounces M vodka
4 ounces Fresh Heirloom Tomato Juice (page 193)
2 grinds black pepper
Pickled Vegetables (page 221), for garnish

In a 12-ounce glass filled with ice, combine the Worcestershire, horseradish, and Tabasco. Squeeze the lime and lemon wedges over the ice and drop the wedges into glass. Stir in the vodka, tomato juice, and ground pepper. Garnish with pickled vegetables, and serve.

Paley's Lemon Drop

Serves 1

2 ounces Absolut Citron vodka
1 ounce Cointreau
1/2 ounce Simple Syrup (page 192)
2 ounces freshly squeezed lemon juice
2 ounces freshly squeezed orange juice
1 lemon slice
Sugar

In a shaker filled with ice, combine all the ingredients except the lemon slice and sugar and shake vigorously until well chilled. Moisten the rim of a chilled 7-ounce martini glass with the lemon slice. Put some sugar on a small, flat plate and dip the rim of the glass into the sugar to coat it evenly. Strain the contents of the shaker into the glass and serve.

Paley's Old Fashioned

Serves 1

1 orange slice (1/8 of an orange), with peel and seeds
6 or 7 dashes of orange bitters
1 sugar cube
1 Housemade Maraschino Cherry (page 194), pitted
2 teaspoons Punt e Mes red vermouth
2 ounces Maker's Mark bourbon

In an 8-ounce glass, muddle the orange slice, bitters, sugar cube, cherry, and vermouth. Add ice to fill. Pour in the bourbon and serve with a straw.

Pear Brandy Kamikaze

Serves 1

2 ounces Clear Creek pear brandy
1 ounce Cointreau
1/2 ounce Simple Syrup (page 192)
1 ounce freshly squeezed lime juice
1 lime slice, for garnish

In a shaker filled with ice, combine all the ingredients except the lime slice and shake vigorously until well chilled. Strain into a chilled 7-ounce martini glass. Garnish with the lime slice, and serve.

Strawberry Lynchburg Lemonade

Serves 1

2 ounces Jack Daniels whiskey
1 ounces freshly squeezed lemon juice
1 ounce Simple Syrup (page 192)
2 ounces Fresh Strawberry Puree (page 193)
Splash of water
Fresh strawberry, for garnish

In a shaker filled with ice, combine all ingredients except the strawberry and shake until well mixed. Strain into a 12-ounce glass filled with ice or a chilled 7-ounce martini glass. Garnish with the fresh strawberry.

Aviation Gin Gimlet

Serves 1

3 ounces Aviation gin
1 1/2 ounces Simple Syrup (page 192)
1 1/2 ounces freshly squeezed lime juice
1 lime wedge, for garnish

In a shaker filled with ice, combine all the ingredients except the lime wedge and shake vigorously until well chilled. Strain into a chilled 7-ounce martini glass or a 12-ounce glass filled with ice. Garnish with the lime wedge, and serve.

Persillade

If there is one thing I cannot do without in my kitchen, it's this simple mixture of garlic and parsley chopped together. Used sparingly, persillade has an extraordinary ability to transform the flavor of any savory dish. It is easy to make and holds well, covered, in the refrigerator for a day or so, although it is best when freshly made.

I developed a taste for it when Kimberly and I spent a year at a small restaurant in the center of France, near Limoges. France has a gastronomic Mason-Dixon Line: in the north, the food rests on butter and shallots; in the south, it is olive oil and garlic. In Alsace (in the north), if you put garlic in the food, people act like you set their mouth on fire. The further south you go, the more garlic you find, with its most assertive use near Nice, close to Italy. It is important to note that garlic is a powerful tool and its use needs to be modulated to suit various preparations.

1 bunch Italian parsley, leaves only
3 large cloves garlic

Finely chop the parsley on a cutting board, then gather it to one side of the board. Finely chop the garlic. Mix them together and chop some more until well incorporated. Transfer the mixture to a small container, cover tightly, and refrigerate until ready to use.

Basil Pesto

Makes about 1 cup

Recipes for pesto have been bastardized through the years, and mine is no exception. In this recipe, I use hazelnuts instead of the customary pine nuts because I do not like pine nuts. Besides, hazelnuts are abundant in our neck of the woods and this pesto presents me with another opportunity to use them. I use lemon juice to balance flavor and brighten color. Neither change creates an authentic version. I find it a healthy practice to take creative liberties, because I know what I like to eat.

If basil is not in season, wait for summer. Pesto will hold, refrigerated, for three to four days. But I prefer to use it within one day as its fresh, grassy flavor seems to disappear quickly. And while I am not a big fan of making and freezing pesto, I have been known to freeze leftovers.

In a small skillet, cook the hazelnuts over medium heat, moving the pan back and forth to roll the nuts until they are evenly colored, about 5 minutes. Watch carefully as they quickly turn brown, then blacken. When the skins start to peel and the nuts give off a toasty aroma, transfer them to a kitchen towel and let cool slightly. Then, rub them in the towel to get rid of as much papery skin as possible.

In the work bowl of a food processor fitted with the metal blade, add the basil, garlic, hazelnuts, lemon juice, and Parmesan and pulse until coarsely chopped. Season with salt and pepper. Pour in all the olive oil and process until smooth. Refrigerate, covered, until ready to use.

1/4 cup raw hazelnuts

2 cups fresh basil leaves

3 cloves garlic cloves, coarsely chopped

Juice of 1/2 lemon

1/4 cup grated Parmesan cheese

Kosher salt and freshly ground black pepper

1/2 cup extra-virgin olive oil

Ketchup

Makes about 1¹/2 cups

Essentially, this recipe makes a great tomato ketchup to slather on your burger or fries. However, with the addition of horseradish, you get the cocktail sauce that we serve with all sorts of seafood from freshly shucked oysters to poached prawns to chilled crab meat (see Variation).

Tomato varieties vary greatly in acidity and sweetness. Judge for yourself how much sugar to add: start with the amount called for in the recipe, and then adjust as the final step if you think it should be sweeter. When the local summer tomatoes are no longer available, we take advantage of good-quality canned tomatoes, which make a respectable version of the sauce.

2 pounds ripe red tomatoes, or 2 (14-ounce) cans good-quality peeled tomatoes	1 tablespoon drained capers
Grated zest and juice of 1 orange	1 tablespoon drained whole green peppercorns packed in brine (see Resources, page 222)
Juice of ¹/2 grapefruit	1 large shallot, coarsely chopped
Juice of ¹/2 lemon	Kosher salt and freshly ground black pepper
¹/4 cup cider vinegar	
¹/2 cup packed brown sugar, plus more, if needed	

If using fresh tomatoes, halve them across their midsection. Squeeze the halves to remove the seeds. Hold the rounded portion of the tomato against your palm and grate the tomato using the largest holes of a box grater set over a bowl. Transfer to the jar of a blender. If using canned tomatoes, add the tomatoes and juice directly into the blender jar.

To the tomatoes, add the orange zest and juice, grapefruit juice, lemon juice, cider vinegar, brown sugar, capers, green peppercorns, and shallot. Season with salt and pepper, then liquefy.

Transfer the mixture to a 2-quart saucepan and cook over low heat until the raw flavor of the shallot has disappeared and the tomato mixture has reduced to the consistency of ketchup, 30 to 40 minutes (longer if the fresh tomatoes are watery).

Ketchup will keep well for up to 2 weeks, refrigerated. Because of its high acid content, the sauce could keep longer, although its vibrancy declines.

Variation

To make **Cocktail Sauce,** prepare the recipe for Ketchup and let it cool completely. Stir in ¹/3 cup Prepared Horseradish (page 202), a generous dash of Tabasco, a generous dash of Worcestershire sauce, and juice of half a lemon and mix to blend. Add additional salt and pepper, if needed. Serve chilled. This sauce will keep for up to 2 weeks in the refrigerator.

Prepared Horseradish

Makes about 1²/₃ cups

As a young boy in Russia, I watched my grandfather stock up every fall on foods like pickles and sauerkraut for the coming winter. Sitting on the balcony of our small apartment, he would spend hours grating fresh horseradish root to make horseradish sauce. I often wondered why he performed this task alone and outside. Now that I prepare it myself, I understand why: when the root is really fresh, it will almost make you cry just looking at it.

The potency of prepared horseradish seems to depend on two things: the freshness of the root and how soon it is prepared after grating. It is most potent if the vinegar, salt, and sugar are mixed in immediately after grating. The sauce is milder if you wait longer, about 15 minutes, to add them.

6-ounce piece fresh horse-radish root, peeled and trimmed

1¹/₄ cups distilled white vinegar or rice vinegar

2 tablespoons kosher salt

3 tablespoons sugar

Grate the horseradish over a bowl. Stir in the vinegar, salt, and sugar. Place the prepared horseradish in a storage container and let it sit at room temperature, uncovered, for at least 4 hours. Covering right away could make it bitter. It will keep refrigerated for about 2 weeks.

Chef's Tip

I always grate the root by hand with a fine Microplane grater, available at most cookware stores. If grated with a food processor, the root gets overly bruised so it oxidizes and turns gray; it also gets bitter and less flavorful from the heat of the machine. To grate the root, scrape against the grater at a 45-degree angle, giving the horseradish a quarter turn every minute or so (the tip will eventually resemble a sharpened pencil).

Aioli

Makes about 1¹/₂ cups

I prefer making aioli in a mortar with a pestle because it yields a sauce with a silky texture that I find incomparable—I think it's actually worth buying a mortar and pestle for. If you do not have a mortar and pestle handy, feel free to use a hand whip and a mixing bowl instead—just be sure to finely chop the garlic first. I like to use a squirt bottle to control the gentle stream of oil. If the mixture becomes too thick or dense and you have a hard time incorporating all the oil, loosen it up by mixing in a teaspoon of lukewarm water.

3 large cloves garlic

1 teaspoon sea salt, plus a pinch more for finishing

3 large egg yolks

1 teaspoon Dijon mustard

1 teaspoon freshly squeezed lemon juice

1 cup grapeseed oil

2 tablespoons extra-virgin olive oil

To prepare the aioli, on a cutting board, crush the garlic with the back of a knife and remove the peel. Add the cloves to a mortar along with the 1 teaspoon sea salt. Using the pestle, work the garlic by press-ing it against the sides of the bowl until it forms a glistening paste, about 1 minute. Add the egg yolks, mustard, and lemon juice, and blend the ingredients until smooth, about 30 seconds.

Dribble 1 tablespoon of grapeseed oil into the mortar with one hand while using the pestle in the other hand to fully incorporate the oil with a swirling motion. Be patient! Repeat, incorporating a second tablespoon until the mixture is emulsified, then once again with a third tablespoon. At this point the emulsion should be ready to accept additional oil easily. Slowly drizzle in the remaining oil with the same swirling motion of the pestle to maintain the emulsion. Be sure that the oil you've added is com-pletely absorbed before adding more. When all the grapeseed oil is incorporated, add the extra-virgin olive oil in the same manner, slowly and carefully. Because salt can make the difference between flavor that is good and flavor that is great, stir in a pinch of salt, taste, and adjust if necessary.

Smoked Bacon

Makes about 3¹/2 pounds

We have smoked bacon for years because it is very easy to do and the results are superior to any other bacon. Though smoking is not necessary, it does give bacon its true and familiar flavor. We smoke bacon in a small stovetop smoker from Camerons Professional Cookware (see Resources, page 222). Wood chips specifically designed for use with the smoker vary in the degree of smokiness they produce. Experiment with all the different types to achieve the flavor you prefer.

Plan on taking five days to cure the meat. Curing salt, an optional ingredient, is a preservative that gives bacon its rosy color and extends its life, but ultimately does not affect flavor. At the restaurant, we observe a strict ratio of one gram curing salt to one pound of meat.

3¹/2 pounds fresh pork belly, skinned

1 teaspoon curing salt (sodium nitrite), optional

¹/4 cup freshly ground black pepper

¹/4 cup ground bay leaves

¹/2 cup packed brown sugar

¹/2 cup kosher salt

To cure the meat, place the pork belly in a nonreactive storage container and rub thoroughly all over with curing salt. Rub the top surface of the belly with half the pepper, half the bay, half the sugar, and half the salt. Turn the belly over and repeat with the remaining pepper, bay, sugar, and salt.

Cover tightly and refrigerate for 2 days. Turn the belly over, cover, and refrigerate for 3 more days. Remove the meat and pat it dry with paper towels. Discard the curing liquid that has formed in the container. At this point, the bacon is ready to use as is or to smoke in a stovetop smoker following the manufacturer's instructions.

Bacon can be refrigerated, tightly wrapped, for up to 7 days or frozen for up to 3 months.

Corn Broth

Makes 8 cups

When I discovered that a broth for risotto could be made from corncobs, it reminded me of a trick that Venetian cooks use when making their classic springtime dish risi e bisi (rice and peas). They boil the pea pods to extract color and flavor and then use this liquid to give the risotto a boost of delicate flavor.

I like the simplicity of this broth and how it utilizes a part of corn that would normally be thrown away. The broth is extremely flavorful when corn is at its seasonal peak. I use only corn, no other vegetables or herbs, to capture its pure flavor.

4 quarts water
8 ears of corn, shucked
2 tablespoons salt

In a large pot, bring the water to a boil over high heat, add the corn and salt, and cook 5 minutes. Remove the corn and let cool. Using a paring knife, slice off the kernels from the cobs, letting them drop into a bowl. Set the kernels aside if using them right away for another recipe, or refrigerate them in a covered container for no longer than 2 days. You can also freeze them for about 2 weeks.

Halve the 8 stripped cobs crosswise and return them to the pot of cooking water. Simmer over medium-low heat until the broth develops a definite corn flavor, about 45 minutes. Strain the broth, discarding the cobs, and reserve if using right away, or let cool and refrigerate in a covered container. It will keep, refrigerated, for up to 3 days, or frozen for up to 1 month.

Veal Stock

Makes about 8 cups

Although cooking this stock is an all-day event (it must simmer for almost ten hours), it is easy to make as you don't roast the bones and vegetables. It gets color from the addition of blackened onion, onion skins, and tomato paste. The final stock is not only lighter and leaner than classic veal stock, but is also more versatile as it does not have the over-powering taste of roasted bones. Therefore it can be used to make sauces accompanying fish, poultry, and game. It can also be added to any meat-based soup for subtle richness. If veal bones are not available, I use beef bones, which are easier to come by.

5 pounds veal bones	1 tablespoon whole black peppercorns
2 onions, papery peels intact, halved crosswise	2 bay leaves
1 large carrot, peeled and sliced into 1/2-inch rounds	8 sprigs of thyme
	1/4 cup tomato paste

In an 8-quart stockpot, add the veal bones and completely cover them with cold water. Bring to a boil over high heat, decrease the heat to medium-low, and simmer for about 1 hour, skimming off the foam as it forms on the surface. Add more water as needed to keep the bones completely submerged throughout cooking.

Meanwhile, on another burner, turn the heat to high, place the onion halves, cut side down, directly onto the burner grate, and cook them, without turning, until completely blackened, about 15 minutes. Set aside.

When the stock stops producing scum and the liquid is clear, add the carrot, peppercorns, bay leaves, thyme, and tomato paste and simmer for 8 hours. Continue adding cold water periodically so all the ingredients stay submerged, and occasionally skim off fat as it forms.

Stop adding water after 8 hours of cooking, and continue to simmer the stock for another 1 1/2 hours to concentrate flavor. Strain, discarding the solids, and transfer the liquid to a clean heat-proof storage container.

Cool the stock quickly by placing the storage container in a sink of cold water or an ice-water bath. Cover and refrigerate.

The stock keeps well, refrigerated, for up to 1 week, or frozen, up to 3 months. We prefer to freeze stocks and sauces in small amounts, which lets us defrost only what we need, eliminating waste.

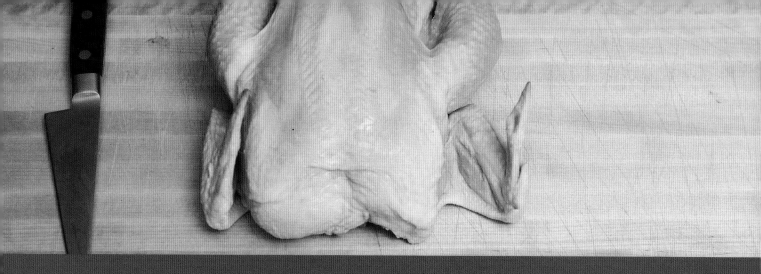

How to Bone a Chicken

This technique is for a do-it-yourselfer. Imagine that shopping for chicken is like shopping for building supplies at a store like Home Depot. If you enjoy that kind of thing, you will come out of this experience saving money, gaining a very useful skill, and having a newfound appreciation for your butcher.

Place a whole chicken on a cutting board, breast side up. Press down on the breastbone to flatten and stabilize the chicken. Using a sharp boning knife, cut through the second wing joint (counting from the wing tip toward the body of the bird). Reserve the wings for making stock.

Pulling on a drumstick with one hand, cut between the leg and the breast. It will separate easily. Press down on the leg to dislocate the joint closest to the body and then continue cutting between the leg and the carcass, pulling at the same time until the joint is exposed. Flip the bird over. Keep pulling on the leg until the joints have separated. Cut to remove the "oyster," a small chunk of flesh along the spine. Finish tearing off the leg and set it aside. To bone the other leg, turn the bird 180 degrees (work with a leg always on your left, if you are right-handed, on your right, if you are left-handed) and repeat the procedure.

To bone each leg, hold the tip of the drumstick with one hand and cut a ring near the rounded tip of the drumstick through the skin to the bone. Scrape down from this cut along the bone to remove all the flesh in one piece. Remove all the cartilage and discard. Reserve the meat and the skin and set aside (it can be used to make the forcemeat for the Chicken Roulade, page 119). Save the bones for making stock (recipe follows).

To bone the breasts, hold down the top of the bird with one hand and with the other, cut along one side of the breastbone from top to bottom. Keep your knife turned inward at a slight angle to get as close to the bone as possible. Using a combination of pulling with one hand and small cuts down the rib cage with the other, separate the breast meat from the carcass. Turn the bird 180 degrees and repeat on the other side. (Fillet on your left if you are right-handed, on your right if you are left-handed.) Be sure to keep the fleshy part of the wing (the drumette) attached to each breast for a more attractive presentation. Refrigerate the boned breasts in an airtight container for up to 2 to 3 days or freeze them. Use the carcass to make stock (recipe follows). If not making the stock right away, refrigerate the bones and carcass for up to 2 days or freeze for up to a week.

Press down on the breast bone.

Cut through the second wing joint.

Cut between the leg and the breast.

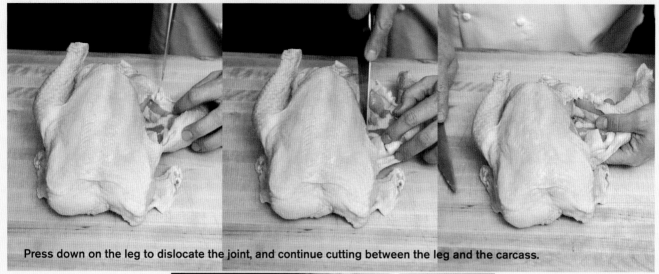

Press down on the leg to dislocate the joint, and continue cutting between the leg and the carcass.

Flip the bird over.

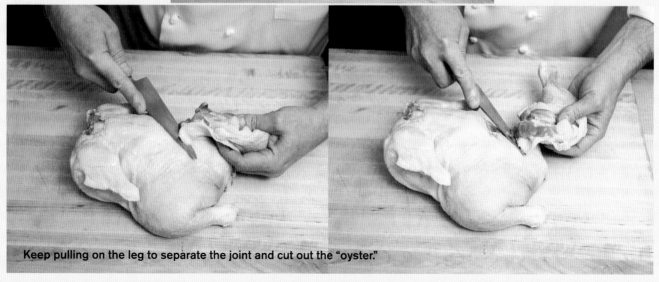

Keep pulling on the leg to separate the joint and cut out the "oyster."

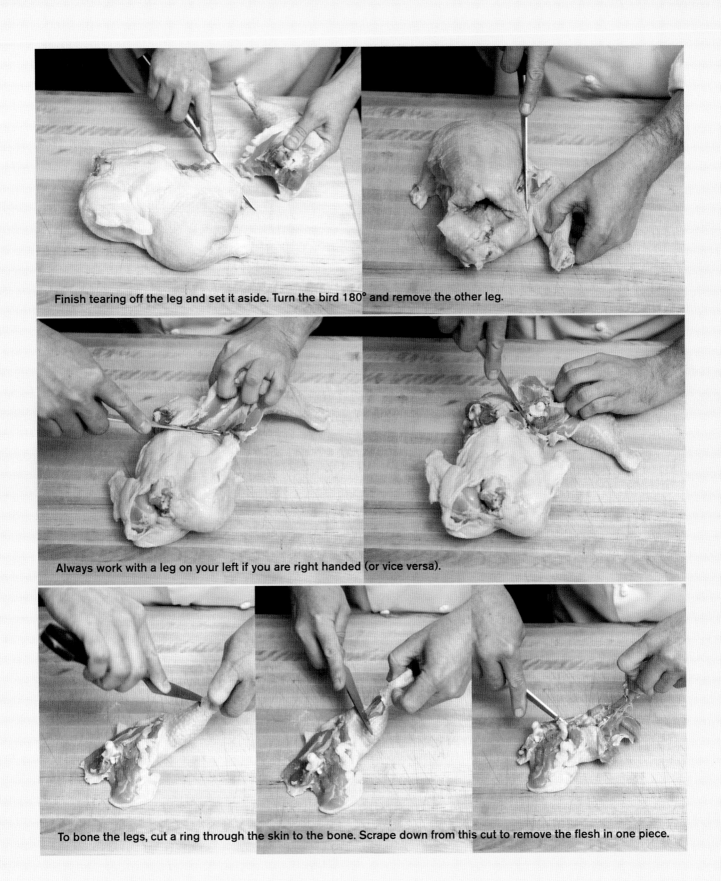

Finish tearing off the leg and set it aside. Turn the bird 180° and remove the other leg.

Always work with a leg on your left if you are right handed (or vice versa).

To bone the legs, cut a ring through the skin to the bone. Scrape down from this cut to remove the flesh in one piece.

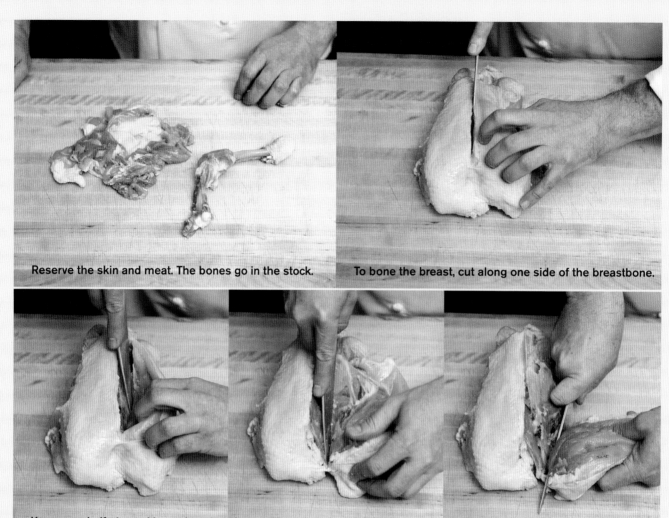

Reserve the skin and meat. The bones go in the stock.

To bone the breast, cut along one side of the breastbone.

Keep your knife turned inward to stay close to the bone. Pull and cut to separate the breast meat from the carcass. Turn the bird 180° and repeat on the other side.

Chicken Stock

This is the version of chicken stock I've used for years. It has never failed me yet.

2 (4- to 5-pound) free-range chickens, boned (see page 208)

1 large onion, papery peel intact, quartered

2 large carrots, peeled and sliced into 1/2-inch rounds

2 large celery roots, peeled and cut into large dice

1 medium leek, including green part, quartered, washed, and cut into large dice

10 whole sprigs of thyme

5 whole sprigs of parsley

3 bay leaves

2 tablespoons whole black peppercorns

1 tablespoon kosher salt

2 cups good white wine

In an 8-quart stockpot, put the chicken carcass, leg bones, neck, giblets, and wings. Reserve the leg and breast meat and the liver for other uses.

Add the onion, carrots, celery roots, leek, thyme, parsley, bay leaves, peppercorns, and salt. Pour in the wine, then add enough cold water to cover the solids by 1 inch. Bring to a boil on high heat, decrease the heat to medium-low, and simmer for 1 1/2 to 2 hours. Adjust the heat so that the stock is always gently bubbling. Periodically skim off the fat and foam from the surface.

Taste the liquid after 1 1/2 hours to make sure the flavor is developing nicely. If the taste seems weak, continue cooking. When the flavor is to your liking, remove from the heat. Strain, discarding the solids, and transfer the liquid to a clean heat-proof storage container.

Cool the stock quickly by placing the storage container in a sink of cold water, or in an ice-water bath. Cover and refrigerate overnight. The next day, remove the hardened layer of fat that has formed on the surface of the stock. If the stock jelled, take pride in having extracted maximum protein from meat and bones, and know the liquid will be flavorful.

Use the stock within 1 or 2 days, or freeze it in small containers for up to 3 months. We find freezing in small amounts lets us defrost only what we need, eliminating waste.

Cooked Crab

Yields about 1^1/$_2$ to 2 cups cooked crabmeat

For a city dweller like me, working with live crabs fresh out of the water feels primal and a little daunting. It's about as close to hunting as I am going to get. Dispatching a live creature does inspire me to make good use of its every part. Once you have picked the meat (which is quite easy), the shells make an incredibly delicious stock.

Hold live, uncooked crabs refrigerated in a roasting pan covered with newspaper or in a large brown paper bag (a plastic bag will suffocate them). The lack of light keeps them quiet. Cook the crabs the same day you buy them and make sure the crabs are alive before you do. If they are not, discard them, as they tend to deteriorate quickly and taste very unpleasant if cooked and eaten. Expect about a 40 percent yield when picking cooked crab, unless of course you sample the goods while picking.

2 live Dungeness crabs
Kosher salt

Fill a 12-quart pot two-thirds full with cold water, cover, and bring to a boil over high heat. Once the water boils, add enough salt to make it taste like sea water.

Handle the crab with your hand or with a pair of long tongs. Pick up the crab from behind, its claws pointing away from you, and submerge it in the boiling water. Let the water return to a boil, then cook the crab for 15 minutes. Remove it from the pot and set it aside to cool. Cook the other crab. Discard the cooking water.

Using your hands, remove the legs and claws of both crabs, working over a large bowl to capture the juices. Using sturdy kitchen scissors, cut the legs and claws crosswise at the joints into more manageable pieces. Insert 1 blade of the scissors into the cut leg sections and snip lengthwise. Pick the meat clean and put the meat in a bowl. Reserve the shells for preparing stock (see page 34).

Next, remove and reserve the large top shell and expose the carcass. Snip with scissors and discard all the black and gray gills along the sides of the body. Cut the crab carcass into quarters, and carefully pick the meat into the bowl with the claw meat, an easy task if you use your hands (the exposed joints where the legs attach are particularly meaty). Pour off the juices into a small bowl and refrigerate, reserving them for broth. Transfer the picked meat into a smaller storage container, cover tightly and refrigerate for a day or two at the most before using. Do not freeze the meat as its texture will change dramatically—the meat will give up all its moisture and become rubbery. The shells and picked carcass will keep, refrigerated, for one day or frozen for about a week.

Sauce Bordelaise, My Way

Makes about 2 cups

In my variation of a classic French sauce, I incorporate balsamic vinegar for additional flavor. We use the sauce with grilled meat, for rich fish dishes like Bacon-Wrapped Sturgeon Bordelaise (page 97), and for Escargot Bordelaise with Roasted Marrow Bones (page 31). It can be made in advance because it keeps well–up to three days in the refrigerator or up to one month in the freezer.

1/4 cup extra-virgin olive oil

4 large shallots, finely diced

1 small carrot, peeled and finely diced

2 cups balsamic vinegar

2 cups red wine

2 bay leaves

5 sprigs of thyme

1 teaspoon whole black peppercorns

2 cups Veal Stock (page 207)

Kosher salt and freshly ground black pepper

In a 3-quart saucepan, heat the olive oil over medium heat. Add the shallots and carrot and cook, stirring, until the vegetables turn a dark caramel color, about 15 minutes. Add the vinegar, wine, bay leaves, thyme, and peppercorns. Cook until the liquid is reduced to a syrupy consistency, about 30 minutes. Add the stock and return to a simmer. Season with salt and pepper and strain through a fine mesh strainer into a storage container. Cool the sauce in an ice-water bath. Cover tightly and refrigerate or transfer to several smaller containers and freeze.

Brioche

Makes one 10 by 5-inch loaf, or 6 to 8 burger buns

Few foods are as enticing as brioche warm from the oven. Learning to master this recipe may keep you from having to buy ordinary white bread. It helps to have a heavy-duty stand mixer with a dough hook attachment for this recipe.

When wrapped and refrigerated, brioche will hold for up to two days. When frozen, it will hold for up to a month.

2/3 cup whole milk	3 large eggs, plus 1 large egg, beaten, for egg wash
1 1/2 teaspoons active dry yeast	1 large egg yolk
3 1/2 cups bread flour, plus extra for kneading	1/2 cup (1 stick) plus 2 1/2 tablespoons unsalted butter waxed (5 1/4 ounces), softened
1 1/2 teaspoons kosher salt	
1 1/2 teaspoons sugar	1 tablespoon poppy seeds, for the buns

In a small saucepan, heat the milk over low heat to 110°F (check with an instant-read thermometer). Remove from the heat, sprinkle the yeast over to soften, stir to dissolve, and let rest to activate, about 5 minutes.

Transfer the yeasted milk to the bowl of a heavy-duty stand mixer fitted with the dough hook. Add the 4 cups of flour, salt, sugar, 3 whole eggs, and 1 egg yolk. Mix on low speed until the dough comes together into a smooth paste, about 7 minutes. Divide the butter into 4 pieces and with the mixer running, add in 1 piece at a time until just incorporated and the dough comes away from the side of the bowl.

Transfer the dough to a lightly floured work surface. Form a smooth ball by kneading with the palm of your hands 6 or 7 times. Place the dough in a large bowl, cover with plastic wrap, and let it rise in a warm spot until doubled in size, about 2 hours. You can also refrigerate the dough and let it proof slowly overnight.

To form a loaf, spray a 10 by 5-inch loaf pan with nonstick vegetable spray. Lightly flour a work sur-face. On the work surface, punch down the dough to flatten it, then shape it into a rectangle about 1/4 inch thick and the length and width of the loaf pan.

Starting from 1 long side, tightly roll up the dough like a jelly roll. Tuck the narrow ends under slightly to prevent the seam from opening during baking. Transfer the roll, seam side down, to the pre-pared loaf pan. Let it rise in a warm spot, uncovered, until doubled in size, about 1 1/2 hours.

Preheat the oven to 350°F.

Gently brush the top of the loaf with egg wash. Bake until the surface is a light golden color, about 25 minutes. Carefully remove the brioche from the loaf pan and transfer to a baking sheet. Return to the oven and bake until uniformly colored, about 25 minutes. The loaf is done if a wooden skewer inserted in the center comes out clean and when the loaf sounds hollow when lightly tapped on the bot-tom. Let the loaf cool on a wire rack for at least 30 minutes before slicing.

To form burger buns, line a baking sheet with buttered parchment or waxed paper. After the first rise, invert the brioche dough onto a clean work sur-face and punch it down. Divide the dough into 6 to 8 equal pieces. For each piece, cup your hand around the dough and roll it until it forms a smooth ball. Flatten each dough ball into a disk about 1/4 inch thick and transfer to the prepared baking sheet. Let the buns rise in a warm spot, uncovered, until doubled in size, about 1 1/2 hours.

Preheat the oven to 350°F.

Gently brush the tops of the buns with egg wash. Sprinkle with poppy seeds and bake until golden brown, about 30 minutes. Transfer to a wire rack and let cool for 30 minutes before using.

Cheddar Cheese Biscuits

Makes about 12 biscuits

This is an easy and very versatile recipe. Enjoy these flavorful, savory breads with eggs for brunch or as part of a wonderfully rustic holiday meal. We frequently serve them with our Dungeness Crab and Corn Chowder (page 34).

1/2 cup (1 stick) plus 1 table-spoon cold unsalted butter, cut into 1/2-inch dice	2 teaspoons baking powder
1 onion, finely diced	1/4 teaspoon baking soda
2 teaspoons fennel seed	1/2 teaspoon kosher salt
2 cups all-purpose flour	1 cup buttermilk
	1 cup grated cheddar cheese

Preheat the oven to 450°F.

In a 10-inch skillet, melt 2 tablespoons of the butter over medium heat and sauté the onions until translucent, about 5 minutes. Add the fennel seed and cook, stirring, 2 more minutes. Transfer the onion mixture to a small bowl to cool.

In a large bowl, sift together the flour, baking powder, baking soda, and salt. Add the remaining 7 tablespoons butter and work by hand or with a wooden spoon until the mixture resembles coarse bread crumbs. Add the cooled onion mixture, buttermilk, and 3/4 cup of the cheddar cheese, stirring until just combined.

Line a baking sheet with parchment or waxed paper. Drop heaping soup spoonfuls of the dough onto the paper about 2 inches apart. Sprinkle the biscuits evenly with the remaining grated cheese. Bake until a wooden skewer or a small paring knife inserted into a biscuit comes out clean and the tops are golden, about 15 minutes.

Fresh Ricotta Cheese

Makes 1¼ cups (about 10 ounces)

If the restaurant had a motto, it might be: "If we can make it better, we will." After trying several commercial brands of ricotta without ever really being satisfied with their flavor and texture, we made it ourselves. It proved a worthy experiment. It had the creamiest of textures with just the right balance of flavors.

If you ever thought about making your own cheese, this is the easiest one to start with. A watchful eye and a well-calibrated instant-read thermometer are the only tools you'll need.

½ cup heavy cream
4 cups whole milk

2 tablespoons freshly squeezed lemon juice
Pinch of kosher salt

In a nonreactive saucepan, combine the cream, milk, and lemon juice and cook over medium-low heat until the mixture reaches 205°F. (Remember, cheese making is a science and temperature is crucial.) Remove from the heat and let rest for about 15 minutes, during which time the curds and whey separate.

Line a strainer with cheesecloth and set over a bowl. Ladle the curds (the ricotta cheese) into the strainer to drain the whey. Cover tightly with plastic wrap, refrigerate, and let drain overnight.

Discard the whey and wipe the bowl dry. Transfer the ricotta to the bowl. Stir in the salt, cover tightly, and refrigerate until needed. Ricotta will keep well refrigerated in an airtight container for up to 3 days.

Preserved Lemon Peel

Makes 2 tablespoons

The conventional way of preserving lemons can be time consuming. I devised this quick and easy alternative.

1 lemon, washed and dried
½ teaspoon kosher salt
½ teaspoon sugar

With a paring knife, remove the peel from the lemon in large pieces, then cut it into julienne strips. In a small saucepan, place the peel and enough cold water to cover and cook over high heat until the water boils. Drain and repeat the process twice more.

Juice the peeled lemon and strain into a small bowl; add salt and sugar, then the blanched peel. Let the peel macerate at room temperature for 1 hour so the flavors marry. Store, refrigerated, in a tightly sealed plastic container. It will keep for about a week.

Bread-and-Butter Pickles

Makes 3 cups pickling brine, to pickle about 3 cups of vegetables

Try these on your favorite sandwich. At the restaurant we serve them next to our burger, with a plate of cured meats, or as a garnish on a green salad. I prefer rice vinegar for pickling because it is milder than others and naturally sweet.

1 large English cucumber, sliced into 1/4-inch rounds

1 medium onion, thinly sliced

2 cups rice vinegar

3/4 cups water

2 tablespoons coriander seed

1 bay leaf

3/4 tablespoon ground turmeric

2 tablespoons kosher salt

3/4 cup sugar

Place the cucumber and onion slices in a heatproof 1-quart glass jar. To make the pickling brine, in a small saucepan, combine the vinegar, water, coriander seed, bay leaf, turmeric, salt, and sugar. Bring to a boil over high heat, decrease the heat to medium low and simmer about 8 minutes. Cover the vegetables in the jar with the hot brine. Set aside to cool to room temperature. Cover tightly and refrigerate. Pickles will hold well, refrigerated, for up to 2 weeks.

Pickled Vegetables

Makes 8 cups pickling brine, to pickle 6 to 8 cups of vegetables

Virtually any vegetable can be pickled, so get creative. Use this recipe, essentially for pickling brine, as a guide for amounts and cooking times for the more commonly used vegetables. It generally takes 1 cup of brine to pickle 1 cup of vegetables. Some vegetables (like carrots) require cooking, and others (like cucumber) will not. Best of all, it is a very fast and easy process that will let you enjoy the pickles within 24 hours of making them.

2 large carrots, peeled, and sliced on the diagonal into $1/4$-inch rounds

1 large English cucumber, sliced into $1/4$-inch rounds

8 asparagus stalks, woody ends removed, halved

5 cups rice vinegar

3 cups mirin (Japanese rice wine)

3 tablespoons whole black peppercorns

3 star anise

1 tablespoon cardamom pods

3 tablespoons fennel seed

3 tablespoons ground coriander

1 tablespoon red pepper flakes

4 bay leaves

6 tablespoons kosher salt

In a small saucepan, place the carrot slices and set aside. Place the cucumber and asparagus in a 1-gallon heatproof glass jar and set aside.

To make the pickling brine, in a large soup pot, combine the vinegar, mirin, peppercorns, star anise, cardamom, fennel, coriander, red pepper flakes, bay leaves, and salt and bring to a boil over high heat.

Pour 4 cups of hot brine into the glass jar, or enough to cover the cucumber and asparagus, and set aside to cool. Pour 2 cups of brine into the pan with the carrots and cook over medium heat until the carrots are just tender, about 8 minutes. Set aside to cool. When all the vegetables are at room temperature, add the carrots and their brine to the glass jar, cover tightly, and refrigerate. Pickles will hold well, tightly covered, for up to 2 weeks. Save any extra brine for future pickling. It holds well, refrigerated, for up to 1 month.

Resources

Here are producers and vendors we like and use (and whose products are available through mail order). In Portland, Ecotrust publishes a guide to local and seasonal foods each year (check out www.ecotrust.org, or call 503-222-1577). Your area may also have one or more good guides to organic, sustainable, or local producers—an Internet search will likely turn up a wealth of blogs, localized websites, grassroots organizations, producer groups, and the like to help you orient yourself to the best produce your locality has to offer.

Mushrooms and Truffles

Peak Forest Fruit
503-324-0117
Wild and cultivated mushrooms and truffles, fresh, frozen, and dried; Oregon wild huckleberries, fresh or frozen

Mycological Natural Products
888-465-3247
www.mycological.com
Wild mushrooms like porcini, morels, chanterelles, and Oregon truffles

Meats and Seafood

Nicky USA, Inc.
503-234-4263 / 800-469-4162
www.nickyusa.com
Specialty game meats like rabbit, elk, lamb, lamb's tongues, lamb and veal sweetbreads, and American Kobe beef; game birds like quail, duck, and guinea fowl

Cattail Creek Lamb
541-998-8505
www.cattailcreeklamb.com
Whole lambs or specific cuts like lamb necks or bone-in shoulders

Viande Meats & Sausage
503-221-3012
www.viandemeatsandsausage.lbu.com

Newman's Fish Market Inc.
503-227-2700 (retail and mail order in Portland)
541-344-2371 (retail only in Eugene)
All kinds of fish and seafood, including halibut, sturgeon, black cod, fresh or frozen at sea wild salmon, mussels, razor clams, and Oregon Dungeness crab (live, cooked whole, and picked)

Oregon Salmon Commission
541-994-2647
www.oregonsalmon.org
For the latest facts on season openings and availability

Oregon Dungeness Crab Commission
541-267-5810
www.oregondungeness.org
General information and source of suppliers of Oregon Dungeness crab in Oregon and elsewhere, and by mail order

Specialty Foods, Cheeses, Grains, and Hazelnuts

Potironne Company, LLC
877-SNAILMAN
www.snailman.com
Escargots

Juniper Grove Farm
541-923-8353
www.junipergrovefarm.com
Farmstead goat cheeses, aged and fresh

Rivers Edge Chevre
541-444-1362
www.threeringfarm.com
Farmstead goat cheeses, aged
and fresh

Rogue Creamery
www.roguecreamery.com
541-664-1537 / 866-396-4704
Oregon Blue and other Rogue
Creamery cheeses

New Seasons Market
503.827-4357 / 360-992-4357
www.newseasonsmarket.com
For crème fraîche, Boschetto al Tartufo
cheese, and Pastures of Eden feta

Steve's Cheese
503-222-6014
www.stevescheese.biz
Retail sales of specialty, gourmet, and
artisanal cheeses

Pastaworks
866-206-1735 / 503-221-3002
www.pastaworks.com
Retail and mail order sales of gourmet
cheeses, crème fraiche, truffle butter, olive oils, balsamic vinegars, saba,
chocolate, cacao nibs, green peppercorns, and verjus

igourmet.com
877-446-8763
www.igourmet.com
Boschetto al Tartufo and other fine
cheeses

Israelikosher.com
718-645-1213
www.israelikosher.com
Pastures of Eden feta

Bluebird Grain Farms
509-996-3526
www.bluebirdgrainfarms.com
Emmer farro and other organic,
heirloom grains

Bob's Red Mill
800-349-2173
www.bobsredmill.com
Polenta and other specialty grains
and flours

Freddy Guys Hazelnuts
503-606-0458
www.freddyguys.com
Hazelnuts

Wine and Spirits

Oregon Wines on Broadway
800-943-8858 / 503-228-4655
www.oregonwinesonbroadway.com
Specializes in Oregon and Washington
wines

Liner & Elsen
800-903-9463 / 503-241-9463
www.linerandelsen.com
An excellent selection of Pacific
Northwest and French wines

E & R Wine Shop
503-246-6101 / 877-410-8654
Retail and mail order sales of a com-
prehensive selection of wines from the
Pacific Northwest and France

Made in Oregon
866-257-0938
www.madeinoregon.com
Oregon wines and artisanal goods

Clear Creek Distillery
503-248-9470
www.clearcreekdistillery.com
Fruit brandies such as pear and Kirschwasser (cherry), grappa, liqueurs, and
whiskey

Bendistillery
541-318-0200
www.bendistillery.com
Desert Juniper gin and other spirits

House Spirits
503-235-3174
www.housespirits.com
M vodka, Aviation gin, and other spirits

Kitchen Equipment

In Good Taste
503-248-2015
www.ingoodtastestore.com
Professional cookware, including
chitarra pasta cutters, food processors,
blenders, knives, mandolines, candy and
probe thermometers, stovetop smokers,
ice cream makers, and cedar planks;
wine and specialty foods like olive oils,
balsamic vinegars, saba, chocolate, sea
salts, verjus, and spices like pimentón
and saffron

Williams-Sonoma
877-812-6235
www.williams-sonoma.com
Stand mixers and attachments; food
processors and attachments

Sur La Table
800-243-0852
www.surlatable.com
Chitarra pasta cutters and other kitchen
equipment

Kitchen Kaboodle
800-366-0161
www.kitchenkaboodle.com
Stand mixers and attachments like pasta
rollers, cutters, and meat grinders

Camerons Cookware
888-563-0227
www.cameronscookware.com
Stovetop smokers and wood chips

Acknowledgments

I would like to thank the following people who helped make this book a reality.

To my wife, partner, and co-author, Kimberly Paley: thank you for standing by my side through thick and thin, for your devotion and unconditional love, and for your ability to get to the core of the matter both in writing this book and in our life.

We owe a great debt of gratitude to Robert Reynolds, who wrote with abandon and whose nimble mind and gentle hand helped shepherd our words into stories.

To John Valls: your tireless eye for detail and unwavering thirst for perfection captured life, energy, and magic in every photograph. Thank you.

To Theresa Valls: thank you for your keen sense of style and for keeping us organized.

To my mother, Genya Paley: thank you for bringing me to this country. Thank you for your tenacious love and undying inspiration. Thank you for helping me remember those few precious tastes of my youth.

To my grandparents Michail and Roza Livshits: thank you for my blissful, carefree childhood and a lifetime of happy memories.

To my dad, Mark Paley: thank you for your big heart and your patience and for letting me pursue my dreams.

To Kimberly's parents, Merle and Jo-Anne Brown, our most constructive critics: thank you for your wisdom, love, and immense support, and for helping us find our bliss.

To Mark Abrams and Michel Bordeaux, Michael Romano and Danny Meyer, Roger Dagorn and David Bouley: thank you for believing in us and giving us our start. To this day you still inspire us.

To all the farmers, purveyors, foragers, fishermen, artisanal food producers, winemakers, and distillers—both those mentioned in this book and all the others who provide us with local and seasonal bounty. We adore what you grow, gather, harvest, craft, and catch. You are the real stars of our show. Thank you from the bottoms of our hearts.

To Mark Gould, vineyard manager at Ken Wright Cellars, and his canine partner, Bandit: thank you for sharing with us your slice of heaven and allowing us to capture you in action. Bandit, we will miss your free spirit.

To Patrick McKee, Benjamin Bettinger, Rebecca Finley, Tom Lindstedt, and Sean Temple, our present and past managers: you gave us invaluable feedback, allowed us to spend time writing, and kept things running smoothly.

To our recipe testers, Rick Lumagui, and Joe Sterling, who came in every Monday morning for a year and a half, rain or shine, tired or not, and tested away: thank you.

To Luis Cabanas, Gavin Ledson, Timothy Wastell, Sean Temple, Misha Pavel, Holly Jimison, Janet Jones, Margaret O'Toole, David Reamer, Robert Reynolds, Timothy Murphy, Daniel Sherman, Willoughby Cooke, and the students at The Chef's Studio: thank you for testing as well. We hope you enjoyed the results.

To Jennifer Packer and Wednesday Wild-Wilson, our two former pastry chefs; thank you for your sweet discoveries. The best of your creations are in this book for all to see. To Lauren Fortgang, our current pastry chef, who advised on and tested recipes in this book as well: thank you for carrying the torch proudly and creating deeply satisfying pastries and desserts.

To Ellen Jackson, a writer, pastry chef, and friend: thank you for your expert ability to convert the sweets down to their present state, test them, and write them out. We could not have done it without you.

To Suzanne Bozarth and Matthew Mount, our two former bartenders extraordinaire: thank you for formulating such flavorful libations.

To our entire staff, past and present: thank you for seeing the world through our eyes.

To our friends and loyal patrons too numerous to mention. Thank you for allowing us to cook for you.

Your friendship and support means so much to us.

To Nancy Fitzpatrik of the Oregon Salmon Commission, Nick Furman of the Oregon Dungeness Crab Commission, Doug Heater of Bornstein Seafoods, John Cleary and Deloris Roorda of Newman's Fish Company, Dave Hoyle of Creative Growers, and Manuel and Leslie Recio of Viridian Farms: thank you for your expert advice.

To Rolly Morse, our milkman: service like yours does not exist anymore. Thank you.

To Phil Wood and Lorena Jones of Ten Speed, who encouraged us and gave us the opportunity to write this book: thank you. We would like to offer a very special thanks to Clancy Drake, our editor. "Be complete, truthful, and impassioned when writing," she advised. We were. Thank you for your ability to understand what we had to say, distill the content to its essence, and see the dots and connect them. Sincere thanks go to all the other great folks at Ten Speed, including Betsy Stromberg, designer; Hal Hershey, production manager; Kristin Casemore, publicist, and Lisa Regul, publicity director; Patricia Kelly, VP of Sales, and Debra Matsumoto, marketing and promotions manager.

Thanks also to the freelancers associated with Ten Speed who assisted in this book's production: Jane Horn, copy editor; Leslie Baylor, proofreader; and Ken Della Penta, indexer.

Finally, to Melissa Broussard and Lisa Hill of Broussard Hill Communications: you are the unsung heroes behind the people you promote. Thank you.

Index